The Entangled Activist

Introducing Perspectiva Press

Soul food for expert generalists

Perspectiva seeks to understand the relationship between systems, souls and society in a time of crisis, and to develop methods, grounded in an applied philosophy of education, to help us meet the challenges of our time.

As part of this broader endeavour, Perspectiva Press will specialise in short books with occasional longer works. These books will be well-presented and distinctive. Their purpose is to shape and share thinking that helps to:

- create a community of expert generalists with skills of synthesis and epistemic agility

- envisage a world beyond consumerism, and pathways for how we might get there

- support sociological imagination in a dynamic ecological and technological context

- cultivate spiritual sensibility; clarifying how it manifests and why it matters

- encourage a more complex and systemic understanding of the world

- commit to going beyond critique, by developing vision and method

- indicate how we can do pluralism better; epistemic, cultural, political, spiritual

- clarify what it means to become the change we want to see in the world

- develop the authority of people doing important work aligned with Perspectiva

It is unusual for a charity like Perspectiva to become a publisher, even a small one, but we value books as dignified cultural artefacts with their own kind of analogue power, and we believe ideas travel further and connect more deeply when they are rooted in the mandate of a publication designed to last for years, not merely moments. We also see a gap in the market for books that specialise in the kinds of integrative and imaginative sensibilities that speak to the challenges of our time.

Already published:

The World We Create: From god to market   *Tomas Björkman*
An entrepreneur offers an historical perspective on achieving a more
meaningful and sustainable world

To be published in 2021:

Unlearn: A compass for radical transformation   *Hanno Burmester*
A compass for societal transformation, arising from the personal testimony of
coming out in the shadow of Nazi Germany

**Collective Wisdom in the West: Beyond the shadows of the
Enlightenment**   *Liam Kavanagh*
A cognitive scientist and contemplative on the nature of 'collective wisdom'
and what we need to do to get there

**The Politics of Waking Up: Power and possibility in the fractal
age**   *Indra Adnan*
A psychosocial therapist on refashioning politics by meeting people where they are

**Dispatches from a Time Between Worlds: Crisis and emergence in
metamodernity**   *Authors include Jonathan Rowson (ed), Layman Pascal (ed), Zak
Stein, Bonnitta Roy, Daniel Görtz, Lene Rachel Andersen, Sarah Stein Lubrano, Minna
Salami, John Vervaeke and Christopher Mastropietro, Tom Murray, Mark Vernon and
Jonathan Jong, Siva Thambisetty, Jeremy Johnson, Brent Cooper*
An anthology of metamodern scholars and writers on our world-historical
context and pathways to cultural renaissance

Anyone who wants to change the world, or considers themselves an 'activist' please read this book for your own sake and for all of us – then we'll have so much more chance of succeeding.
Dr Gail Bradbrook, co-founder, Extinction Rebellion

Our attempts to make the world a more decent place too often neglect the profound implications of the fact that we're inextricably part of that world, with inner lives that can't just be ignored in the quest for social change. Blending politics, psychology and spirituality, this perspective-shifting book is an essential manual for getting better both at activism and being human.
Oliver Burkeman, author of The Antidote: Happiness for People Who Can't Stand Positive Thinking

We need activism today more than ever, to heal our widening divisions, rein in abusive power, and mend the natural fabric. But activism without reflection can never succeed. Anthea Lawson understands from her own experience what this means on the front line. She knows the activist must ask not only 'what am I going to say?' but also 'how do I want to be heard?' This is a manifesto for reflective activism. Anyone who wants to make things better through effective public action should read it.
John Ashton, independent activist and former diplomat

A book of liberating honesty that speaks to the need in our times to move from the splashy end of the pool where much activism necessarily begins, and learn to swim, and then to dive, and even how to breathe underwater.
Alastair McIntosh, co-author of Spiritual Activism and Riders on the Storm

Anthea Lawson's *The Entangled Activist* is the first spoonful of needed medicine gently administered to the exhausted, bewildered figure of the modern activist … you will be introduced to strangely familiar and poignantly articulated questions about agency, action, and the inner turmoil of attempting to enact change in a world that seems prohibitively solid, fixed in place, and mocking of those who seek the otherwise. Lawson's medicine lies specifically in a sublime and molecular series of operations: she shows how our inner worlds are not as 'inner' as we might think; how we are part of the systems we seek to change; and, crucially, why our entanglement with the world affords us opportunities for new moves fitting for stranger times. This book is medicine: now, open wide and say 'aaah'.
Bayo Akomolafe, Ph.D., author of These Wilds Beyond our Fences: Letters to My Daughter on Humanity's Search for Home

It is incredibly unusual that a psychologically informed book can be so practical and timely. Addressing the inner life of activists, including the shadow aspects of political passion, will make it easier for those who fear engagement to make the moves towards action. Shadow is there in the self-congratulation and that twinned contempt for people who are outside. The elitism – for that is what it is – of some activism is challenged with compassion and diplomacy. More profoundly, the book bridges the gap between those who act and those who reflect and analyse, between those who 'do' and those who 'be', in a unique way that itself links psyche and polis.

Professor Andrew Samuels, author of The Political Psyche

The Entangled Activist is a compelling read. Anthea Lawson addresses a great paradox and a deep dilemma which many activists face when they are engaged in social or environmental activism. She addresses it with clarity and audacity, and while analysing the problem she is also indicating the solution which is intrinsic within the problem. I have hugely benefited by reading this book and I can wholeheartedly recommend it to all my fellow activists and would-be activists. This book is asking the reader to be courageous to embrace the paradox, appreciate the dilemma and then move forward with one's own insights, wisdom and commitment. The book is an outstanding contribution in the field of activism.

Satish Kumar, Editor Emeritus, Resurgence & Ecologist

Lawson's wry, observant prose sketches the contours of activism's pitfalls in a way that makes me sigh and laugh with recognition. She undercuts unhelpful utopian thinking, instead providing a sense of how one might cultivate a realistic, self-aware optimism of will. It's a book to be kept at hand for the darker days of trying to change – well, not just the world, but also oneself.

Sarah Stein Lubrano, researcher, Oxford University and The School of Life

This book offers a first step into a hugely neglected area, why is it that political activists are often their own worst enemies? Lawson explores phenomena such as the activist's need to 'be in the right' and the narcissism and simple lack of civility that sometimes infects activism. These investigations will surely begin some much needed conversations.

Paul Hoggett, Climate Psychology Alliance

The Entangled Activist

Learning to recognise the master's tools

Anthea Lawson

Perspectiva Press, London, UK

systems-souls-society.com

First published in 2021

ISBN (pbk) 978-1-9998368-2-5

ISBN (ebk) 978-1-9998368-6-3

The author and publisher gratefully acknowledge the copyright holder for granting permission to reproduce an excerpt from *Parable of the Sower*, © Octavia Butler, 1993

Cover design Studio Sutherl&

Typeset in Baskerville and Akzidenz Grotesk by www.ShakspeareEditorial.org

Printed by TJ Books, Cornwall

To Dad

Entanglement

'Quantum entanglements are not the intertwining of two (or more) states/entities/events, but a calling into question of the very nature of two-ness.'

Karen Barad[1]

'All that you touch
You Change.

All that you Change,
Changes you.'

Octavia Butler[2]

'When we try to pick out anything by itself, we find it hitched to everything else in the Universe.'

John Muir[3]

'Bill Torbert once said to me that the 1960s slogan "If you're not part of the solution, you're part of the problem" actually misses the most important point about effecting change. The slogan should be: "If you're not part of the problem, you can't be part of the solution."'

Adam Kahane[4]

Contents

Introduction

I WENT ON some anti-globalisation marches and protests in 2000 and 2001, dug up Parliament Square in guerrilla-gardening efforts, got kettled by the police and spent my holidays volunteering in an off-grid permaculture community, but I didn't call myself an activist.[5] These were things I was doing in my spare time in my twenties, to feed a growing and experimental sense of what my real values might be. I didn't organise my identity around 'activism' until I stopped the work as a newspaper journalist that I'd recently trained for and began a job as a professional campaigner at Amnesty International.

That's when the reactions began: discomfort, arguments, devil's advocacy, admiration. People were never neutral. There are jobs that, when you are asked that very British question, 'so what do you do?' provoke an 'oh, right' answer, intonation dropping at the end to indicate a conversation over. And there are jobs that elicit the 'oh, really?' upwards-rising reaction, that opens the way to further questions, not always comfortable ones. Campaigning is one of those. It wasn't only the fact of what I was doing that provoked reactions, however. It was also the way I spoke about my work, the intensity of my evident passion. I would get so wound up with righteous fury, speaking so fast and sharply about the people who defended or profited from the bad things I wanted to change, that colleagues, friends and family would regularly be prompted to ask, 'are you ok?' And these were people who knew me, who cared enough to ask. My suspicion is that many of the people I was trying to persuade directly were switching off rather than have to deal with the frenetic force of my arguments.

I used to assume that my speed, forcefulness and fury were part of the territory. I didn't question why I was launching into such frantic behaviour when I went into activist mode, in a way that went far beyond the necessary adrenaline requirements to speak out in public. I thought other people were the problem. I thought that in resisting my rage, they were resisting the political views that lay behind my rage. I assumed that the other problems I noticed in activist circles were part of the territory too: campaigners spending energy fighting among themselves, campaigners treating each other terribly, and endemic burnout.

This is just how it is, activists themselves say. We get emotional and shouty and frantic because it is important and urgent, and we care so much. Our campaigning organisations are badly run and under-resourced, they don't treat staff and volunteers well, lots of people burn out, because we are all so passionate and focused on our task. And that is just how activists are, say observers from outside. They're hypocritical, hysterical, they're often fighting each other, they think they are doing it for love and care but give them any power and they'll be trying to control us all. The fear that activism can lead to the gulag or the guillotine is real: history is full of revolutionaries who became tyrants.

These are bad outcomes, whether on the grand scale of political tyranny or the localised one of toxic working environments that prevent effective work being done. Why do people with good intentions create bad outcomes?[6] The simple answer is that activists are human, just like everyone else. We do not have all the answers, and are as likely as anyone else to shout, to succumb to fear and violence, to try to control others. There is of course a truth in this. Christians might call it sin, which the author Francis Spufford describes, in turn, as 'the human propensity to fuck things up'.[7] I fuck things up regularly, and I am happy to acknowledge our flawed humanity. But to accept this answer without further enquiry is to accept things as they are. And I am an activist; accepting things as they are is *not* what I do.

I wrote this book to explore a question that had troubled me through two decades of campaigning: why are activists unconsciously replicating so many aspects of the systems we don't want? Behind all my busyness and urgency was an insistent feeling that there was something about the 'inside' of activism, its inner life, that we weren't attending to. It was something about our own emotional lives and how our work was affected by our feelings about it and why we were doing it. And it was something about the inner lives of the people we were trying to influence, with questions about the extent to which their behaviour would really be altered by, for example, a new law that restricted their choices. I couldn't put much of this unease into words, though I knew I wanted to ask other activists whether they were troubled by similar feelings of unease. It turned out that many of them were.

I paused my activist busyness and started asking questions about what I had been doing, and these queries about the 'inside' of activism started to change shape. They brought me face to face with our own deep implication in the problems we want to fix. So while I started off thinking that my question was about tracking down and illuminating the inner life of activism that was missing in all of our non-stop action, my conversations with other campaigners, my reading and reflecting on my own experiences led me, inexorably, to seeing how entangled we are. How the damage that is caused by the systems we are trying to change runs through us too.

That activists are part of what we are trying to change, and that the problems frequently appear in us, too, appears on the one hand to be terribly obvious. Yet at the same time it can be hard to grasp. It certainly took me a long time to grasp. It doesn't help that some of the *ways* in which we are entangled – by being subject to the dominant culture's way of seeing things, for example – help to obscure the *depth* to which we are entangled. 'You're off changing the world, then,' people would remark to me when I talked about my work. Or sometimes, for those with an even more inflated idea of what activists might be up to, 'you're off *saving* the world'. It is often just a turn of phrase, but it is revealing. The grammatical structure of that sentence uncovers the heart of the problem. The activist is the subject, and the world is the object. In my experience, activists do not claim to be 'saving' the world or 'changing' the world as often as other people describe us as trying to do so. Nonetheless, activists usually share this implicit view that the 'world' is separate to 'us', and that what needs changing is something or someone 'over there': something that is 'not us'.

To think like this is to share the same deep worldview that created the problems activists are trying to tackle. It is the worldview of separation, dominance and exceptionalism (the latter being the assumption that you, your group, your way of thinking or being is special and therefore superior) that has led to ecological destruction and the subjugation of peoples and other species. However we describe it, this worldview involves a narrowing of perception, a closing down to what we might otherwise see and feel. In the terms of complex adaptive systems theory, which challenges simplistic views of cause and effect,[8] our narrow perception does not allow us to see how the world is made of un-ordered interconnections, complexity and non-linear causality. In the terms of deep ecology, it prevents us understanding how we are embedded in the web of life, not above it. In spiritual terms, this limited perception keeps us from recognising the fundamental ground of our being: our connection to all else that is. And in the terms of depth psychology, it keeps us from acknowledging that we are split and that we project what we disown in ourselves onto others. It is of course very useful, however, this narrowed perception that structures 'normal' reality, in keeping us chained to business as usual.

So this book is called *The Entangled Activist* because it is about how activists are always entangled in the problems we are trying to fix or change, whether we realise it or not. It is about how we are entangled, what and who we're entangled with, why it matters and what we can do when we realise it.

We are entangled activists when we campaign for fossil fuels to stay in the ground to prevent climate change while also living a life whose food supplies and other practicalities almost inevitably depend on those fuels. We are entangled activists when we are trying to protect people from harmful exploitation while we continue to benefit from the political and economic systems that cause the harm. These are forms of entanglement that we might already recognise: entanglements in the moral thickets of industrialised consumer life.

But there are entanglements that are harder to perceive, too. We are entangled activists when we are talking about human rights and yet are treating other people − colleagues, collaborators or opponents − horribly. We are entangled activists when we are burning out in exhaustion from working so endlessly to stop an endless-growth economy from burning out the planet we live on. We are entangled activists when we are shouting loudly to 'save' others from harm while, in doing so, placating our own unacknowledged emotional needs for recognition and security. We are entangled activists when we are getting a kick out of attacking and criticising the people on the 'other side' who we think have got it so wrong. And we are entangled activists when our need to be so right and to sound so certain about the problem we're talking about − and it does feel good to sound certain and right in such a confusing world − prevents us being honest about the complexity of our own position.

What are we entangled in? We are entangled in the stories that our culture tells about heroes and saviours, and hard work, and the value of doing over being. We are entangled in the oppressive effects of systems of power upon us, whether we have suffered from them or benefited from them or both, and whether or not we can perceive that there are other more generative forms of power that are based in partnership rather than dominance. We are entangled in the habits and ways of being that are normalised in a culture where truly feeling − our own pain, and that of human and non-human others − is numbed and discouraged.

All of these entanglements affect how we try to achieve change. We may be projecting unwanted aspects of ourselves onto the people we are busy disagreeing with, and they may be doing the same onto us in return. We may think it is the 'systems', external to us, that need changing, when the problems we are tackling run through us too. And many of the methods we think could work emerge from the same mindsets that caused the problems. But often we don't realise it. I had been a campaigner for 15 years and I didn't.

I've worked on successful campaigns for new international treaties, and launched a prizewinning campaign that has since resulted in changes to the law in dozens of countries. I know how to investigate the misdeeds of banks, oil companies and governments, how to get a story onto the front page of a newspaper, how to get policies changed, and how to bring together global coalitions of support around an issue. And after blocking the road with Extinction Rebellion, I know what the inside of a police cell feels like. I care about activism deeply, have spent much of my adult life doing it, and intend to continue. Yet, through my enquiry, I have come to believe that we need to understand activism better. Not so much what it does or does not achieve in the world – there is already plenty of discussion and writing about that. This is about better understanding activism from the inside, in terms of how it is experienced – both by those who do it and by those who receive it. These questions need airing because activism is not well served if they remain subterranean. If we can look more honestly at what goes on behind our desire to change the world, we are more likely to be able to reach a wiser form of activism that goes beyond our own projections and emotional needs, and that avoids the self-defeating consequences that occur when our righteousness and need to be right overwhelm the subject of the conversation.

But the question that arises then, is: what on earth do we do now? What do we do when we realise we are entangled? Acknowledging entanglement could lead to despair. (Which is, of course, why activists don't like thinking about it. Despair is not good for motivation.) If the problems go that deep, if they run through all of us, then what hope is there of changing them? It can sound like we are being asked to change human nature. I choose to see it the other way. If we are so entangled that the problems run through us too, then we know where to start: with ourselves. And in saying this, I am not proposing that activists only retreat to the meditation cushion. Many activists sense that personal transformation alone is insufficient when the problems are structural, yet we also sense that carrying on as we have been, replicating the habits of the dominant culture until we repeatedly burn out, is not going to work either.

We can do both reflection and action, as long as we acknowledge that the reflection may profoundly alter what we think the task of the action is. Appreciating the depth of our own entanglement is a useful guide to what needs doing. Yes, it is unchangeable that we humans have some psychological habits, like projection and scapegoating, which, mishandled in the collective, have negative social consequences. But the reverse is also true: many of the psychological and spiritual difficulties that we experience as individuals arise from the ill effects of an unhealthy culture upon us. If activists are able to notice what is unhealthy about our own ways of being, we have a compass that points to what needs to shift in the wider culture.

And the world needs activism more than ever. Old abuses and injustices that have never gone away are still causing pain and difficulty, while new dangers continue to emerge. Even when ecological catastrophe isn't in the foreground of what campaigners are talking about, it is now always somewhere close by. Whatever happens to the earth and to us as humans living on it, I don't think we will ever have a human world where activism is not needed. Even if we can mitigate the worst climate change outcomes, human nature – indeed, every human – contains good and bad. We do not reach utopia. Activism is the constant task of trying to mitigate against the worst of what we humans are capable of, while orienting our societies towards the flourishing of the best.

So this book is for anyone who thinks they are doing activism. It's for anyone who is trying to make things better but doesn't call it activism. And it's for anyone who is interested in the world being better than it currently is, but who really doesn't want to be an activist. I say that because it's hard to define what counts as activism and what doesn't: such divisions are often part of the problem that this book describes. Activism is trying to do something to make the world better, whether noisily or quietly, on our own or with others. It can be done in our spare time in our community or as a job with a professional organisation. It can be on a small local issue or as part of a national or global movement. It can be speaking out in one moment, or the commitment of a lifetime. It can be done through one-on-one acts of supporting others or through big performances of resistance and confrontation, along with everything else that lies in between.

While I have been thinking about how deeply my activism is entangled, I have also continued to be involved in it. I have tried to 'stay with the trouble', to borrow Donna Haraway's phrase.[9] Lying in the road in the dark with Extinction Rebellion, then spending a night in a police cell and a morning in court are opportunities to reflect on the meaning and community generated by such a powerful experience of agency, even while it alienates some of those it is trying to speak to. A local constituency meeting at which feelings are running high about how best to prevent votes for the Conservative candidate when the anti-Tory vote is profoundly split between Labour and the Lib Dems is an opportunity to observe, close-up, the enormous difficulty of holding and articulating passionate views while still communicating persuasively with those who do not share them. All of us in that hall, the week before the 2019 general election, had the same goal: to prevent a Tory MP being returned. Yet one party activist after another succumbed to urgent shouting, oppositional moralising and exhortations that took no account of the likelihood that their listeners would have some views in common, or of what this was doing to everyone's nervous systems. It wasn't the only reason we failed and now have another Tory MP: I live in a conservative rural area. But in terms of my enquiry, it does make me question the effectiveness of this approach.

I have done the same, so many times: failed to see that the starting place does not have to be me and my views; failed to see that starting with me and my pressing desire to speak may not be the best route to the fairer world I want to help create. I am still not yet always able to stop myself doing it. I am quick to anger, quick to find words ready formed in my mouth, words which want to come out. But now I observe it happening in others and I see its limitations. I have also, while writing this book, continued to do my other job: sharing with my husband the job of looking after our two small children, including through the pressure cooker of spring 2020's coronavirus lockdown and school closures. When the mood is turning fractious, as it so often does when tea is still half an hour from being on the table, I have begun to observe, in my own nervous system, the switch from calm functioning to escalation. I have observed the strength of my instinctive desire to exert forceful control when things feel uncomfortable and I am moving into that quick-fire heightened state. I have observed the difference in outcome, in the reaction of these small, tired people to the way that I am comporting myself, when I can find a way to drop back down into calm functioning and not act or speak from what I call 'the heightened place'. These are valuable daily opportunities to reflect on where the stridency in activism can come from and to consider the risk of unleashing the inner authoritarian in all of us.

So this book has an autoethnographical aspect: it is an analysis of personal experience in order to help understand a cultural experience.[10] That cultural experience is the attempt to bring positive change while being part of the unhealthy culture that needs changing. Most of the activists I interviewed were in the UK, though I also spoke to people from Brazil, Ethiopia, Germany, Uganda and the US. Some worked in NGOs, some in community initiatives. These interviews did not span every issue that activists work on, nor every context in which they work, and I will inevitably have heard their experiences through the filter of my own, however openly I have tried to listen.

I am talking, unless I say otherwise, about activism in the UK. Some of it may be applicable in other countries and I look forward to conversations about what resonates and where. Throughout this book, when I say 'we' it is deliberate: unless I specify otherwise, I mean anyone who thinks they are doing activism, anyone who thinks they are working for positive change in the world whether or not they call themselves an activist, and anyone who is thinking about making the world more just. Yet even within the context of the UK, I am making inevitable generalisations about who 'activists' are. There are times when I am painting in broad strokes and, at any point, I may not be speaking for everyone who considers themselves to be doing activism. I am willing to take this risk, for which I apologise in advance, because I think there are some things that are worth saying about activism as a phenomenon. (Nor, indeed, am I speaking for right-wing activism, though perhaps some of my observations might apply to it.)

That said, if I mean specific types of activists, or activists in specific places or engaging in specific behaviours, I say so. I acknowledge the profound differences between fighting for our lives, with lived experience of the problem that we are campaigning on, and intervening on principles of justice because we want to help others. The difficulties that arise when activists coming from these different starting points encounter each other are at the core of many of the entanglements in this book. One of the many challenges in writing this book was the articulation and differentiation of its 'voice'. Who is it that I am speaking for when I say 'we'? The challenge was to be clear when (a) I am speaking for myself, when (b) I am speaking for other people like me who have approached activism, however unconsciously, from a white-saviour perspective, when (c) I am speaking more broadly for anyone who is trying to do activism or is thinking about it, and when (d) I am speaking about our universal human nature.

The universalising tendency which presumes that the experiences of one's own 'we' are more worthy of attention, or can encompass and speak for the experiences of anyone else's 'we', is one of the foundational assumptions of whiteness. And as a white woman, whiteness has been foundational to my experiences, upbringing, education and perspectives. I have learned, through the process of writing this book, that whiteness is not, as I used to think, 'only' a suite of implicitly held racist assumptions and a related tendency towards defensiveness and fragility when confronted with evidence of them. Whiteness encompasses, at its broadest, an unconscious approach to perception, epistemology (how we know what we know), our approach to our work, and our encounters with everyone we meet. It underpins the dominant culture in which I'm entangled, as I explore throughout the book. This means that it doesn't only affect how white people relate to people of colour. I have noticed, for example, how the lessons that I am learning about the dominance tendencies and subject–object perceptions of whiteness are applicable, in certain ways, to class privilege and prejudice, which remains a live issue in many types of helping-others activism and politics within the UK.

I would not have been able to 'see' aspects of the systems of power I want to change – those aspects in which I am particularly entangled by my own starting position of being white and middle class – without learning from the writing of activists and thinkers who have been marginalised by those systems and can thus see them more clearly from 'outside'. I'm profoundly grateful to all of the activists and thinkers whose work informs my explorations of my own entanglement, perhaps especially to Black feminists such as Audre Lorde, who raised these same issues that I have only now been waking up to, in the years before I was born. The subtitle of this book comes from Lorde's essay, 'The Master's Tools Will Never Dismantle the Master's House', and I am using it both because of its astuteness and relevance, and also to pay tribute to the legacies of critical thinking about activism on which I am drawing. I encountered Lorde's essay in the months when I was first allowing myself to think about the limitations of the activism I had been doing. Her words were from a speech criticising white feminism and its reinforcement of racism, and they remain applicable not only to that ongoing problem but to any form of activism that cannot perceive what it is reinforcing.[11] They rang through me, and grew in profundity and resonance throughout my enquiry, throughout my realisations of how I had repeatedly been wielding the master's tools, had sometimes myself been one of those tools, and throughout my slow process of learning to recognise some of them.

The Entangled Activist begins, then, with how I stopped doing the form of activism that I had been absorbed in for so long. Chapter 1 describes my experiences in campaigning, my growing unease with my job at an NGO, and the questions that were forming as I decided to turn away from it. Chapter 2 offers several answers to the question of 'why?' Why should we even stop to think about how we approach activism, when the tasks activism takes on such as halting ecological destruction, and threats to democracy and justice are so very urgent? Chapter 3 introduces some of my own entanglements, to open up the topic of how our starting points affect the ways in which we try to create change.

The following two chapters look underneath the surface of classic activist behaviours. Chapter 4 explores how activists are entangled with our opponents. It makes the case for examining our unconscious motivations, and looks at what lies underneath the projections that often occur, in both directions, when an activist speaks. From the activists: anger and righteousness. From their audience or opponent: guilt and resistance.

Chapter 5 investigates three further activist tendencies: trying to carry the world on our shoulders, saviour heroics and status-chasing.

Part 2 then explores more deeply what it is that we are entangled with. Chapter 6 goes in search of an appropriate language which we can use to speak about the overarching framework of unconsciously held ideas and assumptions that condition our thinking and actions. How do we describe what it is that has to change if we too are part of what has to change? That it is hard to find the right words is an indication of the problem: we are not accustomed to seeing ourselves as part of the world. Chapter 7 is about our entanglement in the stories of our culture and how we react to them. Activists may develop a critical stance on some aspects of a story, while other aspects hold them firmly, which leads to some of the contradictions. I look at what happens when activists try to disentangle themselves from an ideology.

Disentangling ourselves from stories and ideology is, however, a tall order when stories have been made concrete in the institutions that govern our lives. Chapter 8 looks at the ways in which activists are entangled in the practical effects of the political and economic structures they are trying to change. These can alter activists' strategies, behaviours and even perceptions. Responding to the challenge of decolonial thinking, I reflect on my experiences of doing forms of activism that try to 'help'. Chapter 9 turns back to our inner worlds, and the deep ways that we have been shaped, at the level of our nervous systems, by the effects on us of the systems that we are trying to change. I introduce trauma-informed thinking, which allows us to see collective cultural patterns, including unhealthy habits that shape activism, in a new light.

Chapter 10 explores activist 'over-forcefulness', which is what can result when activists sense the depth of the wounds in themselves and at the heart of the dominant culture and launch themselves with heightened efforts over the gap between how things are and how they want them to be. Other sources of forcefulness include the need for certainty and the need for meaning, human traits that are heightened by the effects of the systems that activists are trying to change.

Part 3 is about next steps and the future. We are not going to disentangle ourselves from the problems we are working on. But we can become more aware of our entanglements. This allows us to start our activism in a different place, and Chapter 11 offers some outlines of what this different place feels like. It is an approach to activism that includes time for stillness, embodied practice, reflection and self-honesty.

The book ends with some questions for entangled activists to use in their own reflections. If, by this point, I have encouraged any reader to think differently about how they engage with the problems of the world, whether or not they call themselves an activist, then I will be pleased.

Part 1

How activists are entangled

1 Let's get the bastards

THE GREEN room was low-ceilinged, hot and crowded. People coming in or leaving had to squeeze themselves through the narrow space inside the door that led to the stage, and I was perched, surrounded by other people's bags and jackets, on a chair just inside it. Someone with a headset and clipboard was busy checking names and organising microphones. I scanned my notes in a dull panic, aware of how pointless it was to do so. If I didn't know my words by now, it was too late. Doing TED talks isn't the same as giving a regular presentation. There's no table or lectern to stand behind, nothing to lean on, nothing against which to steady your hands when their involuntary shaking threatens to betray your nerves. And crucially, you're not supposed to use notes. You simply have to know your words, speaking for about 15 minutes on the subject you're excited about. I didn't want to freestyle, because I would be making defamatory statements and needed to get the wording right. So I'd practised this talk several times with my Dad over Skype from his hospital room, and had reached a point where I could get through it without reminders. I did usually like public speaking. But the thought of the live webcast was making me feel unsteady, and I had an emergency index card with headings folded up in my back pocket in case I lost my way.

I didn't need it. Once my name was called, once I walked onto the stage and got over the awkwardness of the first few words, I took in the room in front of me, and realised that I had spoken to larger audiences before. And this one would be friendly. They weren't experts in my topic who'd be pulling angry or agonised faces when they thought I was off-point; they were interested members of the public who wanted me to do well. This was TEDx Westminster, one of many spin-off events from the original TED talks, and I was in a conference room in the heart of Whitehall. And the words were coming. Of course they were. This was what I had worked on for most of a decade. The video shows me leaning forward earnestly as I explained how banks headquartered in London were ripping off the people of impoverished countries by accepting, into the accounts of their rulers, corruptly obtained funds that should have been in public budgets. I was describing the creation of poverty by some of the most powerful institutions in the world, and what should be done about it. I knew what I was talking about because I had been investigating it myself, and I really cared. 'You smashed it,' was the gleeful response when I returned to the office of the anti-corruption campaign group I worked at, where several of my team had been watching online. I was told, too, by colleagues there, that it was a minor hit in Nigeria, one of the countries whose pilfered oil revenues I'd been talking about. And the numbers of views online ticked up over the next few days.

Why, then, did I feel so flat? I couldn't quite understand my gloom, but I sensed it was something connected to what I *wasn't* able to say. Because I was representing the organisation for which I was a campaigns director, I needed to keep within the lines of our campaigning 'asks': the changes that we viewed as necessary and that we were agitating for. Those 'asks', which on this topic I had devised myself, were that banks be properly regulated to prevent them fuelling corruption and the hollowing-out of public funds. And I still stand by the changes that I was recommending in that talk.

Banks do need to be carefully regulated to prevent them fuelling corruption and tax evasion. It is because they are still not regulated appropriately that new examples of the financial and legal sectors' contribution to poverty and the degradation of the public sphere keep emerging with each new leak of data from a whistleblower, even as the examples I gave from our investigations up to 2014 are now beginning to age. So what was it that I couldn't say?

Here's what I was starting to see, but couldn't say. 'We need an economic system that isn't based on economic growth, one that puts care at the heart of everything. We must regulate banks, sure, but we also need to alter the way that money is created and used. We need to live in a way that isn't so dependent on extraction from other people and other places, and if we don't find a way to do these things, worsening ecological destruction and worsening injustice are guaranteed...' But because I was only starting to see the depth of the problems we face, I couldn't craft these despairing feelings into a 'clear message' with a positive pay-off. Even if I had been able to, these points did not relate to my work on the specific campaign about which I had been offered a platform at that event. Perhaps the hovering presence of this unspoken material is why my talk never really took off online like some TED talks do. An acquaintance who works in communications offered the frank feedback that I hadn't done what the really successful talks do. They make it clear right from the top that there is something that can be done differently, a positive vision which is then woven through the discussion of the problem. I had started with the problem, described it clearly and passionately. And then I'd put some suggestions for change – in this case, 'more regulation' – at the end. I sort of knew it wasn't top-notch campaigning. That feedback, which I welcomed, wasn't a huge shock. But the reason I'd put my proposals for change at the end, rather than foregrounding them, was because I had become so painfully aware, despite their necessity, of their insufficiency. And that felt very uncomfortable. Activism doesn't really work if we're not fully behind what we're saying.

What do I mean by 'activism'? I am talking about efforts to turn the world towards what I regard as justice, equality, peace and ecological sanity, though of course the word is not owned by those who work for these goals as I construe them. Populist and far-right movements expressing very different values are also doing 'activism'. In the widest sense, it is being pro-active to try to create change. But even assuming that we are talking about the justice, peace and ecological sanity version, reactivity to the word means that there may be no neutral place from which to answer the question of what activism actually *is*. The term is loaded. It has martial origins: the Swedish 'activists' who tried to pressure their country to join the First World War.[12] To many, it sounds sharp and aggressive. And, because it polarises identity, it is hard to talk about 'activism' as a particular type of activity, without getting into the question of who is an activist.

There are people who appear – fairly clearly, to many of those who observe them – as if they are doing activism, yet they don't want to call themselves activists. There are people who would like to do something to make the world better but hesitate to begin, because they feel allergic to the very idea of being an activist. In their minds it carries an uncomfortable image with which they do not identify. Then there are people who are keen to call themselves activists, to the extent that they unwittingly erect barriers against those who do not – even towards those on their own 'side' who might pursue a different approach. These powerful questions of self-identification as activist – or not – overwhelm and obscure other ways of looking at what activism can be. If activism is trying to make things better, then many people are involved, in many public and private spheres, both within and outside of their day jobs. If it is a mindset, that the world can be improved, on whatever scale, then it is something open, potentially, to everyone, and many are already doing it. If it is a tactic of speaking up and confronting people about what matters to us, then it is not only those who are in the streets, getting in the way, or who are able-bodied and can turn up to the place where the confrontation is happening, who are being activists. It is not only those who are patiently collecting signatures, knocking on doors, writing emails and standing up at public meetings, explaining the problem over and over again. Activists are also the people who make themselves uncomfortable and don't mind making other people uncomfortable. They are the ones who initiate difficult conversations in public spaces, who don't let things slide: in the pub, at their workplace, on social media, at the family table.

On all of these scales, I was an activist. As a chosen identity, I liked the fuck-you approach to those in power that it seemed to convey. I wore that identity as armour and behaved accordingly, comfortable with the idea of campaigning as combat. As an attempt to make things better, there was nothing else I wanted to do. As a mindset, there was no question: of course I should try to improve the world. And as a tactic of speaking up and confronting, that was who I was. I had been confronting and arguing since I was a child. My parents would be torn: between glee at my brutally articulate, vicious shredding of anyone exhibiting pomposity, lack of analysis or right-wing views at their dinner table, and exhaustion and defensiveness at my attacks on their own right-wing views. In practical terms, I had a professional job as a campaigner for a decade and a half, at organisations both well known and unknown. I worked, on staff, freelance or sometimes as a volunteer, for Amnesty International, Landmine Action, the International Action Network on Small Arms, Christian Aid and Global Witness, as well as at an undercover research agency that investigates the arms trade for human rights campaigners, a UN disarmament agency and a small child-protection charity in Sierra Leone that has since closed. I did research, writing, strategy planning, coalition building, political lobbying and press liaison.

I worked on campaigns that resulted in a treaty to limit international weapons sales and the treaty that banned cluster bombs. I gave testimony to a US congressional inquiry and submitted evidence to a parliamentary inquiry in the UK. I launched a campaign to tear down laws allowing secret company ownership in tax havens and major financial centres, that has resulted in changes to the law in – so far – 81 countries.[13] I became a campaigns director, a portentous-sounding title for a job that entailed responsibility for a fairly generous budget and a team of 20 investigators and campaigners who were publishing relentlessly defamatory material about the facilitation of grand corruption and ecological devastation by oil and mining companies, banks and tax havens. The task was a mixture of strategy, editorial, whistleblower-management, source-protection, motivation and agony aunt. I had to keep everyone safe while on undercover exploits, out of the libel courts, and in the pages of the *Financial Times* and *The Economist* where our investigations and recommendations would be seen by those in charge.

Joanna Macy, a philosopher, activist and trainer, sees an ecology of change-making activity in which there are three types of interventions necessary to bring about the 'great turning' towards justice and ecological sanity. Opposing abusive power directly is the first: the 'holding action' to prevent further harm. This is the classic oppositional 'no!' of activism, the one that is most obvious to the outside observer. Second is the work to create new alternatives, and third is the 'inner' transformation necessary to envisage a world not built on violent domination.[14] I was in the thick of the 'holding actions', and for many years this work felt good. I was using the journalism skills I had originally trained in. It felt more effective than going on marches (though I did those too), like the huge anti-Iraq war one in March 2003 that was so roundly ignored by the warmongers in Downing Street. I was working on something I cared about, the responsibility of companies and banks, headquartered on my doorstep in London, for the awful state of economies that were dependent on natural resource revenues. This felt especially important after living in Sierra Leone for six months, working for a small aid agency in the aftermath of a recently ended civil war that had been fuelled by the diamond trade.

At Global Witness in particular, there was a rough glamour to the scene that appealed to the side of me that had, before I turned away from newspaper journalism, aspired to be a foreign correspondent. It started from the moment I was 'interviewed' for a job by a dishevelled, cowboy-booted enthusiast who appreciated my tales of trying to outwit National Rifle Association lobbyists in the corridors of the UN in New York during negotiations towards a (failed) agreement to control the second-hand gun trade. We ranted about the ghastliness of various arms dealers whose efforts we had tracked, and traded stories about unpleasant members of the *Blood Diamond* film production crew whom we had each encountered in Freetown. After a couple of hours of this I was offered a job investigating the role of banks in facilitating conflict and grand corruption. (Recruitment processes improved slightly in the years after that.)

I spent months talking to policemen (for they were all men), anti-corruption investigators, lawyers, money-laundering experts, journalists, authors, spooks, ex-spooks, corporate intelligence spooks, mercenaries, academics, pedlars of offshore finance, sanctions administrators, UN human rights investigators, and staffers on a US Senate committee that for a few precious years under the now retired Senator Carl Levin used its hefty subpoena powers to investigate the financial sector. I was trying to understand how global banks were managing to behave so badly in plain sight. This was in 2006 and 2007, before the financial crisis made clear how unregulated the banks were. Some of these contacts tried to be helpful, some were alarming, some were sleazy, and some were all three, including the man who offered me his satellite-phone number and suggested that if I was ever in a spot of bother somewhere 'tricky', I should give him a call and he would send a helicopter and some 'friends' to come and get me.

I had a file of documents from the hard drive of one of the entourage of former Liberian president Charles Taylor, procured in Monrovia in the chaos as Taylor's regime fell in 2003; and had seen another that anatomised strands of a complex web of tax haven front companies purportedly used by the oligarchs Roman Abramovich and Boris Berezovsky when they profited from some of the billions that flowed out of Russia, as the Soviet Union fell and its industries were chaotically privatised.[15] Not all of it could be published and not all of it, including that Russian example, was relevant for our purposes, but eventually we started making the case – the first time, as far as we could see, that an NGO had done so in this way – that thanks to ill-designed and ill-enforced money-laundering laws as well as the morally unhinged pursuit of profit, banks were actively helping to create poverty by accepting corruptly gotten wealth.

We spent a summer in court battling a dictator's son who wanted to prevent us publishing evidence of him spending his country's oil revenues on designer shopping in Paris (he failed), and another summer exchanging lawyers' letters with a mining billionaire who was trying to misuse data protection laws to force us to disclose our sources for the corruption allegations we were publishing about him (he failed too). We passed on various offers of whistleblower material that we couldn't verify, a request to investigate toxic waste aboard a pirated vessel off the Somali coast, and many other interesting avenues that we did not have the resources to pursue. In 2014 the company ownership transparency campaign I had launched won a huge prize from TED, and I was invited to do that TEDx talk in London.

9

That was when I hit the wall with a form of campaigning that, for years, I had seen as an extension of myself. It wasn't only the straightforward exhaustion that comes from hard work, although goodness knows, I now understood just what it took to get even one law changed. It was something deeper. The investigations I had done on banking and secret company ownership had radicalised me. I had always known there was something wrong with the global economy, but now it felt that I could see into the very heart of it. I could see that it could never be anything but extractive and predatory. There were no natural resource contracts that didn't involve some form of corrupt influence, even if the law didn't designate it as such. There were no people or species who were immune from a system – capitalism – that was designed to turn living things into money. The financial system itself was systemically criminogenic, a fact that has now been compellingly written up by the journalist Oliver Bullough in his book *Moneyland*. There are many people who, through living in a class, or a racialised identity or a geography that has been subordinated by capitalism, have always known some version of this. But I was white and middle class and from the southeast of England and had reacted against my family to become an activist. I knew there was something wrong with the world system and that it needed changing. But it was new to me to acknowledge this quite so explicitly: that extractive capitalism in the form we knew it was essentially unreformable.

And now here I was, doing a TEDx talk on behalf of the organisation I worked for, an organisation that operated, although we wouldn't have said so explicitly, on the basis of *reforming* capitalism.[16] We were engaged in the first of Macy's three interventions: a holding action, of sorts, to stop capitalism being quite so abusive. We called for new laws, new international agreements, for punishment of offenders. I had even achieved some new laws. We talked about making the system work for the poor: if natural resource revenues could only be transparently handled, then the countries involved would benefit. Our willingness to name and shame the companies doing wrong, to risk the draconian English libel laws that could shut us down, made us feel we were ever so radical – and compared to our peers in the NGO world who were quiet on the causes of poverty while continuing to hand out aid, perhaps we were. But fiddling with the superstructure of capitalism while it continues to consume the earth and its people was not radical, in that word's true meaning of getting to the roots, and now I knew it. And I no longer believed that the 'solutions' I was parroting – regulating this, regulating that – were enough, when the mindset of relentless extraction was going unquestioned. I could no longer live with the cognitive dissonance of talking about a small part of the solution without openly acknowledging that it was only a small piece of what was needed. I left my job a few months later.

I wasn't only tired of proposing changes to our economic system that didn't take account of the fact that our economy is a subset of our biosphere. I was tired, too, of arguing aggressively, with men, about things that their privilege, position and role made it so hard for them to contemplate, and tired of being so patronised by them. ('If you were an economist, Anthea, you would know that what you are suggesting is impossible.' Though what I was suggesting is now law in dozens of countries.) I was tired of trying to tweak a system that systematically left the family, the social, and women's childbearing role out of economic calculations – a system that had, in Katrine Marçal's excellent book title, forgotten 'Who cooked Adam Smith's dinner?'[17] (It was his mum.) I was tired of putting carefully sourced, carefully checked facts in front of policymakers and expecting them to respond rationally. It seemed redolent of the rational-actor assumptions behind the flawed *homo economicus* model at the centre of the economic thinking I wanted to undermine. This was before the Brexit and Trump elections of 2016 that revealed, unequivocally, the limits of assuming that people made decisions through rational thinking. I was also tired of the relentless treadmill of activity, of always taking on more than we could handle, of leaning into the media noise, because it was all so urgent. I was tired of a culture of feeling superior to other campaigners with different tactical approaches. I was tired of having to be so sure I knew the answer. I wasn't suffering the form of 'burnout' that looks like total physical exhaustion and illness, which was something that had happened to me years earlier when I was a journalist. But I was perhaps experiencing one of the earlier, subtler symptoms: that nagging message from within that something needs to change.

I was tired, too, of demonising the other side. Our unofficial motto was that we were going to 'get the bastards'. I did have colleagues with a more inclusive, participatory sense of the task, one perhaps more grounded in experience of the struggles of our collaborators in countries affected by corruption, who didn't feel so comfortable with that phrase. But some of us did like it. I liked the idea of 'getting the bastards' because it fitted with my punchy understanding of what activism was about, as well as with my journalist's sensibility. I was taught at journalism college that reporters must ask themselves: 'why is this bastard lying to me?' I'd even had thrilling little moments of acknowledgement, from some of the bastards themselves, no less, that we might be getting to them. On one of these occasions, a lawyer, a paid representative of offshore tax havens, invited us to his office for lunch so he and several colleagues could grill us about our campaign – which was starting to be noticed (and would soon be acted on) by MPs and Downing Street – for an open register of who owns companies in every country. The meeting went on for hours. 'Can I ask something?' I eventually said. 'You're probably all on several hundred pounds an hour, so we've taken a few thousand pounds of your time already. Why are those who pay you willing to spend that?' 'Because,' he replied, with a sudden show of rather unlawyerly anger, 'what you are calling for will cost our clients a lot of money.' And there, he said it, what so often stayed hidden: that we would impede their profits if we won.[18] (This sentiment was more usually expressed blandly and without mentioning money, by saying that their clients would find whatever we were proposing 'difficult'.) So if I was now getting tired of painting the 'other side' as the bastards, it wasn't because the people and companies we were investigating had stopped doing awful things. They hadn't. In fact, the more we investigated, the worse we realised it all was. But after participating in it for so long – this denunciation of what and who was wrong – I started to feel this was an empty ritual, one that might also be obscuring other truths, including about ourselves.

Donella Meadows, a systems thinking expert and author of the Club of Rome's 1972 *Limits to Growth* report, observed: 'Psychologically and politically we would much rather assume that the cause of a problem is "out there", rather than "in here". It's almost irresistible to blame something or someone else, to shift responsibility away from ourselves, and to look for the control knob, the product, the pill, the technical fix that will make a problem go away.'[19] It can be irresistible, too, for activism to see the problem as those bad guys over there, or that faulty legislation over here, and to seek to pull levers of power and influence to stop the bad guys and fix the faults, without looking at ourselves and what is known about human nature. If we looked at ourselves, we would have to acknowledge that many of us, as activists, are as damaged by the unhealthy human culture we live in as the people we want to change.

The very idea that the only problem is 'those bastards' who are 'over there' emerges from the same form of thinking that created the problems we are trying to tackle: the extractivism, at the heart of the economy, that says we can obtain resources or labour or dump waste 'over there' – anywhere but here. As activists trying to tackle the 'over there-ness' of an abusive economic system, we are prone to thinking in 'over there' terms about those who are responsible for it and those who benefit from it. 'Over there' thinking also contributes to the saviour syndrome, in which those who are being 'saved' or 'helped' are made the repository of projections and assumptions from those doing the 'helping', denying them their humanity and agency.

When activists do not see that we are part of what we are trying to change, it is hard for us to see the ways in which the problems that we are trying to tackle end up manifesting, too, in us. We can see that the logic of endless economic growth is not good for the biosphere and we are busy arguing for alternatives, but it is harder to see the connection to our own logic of endless activity that leads to frequent burnout. We can see the urgent necessity of protecting people from conflict, violence and human rights abuses and are working at some cost to ourselves to try to do so. It is harder to see, however, that the conflicts we have with our colleagues and collaborators, the divisive barriers we unwittingly erect around our activist identity, may share psychological roots with the abuses we are fighting. We can see the centuries of damage and horror caused by colonialism and enslavement and are working to overturn these histories and their current manifestations in inequality, poverty and racist policing and border policies. But for those who have benefited from these histories, it is harder to see how the racist and hierarchical thinking may be manifesting in our own interactions with the people we think we are trying to help – or, indeed, that the entire frame of 'helping' is suffused with unhelpful notions. We have developed the sharp eye to observe abuses of power wherever we look, yet do not want to see the internal forces that drive our own will to control.

And if activists cannot see that the problem we are trying to solve runs in us, then we cannot see the extent of the problem. When we understand the extent to which we are entangled, the real task of activism comes into view: to change not just the rules of the system, but the perceptions and thinking behind the system. Unless we can 'see' this perception and thinking, and get a handle on it, we remain in its thrall, seeing 'through' it, as a lens colouring our vision. As long as we continue to insist that 'the system' – whatever is 'out there' – is what needs changing, we turn away from seeing the perceptions that we still share with the people who run it: that we are above nature, that rational analysis is the only tool we need, that control is the answer, that anything we do can have simple cause and effect.

'Over there' thinking affects our dealings with the bastards, the people we think we are trying to help, and even the people who are mostly like us but who don't seem to appreciate the issue as well as we think we do. 'Over there' thinking is, perhaps, what is going on when people who are campaigning in support of the identity rights of others (i.e., we are campaigning in solidarity, rather than for our own identity to be recognised) become vociferously focused on the wrongs of others *like us* who haven't yet learned what we have learned. It can be easier, as a white person doing anti-racist activism, to get noisily angry at other white people who are being obviously racist, than to do the quiet and difficult work of acknowledging our own ongoing implicit racism. It can be easier, as a cis person supporting the rights of trans people, to weigh in against the views we don't like of other cis people, than to acknowledge just how recently we might have come to our own views. 'Over there' thinking of any kind makes it all too easy, when we are dealing with the nasty things that the 'other side' does – however we are conceiving of the other side – to forget that everyone is capable of it, in ways that start to break down the very distinction between 'us' and the 'other side'.

'Over there' thinking emerges from the human tendency to split ourselves and project the features of ourselves that we don't like onto others; to try to control others as a way of feeling psychologically safe; to create walls around our identity that give us that lovely group feeling but prevent effective communication with those outside the group. While these habits emerge from our human condition, there are ways – with experience, guidance and much practice – to tame them, opening the door to more peaceful relations with each other. In a healthy culture that offered support and role models for this learning, these habits would not be such invisibly inevitable ways of structuring communication and relations in the shared public realm. But we are not in a healthy culture; we are entangled in the damaged and damaging culture that we are trying to change, and these habitual ways of seeing and behaving help to shape what we think activism ought to be. So we hold back from challenging ourselves in case we are the ones who are found wanting. We sound extremely certain about the people who we think are getting it wrong, because it feels that the worst thing, for an activist, would be to sound not quite sure. It was no longer being sure about the sufficiency of what I had for so long presented as a solution that led to my discomfort after doing that TEDx talk.

An alternative to 'over there' thinking is to attend to ourselves. But that doesn't often feel like the right thing for activists to do, as the next chapter explores.

2 Why does it matter?

'THERE'S SOMETHING about the nature of the campaigner that makes them averse to reflection,' an organisational development expert told me. This was a person with two decades of experience in management training and coaching for senior staff in campaigning organisations. 'What I've observed is that the people who run campaigns aren't the people who stop and reflect. It's all go go go, thinking at 100 miles an hour. The general mode for campaigners is adrenaline overdrive. Reflection is really very rare.' And there is a reason for this, many of those campaigners might say. The job we are doing is important, and it is urgent, and we need to get on with it. Does it matter, then, if activists are mirroring the system we are trying to change? Isn't it more important to get on and tackle the urgent problems, including confronting the bastards who are still busy causing them?

Yes, it matters if we are serious about making effective, lasting change. If activists are recreating or reinforcing the thinking behind the problems we are trying to solve, then the real source of the problems remains untouched. We risk applying their efforts to change what we think is 'the system', but which may only be the symptoms of the system, the ice above the surface. We risk, potentially, making the problem worse. Meanwhile, the system still has us firmly in its grip. To take a pressing example, climate change can look like a problem of carbon emissions and is often tackled on that basis. At a deeper level, however, it is about an economic system that requires endless growth and distributes the proceeds and harms of that growth very unfairly. Underlying that growth are perceptions about the world, perceptions that can lead us to see, for example, nature as a resource to be extracted, and the 'environment' as something separate to us. What really needs changing are the *perceptions and behaviours that give rise to* the systems that activists say we want to change.

So activists mirroring what we are trying to change matters for strategic reasons. If the people who are trying to change the system cannot see the perceptions and behaviour that underlie it, there is no chance of us changing the system at its root. But activists share these perceptions and behaviours with everyone else; they are the water in which we all swim. There may be very little clear ground from which an activist can say they have stepped far enough 'outside' a problem, outside how everyone else perceives it, in order to see it clearly and change it. Indeed, the search for such a location may be a symptom of the same binary, us-and-them, subject–object thinking that has caused many people to treat the world and other people as objects. Where does this leave the activist, this person who so keenly wants to make things better? It means that the problem we are trying to tackle can be manifested by us, the activists, as much as it stems from anyone else. And this in turn means that some of the task of change is located within us. If we as activists are doing the things that need to shift, if we are stuck in the perceptions that are at the root of the problem, then the route towards change must include our willingness to do something differently ourselves, as well as seeking to influence others. This is unlikely to happen when we are in action-panic mode, focusing all the attention outwards on the thing or person to be changed, or the people who need saving or helping.

These questions also matter because they are timely. There is more activism going on. It can certainly look like that to those who are joining in or who are noticing activism for the first time. I have been thinking about and writing this book during the years in which the fog of consent around the issues of sexual violence, racism and ecological breakdown has been lifting, thanks to activism: movements like Me Too, Black Lives Matter and the school strikes and Extinction Rebellion. And when that fog of consent clears, we can suddenly see them. There they are: the activists who have always been there, who hadn't waited for the issue to become topical or gain more traction.[20] They had never stopped. Still, political upheavals, democratic deficits, growing awareness of ecological breakdown, and the coronavirus pandemic of 2020–21 *are* creating new activists. The public sphere is being revitalised with the emergence of multiple initiatives, movements and organisations as the failure of politics-as-usual becomes more and more evident. And it is easy for newcomers to activism to step into established understandings of what activism is. Doing it for the first time, it is easy to pick up the established script, the one that identifies the problem as separate to the activist.

These questions are also timely because big shifts are underway within activism. Social media, in practical terms, has widened and sped up movement formation, recruitment, organising and communicating about any issue and what activists are doing about it. In short, it has altered almost everything that happens in the campaigning process. Social media is also where people who are not doing activism are most likely to encounter it, and it makes them more likely to encounter activism than they were before. Many people already sense that posting, liking and re-posting can indicate genuine concern or a desire to perform the right moves and opinions (or, indeed, both), and that these various possibilities operate independently of the liker or re-poster's likelihood of going out and doing any actual real-life activism. And social media's outrage-amplifying and division-widening function is increasingly recognised to be a huge political problem, and evident beyond any questions about how activism is done. But its outrage and polarisation functions are a problem for activism, too. If the social platforms make it easy to look like we're doing activism by saying certain things, they also make it easy to make ourselves feel better by criticising those who don't get it ('it' being whichever issue is in question) as much as *we* do. They make it easier to do activism, but they also make it easier to do activism badly.

Another change in activism is that the form of campaigning I had long done – professional funded charities and non-governmental organisations – is in crisis. Many of the big and well-known single-issue campaign groups grew into their current form during the 1990s and 2000s, when Clinton and then Blair were in power. These non-governmental organisations, or NGOs, were the children of the 'new social movements' of the 1960s, which themselves had turned campaigning away from the parliamentary arena and explicit class struggle, towards human rights, the environment and peace.[21] The NGOs were being well funded in a broader context of privatisation of aid and the use of charities for social provision previously undertaken by the state.[22] Under broadly centrist governments it seemed possible for these professional campaigning organisations to bring some change through incremental technocratic policy interventions. It seemed possible that such policy interventions could be achieved through close alliances with bureaucrats 'inside' the system who wanted the same changes that we did, and who needed us to make a noise 'outside' to help them make the case to their masters. We would choose our target carefully, provide the facts and make the uncomfortable noise outside the walls, and under the rational-actor model, those in power might weigh things up and respond in our favour. We were Fukuyama's children, to borrow my colleague Jonathan Rowson's phrase. This was a form of activism for a particular form of politics – liberal, centrist – and it bought into the political economist Francis Fukuyama's ever so nineties idea of the 'end of history'.[23] Capitalism had won the Cold War and now we were just improving things without attempting deep changes. New Labour in the UK helped lift people out of poverty at one end of the inequality spectrum without tackling the real motor for inequality at the other: the growth of extreme wealth by an uncontrolled financialised economic system. And the NGOs that treated with New Labour were doing their own version of the same thing: taking its money to help out in particular places and get selected rules changed, but without challenging the foundations of the system.

In this pre-2008 crash model, NGOs saw themselves as bridging the gap between power and people: those whose situation needed improving. But the bridges creaked, stretched and broke when power moved to the right from 2010, and those at the grassroots – and some in the Labour Party – responded by becoming more radical.[24] The big NGOs mostly stayed closer to power and carried on working on technocratic and incremental policy change, on the other side of a widening gulf from the ferment of grassroots activism that is now bubbling amid the increasing anti-government radicalisation revealed by the Brexit vote and fuelled by a decade of austerity.[25] The NGOs have been slow to respond: the apocryphal frog in the slowly heating water that doesn't see what is happening in time to jump. Now that the extent of their strategic difficulties is clear, they face a path-dependency problem. They are set up and funded to achieve single-issue incremental policy change, in a world where it is now more evident, to more people, that much more is needed.

People who work for NGOs may acknowledge, privately, that the model is not working so well, though publicly they are still committed and they are still putting their energy into it. I have heard about people still working for NGOs because that is their source of income, while campaigning with grassroots groups in their remaining free time because, they feel, that is more effective. More fundamentally, however, the rise of authoritarian regimes, the normalisation of far-right views on immigration and extreme neoliberal views on the role of the state, as well as the ongoing failure of current political systems to respond to the evident need to cut carbon emissions, are undermining the impact of single-issue, elite-access campaigning NGOs. It's not only because, as Audre Lorde put it, 'there is no such thing as a single-issue struggle because we don't lead single-issue lives',[26] but also because it is becoming clearer that we need an altered political system that can produce a different kind of government, not merely a more successful way of asking or pressuring whoever happens to be in government to do what we want.

With NGO purpose in crisis, then, and with new forms of activism emerging as the world experiences more political, social and ecological crises, there are many activists thinking and talking about *how* we do activism. And there are many initiatives within activist movements and organisations that are focusing on how activism is done, as well as on *what* actual changes are needed. Scholars call such efforts 'prefiguration', because they are trying to prefigure – to create, within their own efforts, the reality they are trying to achieve as a result of those efforts. Some of these efforts have been around in activism for decades, such as non-hierarchical organising and consensus decision-making.[27] Others, such as training on power and privilege, have flowered within the last decade, partly as a result of anti-racist and intersectional activism within activism. There are funders, such as the Guerrilla Foundation and the Chorus Foundation, and networks such as the EDGE Funders Alliance, that have come into existence to support new forms of activism, explicitly acknowledging that the goal is, as the Guerrilla Foundation puts it, 'dismantling the industrial-charitable complex along with the rest of the old paradigm – to create a world where there is no need for Foundations to exist in the first place'.[28] Such 'progressive' funders have been influenced, says Romy Kraemer of the Guerrilla Foundation, by 'realising that the traditional NGO campaigns are winning campaigns but losing the planet'.

It is hard, though, to find ways of doing activism that take into account all of the ways in which we are entangled in and affected by the problems we are trying to solve. Different groups and movements attempt to extricate themselves from particular entanglements, while remaining in the grip of others. The Occupy movement in 2011 was strong on consensus processes and participatory democracy, but researchers have documented multiple accounts of gendered and racist power relations being reproduced in the camps, with white, male voices heard most loudly, dismissals of feminist viewpoints, racist harassment and, at Occupy Glasgow, a rape.[29] Extinction Rebellion, which has emerged while I have been writing this book and on which I have had a participant's view, has been explicit about some aspects of what it calls 'regenerative culture', which is its way of describing prefiguration, or that *how* they are doing what they do matters as much as *what* they are doing. It has set a clear intention – not always followed through in practice – about the need for rest in order to avoid burnout, and the need to avoid blame that can be a cover for our own projections. And by encouraging grief and the use of emotion, it has successfully recruited many people who could no longer – or who had never been able to – take part in activism about our ecological crisis on the basis of appeals to facts alone. But it has failed to take account of the embeddedness of its majority white founders and participants in a culture that systematically marginalises people of colour. While it has been trying hard to reconstitute itself to include wider perspectives, a tone was set early, and a clear perception is in place, for many people, that this is a movement caught up in privilege. This isn't only about who gets to participate, but about Extinction Rebellion's chances of success while remaining unembedded in the communities where it is causing disruption, such as the east London station where angry commuters dragged a protester from the roof of a train in October 2019.[30]

Activism can be a crucible for learning how we all hold, within ourselves, the sickness of the structural systems we are trying to change. When these unhealthy patterns get in the way of our activism, it shines a light on the real nature of the problems that we're trying to heal. Activism can offer opportunities to perceive the extent of the connection between our inner worlds and the social, political and economic world that we share; for realising that shifts in our inner worlds would make a difference to the state of the outer world. This understanding is needed, of course, beyond activism. It is needed in politics, in business, in academia, in healthcare, in education, in technology. It is needed everywhere. In some ways, activists are in a better position than others to realise this necessity. Because we are deliberately trying to improve things, we are likely, sooner or later, to run into the limitations of trying to change the system on its own terms. When we hit this wall, we may come to realise – if we didn't know it already – that the task runs deeper; that it engages our inner worlds, our deep psychology and, as some see it, our spiritual commitments.

Yet progressive activists also want to identify with being 'good'. Our goals are equality, justice and peace, and so, focused on these worthy values, we have an added incentive to push the 'shadow' in ourselves out of sight. We have an incentive to disavow the parts of ourselves that are the opposite: dominant, unjust and violent. We may be defended against acknowledging that the potential for violence, verbal as well as physical, is in all of us, and is much more dangerous if we don't acknowledge it. So we are in a position to see that inner work is necessary for a more peaceful world, yet, identified with the 'good', we may be more invested in not seeing the full implications: that we need to do this work too. We might even want to turn away from it. This contradiction can run at a high temperature in activists. It helps to create the stridency, the righteousness, the lack of nuance … especially when added to our genuine passion for the issue, and the high pressure of the other emotional material that we may be using as additional fuel for our work.

Being invested in avoiding our own shadow is not the only thing that prevents activists appreciating the necessity of inner work to our work in the 'outer' world. Like everyone else, activists are subject to our culture's polarising distinction between inner and outer. We resist seeing the external world and the contents of our internal experience as facets of the same reality, as many Eastern traditions and indigenous cosmologies have long understood, and as a systems theory view of life can describe in Western terminology (by seeing mind and matter not as two separate categories but as 'two complementary aspects of the phenomenon of life – process and structure'[31]) because we are usually taught, implicitly as well as explicitly, that they are not. That said, there are activists who are conscious of the need to pay more attention to their inner worlds. There are guides to 'the inner', whether they are therapists, religious leaders or teachers of practices like yoga or meditation, who can help to develop a spiritual sensibility or mindfulness, and who are conscious of the link between their work and the world of politics and social change. One activist I spoke to while writing this book put it as follows: 'we need to get more people off their yoga mats and into lock-ons, and more people out of lock-ons and onto yoga mats.' (A lock-on is a technique or technology used by protesters to make it harder for the police to move them, ranging from a firm hand grip with the next person, to specially designed hardware.) Retreat to the 'inner' can be a way of avoiding the politics of the 'outer' world as well as a way of reproducing them, too, as the critics of whiteness in yoga culture point out.[32] Too often, attempts to bridge the divide can end up with one side being framed as the antidote to the other. Nor does it augment the appeal of 'inner' work to activists that the idea of a more conscious, inner-focused approach to life is rapidly being co-opted and turned into superficial imagery by commercial brands in their marketing and advertising.

Activist movements that do not emerge in the Eurocentric imaginary can get less stuck in this split: Paolo Freire, the Brazilian educator and philosopher, insisted on the need for both reflection and action, for attention to both subjective experience and the objective world.[33] But our mental structures make it hard to see 'inner work' not simply as a tool to improve our own interpersonal health but to do so as an inextricable part of the health of the system we are trying to change. The theory and practice of non-violent communication, for example, was developed by Marshall Rosenberg as an interpersonal social technology that could be a route to social change, but, co-opted by an individualist culture, it has become more usually seen as a tool for personal development.[34] The Transition movement's 'inner transition' component holds the potential to transform the entire task of developing community resilience to climate change, but it is often relegated – if it is practised at all – to a way of supporting exhausted and fractious activists. Transformative possibilities become downgraded to the tool of personal transformation only, because we put them in a category of 'personal' or 'inner' that separates them from the possibility of change in the outside world. Because of the way we have been taught to separate inner and outer, we don't see that methods of 'inner' attention for activism are not only a tool to protect activists from burnout and to transform conflicts within activism, but could be a tool for the transformation of wider problems. Burnout and conflicts within activism are a feedback mechanism for the system as a whole.[35]

Another reason that activists are reluctant to consider the shadows of our own activism is that it sounds like adopting the classic conservative criticism of progressive campaigning. They call us righteous, hypocritical, angry, bullying, totalitarian, because they want to distract attention from how *they* benefit from the status quo. When our opponents are implicitly questioning the ways in which we might be speaking from our own inner stories, and they are doing so to discredit and downplay our structural critiques of the system, it can feel like a political failure to look at the same material. Aren't we colluding in their attempts to draw our activist attention away from their workings of power? And aren't we giving them ammunition to use against us? It is true that we cannot reduce to personal psychology everything that is going on as activists speak and as those who hear us react. But maintaining a purely political, or purely material account of what is going on strengthens the status quo too. To be resistant to looking at our inner lives because we must urgently focus on the workings of power is to reinforce *once again* the dominant culture's insistence on separating them. We can explore ways to consider our inner lives *together with* thinking about power. This book proceeds on the basis of recognising that the abuse of power we fight against has also impacted our inner lives, and that transformations in our inner lives therefore hold the potential to transform the workings of power. It is a means of resisting oppressive power, not a subjugation to power, to look at how it runs within us, how it makes us its agent.

Also, just because this criticism of activism is being voiced by our opponents – just because, to misquote Mandy Rice-Davies, 'they would say that, wouldn't they' – does it mean that their observation has no truth in it? That activists are never righteous, hypocritical or controlling? The accusation that 'inside every progressive is a totalitarian trying to get out' is an animating one for some conservatives. As an accusation that progressives lust for coercive power, it speaks to conservatives' avowed valuing of freedom and desire to guard against potential state oppression. According to the terms of the psychologist Jonathan Haidt's 'moral foundations' theory, the left makes its moral judgements primarily on the narrow foundations of 'care/ avoiding harm' and 'fairness/avoiding cheating', while the right is more likely to base its moral judgements on a wider range of foundations that include freedom/oppression, authority/subversion, sanctity/degradation and loyalty/betrayal, as well as care and fairness. Haidt's argument, based on his observations of US politics, is that conservatives are more effective at the polls because they are appealing to a wider range of moral 'taste receptors' in the electorate.[36] His theory is helpful, too, in casting light on the things that progressives do not always want to think about. That we are animated by care and fairness does not mean we don't have other instincts. The desire to help and protect others is genuine, but it does not rule out the will to power.

Progressive activists often have a messy relationship with power and are as likely to disavow it as try to seize it. The very idea of power can look dirty when the only form of it you have ever known is the dominator form of power normalised and practised by an oppressive and violent culture. With so few good models, it can be hard to remember that there is also power-with, and power-to: power that looks like agency and empowering and supporting others. The not-uncommon disavowal of all forms of power, because of a fear of the unhealthy form that has framed our understanding of the world, poses a practical problem for progressive activists. We don't always push as hard as the other side to get *into* power; for the opportunities to bring our visions to fruition. But the disavowal poses an additional and different set of risks if our own will to coercive power – 'the fascism in us all'[37] – is kept in shadow, from where it can erupt, unbidden. It is healthier to own it, to acknowledge the different possible sides of power and that the coercive version can run in all of us, especially when we are fearful and stressed by urgency and our nervous systems are aroused. That way, when we are under pressure – or have even managed to get ourselves into power – we can be more certain that we will be exercising the kind of power we want to exercise.

This enquiry is timely, then, but do we have time to do it? To keep the rise in global temperatures below 1.5 degrees, carbon dioxide emissions must be reduced by 45 per cent by 2030, and should have been dropping by 2020, the IPCC conservatively estimated in 2018.[38] But the massive necessary global and national action to transform transport, food systems and infrastructure is not yet happening, which is why so many of us have been taking to the streets. What, then, is the point of looking at *how* we do activism, when carbon deadlines are so pressing, when ecological collapse is already occurring, when politics is already convulsed? When democracy everywhere is under threat from authoritarianism and the negative impacts of the online revolution? The urgency is undeniable and almost unbearable to quantify, but it's what we do with it that matters. The activist's instinctive response, faced with an urgent problem, is to move into action-panic mode and campaign more furiously than ever. But whatever the urgency of the situation, the heightened place of nervous system arousal that comes with urgency and panic is not an effective place to begin. It doesn't encourage clear thinking. It is not sustainable, leading to quick burnout. It creates a stridency that makes us hard to listen to and closes doors for dialogue. And it perpetuates the collective trauma that may already be running through us, conditioning us towards reactivity rather than response. If activism in calmer times already risked recreating aspects of the existing system, then urgent activism at a time of more pervasive fear, anger and awareness of breakdown, risks spreading the fearful states that are linked with attraction to authoritarianism.[39] There are good strategic reasons, therefore, to reconsider how we respond to an urgent situation. But it goes beyond strategy.

We are making assumptions when we ask questions about whether there is 'enough time' to look at anything beyond the urgent tasks in front of us. We are assuming that *we* have enough information to know what the most urgent task actually is. We are assuming, too, that there will ever be a clear point where we can say that we have done what we can to prevent runaway climate change and societal collapse, done what we can to create resilient and sane economies, and so *now* we can turn our attention to these other matters of human development. These assumptions do not stand. The tasks we face are never going to be 'done' per se. There are people living with war, drought, flood and fire who are already experiencing collapse. However much more of the already-underway ecological collapse it is possible to prevent, the task of mitigation, adaptation and survival will remain. We will still have to create liveable communities. Migrants and refugees will still need support, and there will be many more, as well as more contentious border politics. The task of sharing available resources more fairly will still be there and will be ever more fraught when food supplies are threatened by the weather in countries where they have previously been stable. The task of finding healthy ways to relate to each other amid increasingly polarising, fearful and violent political cultures will remain. The need for activism is not going to go away. Activism is the task, in each moment, of making things better than they are. If we can acknowledge that we are never going to reach a point where we are 'free' to attend to questions of how we do activism, then we can see that we are already free to have a go at doing it differently now.

3 Some of my own entanglements

I F WE are all entangled in what we are trying to change, then I am, too. I grew up in the eighties and early nineties in Metroland, the outer suburbs of northwest London, where mile upon mile of 1930s sprawl is cut through by the Metropolitan line tube trains that rattle overground from Baker Street out to the chalk and beech woods of the Chilterns. My parents were socially liberal and relatively cosmopolitan. There was conversation about what was in the news and some of what was going on in the world. My mother was in London several evenings a week singing in a big choir, and they had lots of gay friends. They also voted Conservative and thought Thatcher was just what the country needed, and that the striking miners were on the wrong side; my earliest political memory is of them tutting at Arthur Scargill on the news. I formed myself partly in reaction to their politics and in the late nineties removed myself to a different bubble in north London, surrounded by friends from university who worked in public services, government, journalism, campaign groups or international development and humanitarian aid. I had applied for newspaper trainee schemes and obtained a place at *The Times* which led, two years later, to a staff reporter post. I wasn't fond of the paper's politics nor of its owner, Rupert Murdoch, but it was an extraordinary opportunity. I wanted to change the world, I thought, by being a foreign correspondent and reporting on major stories, and here was an opportunity to begin. But I barely had time to get started on that self-important goal before I burnt out in my mid-twenties with an intense and chronic fatigue that took more than a year to recover from. I was unable to work, and the enforced reflection time led me to follow my emerging values more closely. I worked as a campaigner and researcher at various NGOs for 15 years, and in the middle of that time I lived in Sierra Leone for six months, volunteering for a charity that was supporting children in the aftermath of the civil war.

Two of my key entanglements are already visible in this brief summary. (Others will emerge later.) One is having experienced burnout. It happens a lot among campaigners but the wider culture sets us up for it too. It was incomprehensible while it was happening: a flu-like bug that just didn't lift. I couldn't work. There were many days when I couldn't get out of bed. It took several years after I recovered, and a course of therapy, to understand the personal dynamics in play: how I had been raised and educated to perform and achieve for the sake of performance and achievement. I had no idea how to stop when I was tired. I was incapable of just 'being' without discomfort that I should be 'doing' something. I didn't know how to heed rather than ignore and discredit the voice from within that speaks our real desires. It would take many more years, and witnessing my friends repeatedly burning out as campaigners, to see that I had been participating in a cultural pattern, too; of valuing constant activity, work and achievement. Burnout happens to the people working for the companies that cause ecological destruction, as well as to the people trying to persuade the companies to change their behaviour. The people working to undermine capitalism find themselves working like ... well, like people living under capitalism. My previous experience of burnout meant that I could avoid a repeat of the worst outcome. Campaigning never caused me to become so ill that I couldn't work at all, because I had learned the warning signs as a journalist, and stepped back from the edge in time. I would slow down a bit, take a break, or leave the job I was doing that had become a crushing weight of impossible demands from impossible people. (I had to do this more than once, though I realise now that I would repeatedly take on such jobs.) But several times I came very close to burnout. The underlying pattern, in which I pushed myself in relentless work, had not really changed.

My other entanglement visible here is a materially comfortable, white middle-class life. I want to change economic and political systems that I also benefit from. Imperialist and then globalised economies of extraction have contributed to my material comfort. Whiteness and class privilege have laid down a path relatively free of external obstacles to my progress, and being straight, cis and able-bodied has further smoothed that path. So my background and experiences affect how I do activism, as well as the questions I ask about activism. As mentioned in the introduction, there is turning to activism by challenging and criticising one's community, societal norms and expectations in order to change them (which is what I did when I left journalism to campaign); and there is being radicalised into activism by living a life directly on the receiving end of race, class, gender, sexuality or other oppressions. As intersectional theory shows, people often suffer from a combination of different forms of oppression, and specific problems occur at the points where these oppressions intersect,[40] so there is not always a simple binary between groups of activists who are 'oppressed' and activists who are 'not oppressed'. Similar dynamics tend to recur when people who lack lived experience of an issue seek to help those whose lives are inherently shaped by it. And one of these dynamics, as Chapter 5 will unpack, is that the people who are trying to help instead end up centring themselves in the struggles they're fighting. So this book could look like yet another centring of a privileged viewpoint.

Haven't we had enough of those? But I am not speaking from my own viewpoint because I have failed to realise that there is a world beyond me. My intention is not to centre myself for the sake of it or because I assume it's the natural thing to do. I have thought deeply about the evident tension that runs through my use of my own story in order, ultimately, to de-centre myself. I am writing about my own position as a form of taking responsibility, and because telling our own stories can sometimes have the profoundest effect. The entanglements that come with a viewpoint like mine speak precisely to a key problem that this book addresses, namely, the limitations of trying to change the world from a position of entangled privilege. When I first embarked on my enquiry into the 'inner life' of activism, I wasn't anticipating that this question of my own starting point would run through so many of the other questions I was exploring. Sure, I had some concerns about the naming-and-shaming, policy-fixing activism I had been doing, and I was curious to explore if others perhaps shared them too. But the more I heard from people who were drawn to activism for reasons different to mine, the clearer it became that I couldn't just speak about 'activism' as if it were something that existed independently of my own – or indeed, anyone else's – particular experience of it. I would have to become aware of my own starting point and observe how it is entangled in relation with others' starting points. Yet precisely because whiteness had shielded me from probing into the implications and complicity of my own position, I wasn't accustomed to doing so. I felt shame in realising this, but shame was also the seed that would develop into a sense of responsibility.

Here is what my starting point looked like, once I looked at it really and truly. There are things I share with the majority of those in power. When I say 'in power' I do not only mean the power of government, political decision-making and the judiciary. The real power in the UK is now financialised capital and its owners, who control politics through their donations and the media through direct ownership, and whose true ownership of land, assets and companies is still hidden in tax haven secrecy.[41] What I share with any of these people, or their quotidian enforcers in government departments or senior editorial positions, is not an upper-class form of entitlement, that sense of being born to rule. But I was educated and raised with an unquestioned assumption that if I worked hard there was no reason I couldn't aspire towards ruling. My grandmother left school at 14 to work in a shop; Mum, with her enormous capabilities, left school at 16 to train as a secretary. Dad had a degree, worked in marketing for a publisher and then set up his own management consultancy. I was sent to a private school. I used to prefer to say 'on a scholarship', which wasn't untrue, but it obscured the further truth that my parents would probably have paid the fees if I hadn't won that award. The ambient feeling both at school and at home was that I had choices. This wasn't politically explicit; there was no discussion of the gains of 1970s feminism that had put such a gap between my mother's experiences and my own, let alone of the possibility that any of my beckoning opportunities had anything to do with class and race privilege rather than random luck and my parents' striving. (Nor was there any talk about any aspect of ongoing patriarchy. I knew that Mum had been repeatedly propositioned and groped at work in the sixties, and when I started work in the late nineties I quickly learned which male journalists were NSIT: Not Safe in Taxis. I learned which senior editor liked to play power games with me that I didn't observe him engaging in with any young male reporters, and that made me uncomfortable in ways that I couldn't begin at the time to articulate. In my largely unpolitical family and the largely unfeminist nineties, this wasn't patriarchy, though, it was just how some men are.)

So I share, with many of those who rule, my whiteness, a Cambridge degree and the friends in influential jobs that came with it, and the ability to turn up the volume on my RP accent and pass as one of them, all of which are forms of access to power. That traineeship I did at *The Times* is the same one that Boris Johnson got sacked from a decade earlier for making up a quote. A clever up-and-coming journalist called Michael Gove sat on the news desk, near my lowly hot-desk in the reporters' pool. The current editor of the right-wing magazine the *Spectator*, Fraser Nelson, was another ambitious junior reporter. If I had chosen to stay on that path, who knows, perhaps I might have been in some form of power, not needling at it from NGOs on the 'outside'. (I am putting 'outside' in quote marks because from many perspectives, an NGO *is* part of the elite.) I chose not to stay on that path. I chose not to try to find a similar job when I recovered from the chronic fatigue I developed while doing it. I didn't want to administrate the existing systems of power because I thought there was something wrong with them. But I always felt the equal of those who did. Let's leave aside, for now, the way that sentence betrays my adoption of a status-driven frame that says such achievements are necessary for 'equality' with those in power, when really we are all equal in human worth whatever job we do. Nonetheless, that feeling of equal status felt helpful, as a campaigner, in obtaining access to the rooms where those in power gather; to senior journalists; to the offices of senior people in banks and multinationals.

I had some access to power, then: both practically, in the form of contacts or the ability to track them down, and in my mind, in the sense of feeling entitled to be in communication with them. As described in Chapter 1, my initial response to realising the limitations of my activism was despair and overwhelm. Once I began looking deeper, I felt that inner surge of energy that comes when, with my activist's nose, I feel I might be sniffing out a story: something that needs attention. I would say to former colleagues, 'Hey everyone, there's something wrong with our activism! We're trying to change rules and policies while replicating the methods that created them, and without looking at the attitudes and perceptions that created them: surely we need to look deeper, including at our inner lives?' When I began to interview other activists, however, I noticed something. The campaigners I spoke to who were white were saying, 'Yes! You're really onto something here, I've been feeling that too.' And the campaigners of colour were saying things like, 'You're not wrong. The policy change we need doesn't work on its own … but come on, this isn't new: *of course* there is something wrong with the way an oppressor culture frames things. You're catching up, not realising something that is *new*.'

My implicit sense of what I had shared with those in power, that gave me access to some of the people in power even though I disagreed with their worldview, had obscured the ways in which I saw the world in the same ways as them. I was too embedded in the dominant culture to see what those on the outside of hegemonic systems have been able to see more clearly. I was entangled in power, and was now starting to see that being closer to power affects how we think it can be changed. Whiteness is one form of privilege, and there are others that I have benefited from, particularly class. This might be a different book if I were working class, or if my experience of activism were in trade unions or party politics rather than middle-class NGOs (and there will be parallels and differences between the forms that activist entanglement takes in these environments). But it was by starting to wake up to whiteness, in particular, that I started to perceive my entanglement in power. The latest reckoning with privilege is well underway, in #MeToo, and in a new generation of anti-racist activism. Yet not enough of the reckoning, which is so very overdue, is yet being done by those who have benefited from privilege. The work should not have to be done by those who have borne the burden so others could live in unwitting comfort. By sharing my experience of coming to see how my own entanglements have affected my activism, I hope that among the activists I touch will be people who have approached activism from similar positions to my own.

This matters because more people are now turning to activism, including people who have benefited most from intersecting forms of privilege like being white and middle class. People I've known for 25 years who have never done activism of any kind are now getting involved. They are motivated to act out of horror at the numbers of people who have been made homeless and who are dying on the streets of Britain. They are becoming activists because they see children lying on hospital floors as a decade of austerity continues to shred the social fabric, and as life is turned upside down by the Covid-19 pandemic. But from what I have observed, they are also doing so out of fear for themselves and their families: as generational inequality turns notions of generational progress on its head; as neoliberal capitalism starts to eat away at long-assumed middle-class comfort;[42] as the drawbridges of Brexit limit their children's futures; as mendacious authoritarianism takes hold; as ecological breakdown and climate change threaten everything. They are turning to activism as activists fighting for their lives, even while they maintain many of the assumptions of activists who are trying to help threatened others. One of these assumptions, for example, is that 'fighting for our lives' is anything new. An American climate activist, Mary Annaïse Heglar, expressed her frustration at white environmentalists describing climate breakdown as the first 'existential' threat, in a blog post headed with a photograph of two lynched Black men hanging from a tree with a crowd of laughing white people below. For Black people in America, she was having to point out, an existential threat to life has always been present.[43] Unexamined assumptions that come with whiteness have been endemic in the environmental movement, and are just one deep entanglement in existing structures of power.

4 Entangled with everyone else

THREE OF us are on the street outside a supermarket on a Saturday morning, handing out leaflets about an environmental campaign. The long, dark days of winter have recently transformed into cold but bright early spring, and a few people stop to take a leaflet. But the majority of those approaching drop their heads when they spot us; try to walk past without contact. There's no reason to assume they're opposed to what we're leafleting about, since they don't even know what it is. We're not festooned with logos, nor are we stationed behind a table strung with a banner. It's possible that they are just being British: averse to a conversation with strangers so early in the day. We greet them brightly and try to catch their eyes. Maybe they think we are Jehovah's Witnesses. A few more stop to talk and realise it isn't so bad once they do, but many others shake their heads and keep going. This is a reasonable success rate for such an activity, but one of the other leafleters audibly launches into sarcastic comments to the departing backs. 'Off you go then. You weren't ever going to stop, were you?' she says. While I remain silent, in my head I'm tempted to do the same thing. I'm trying not to form ideas about who will respond, or about those who walk on, trying not to acknowledge us. I'm trying not to feel superior.

Activists are prone to overestimating how different we are from everyone else. We often see ourselves as apart from the people we are trying to change or influence, as well as from those who are not obviously trying to change the world. We are right, and the other people are wrong. At best, they are 'asleep' or they do not 'get it'. I spent years thinking my job was to 'get the bastards' who were responsible for the environmental and human rights crimes that we were investigating. They were the bastards, and they were in the wrong. We, of course, were right. Or my task was to 'wake people up'; I was conscious, and they were not. The same sort of feeling of superiority, of apartness, has been present – more or less aggressively voiced, more or less explicitly acknowledged – in every form of activism I have been involved in, over 25 years.

What I now see, however, is that activists are not as separate from everyone else as we like to think. We are entangled with the people we are trying to change or influence, to the point where the interactions that take place may be helping to cement each 'side' in our identity of 'activist' and 'not-activist', which ends up making us less effective, less likely to be heard. I am using the distinction between an 'activist' and a 'not-activist' as a tool to investigate the reactivities around activism – the reactions that people have to activists, as well as the reactions that activists have to other people – rather than as a statement of how things actually *are*. There may be more variation within the categories of both 'activist' and 'not-activist' than between them. And surely, there is no such thing in reality as a 'not-activist'?[44]

Or is there? Somebody might not consciously think of themselves as 'not an activist', yet that is effectively what is happening when they look at activism and – for whatever reasons – think, 'that's not for me'. And activists might not explicitly describe the people they are reacting to as 'not-activists', but they are seeing them as something 'else'. It is a 'something else-ness' that encompasses the observation that those people are *not doing activism*. When we are speaking as activists, the not-activist is anyone who is disagreeing with us, anyone we are trying to persuade. It is the other side, whether we are in a confrontation or not. It is the official whom we are meeting to advocate for a change to the law. It is the sceptical journalist whom we are trying to convince to run our story. It is the bystanders looking irritated, perplexed or blank as we march or stand in the street. It was my Dad when I was arguing with him about the Iraq war or endless economic growth or whatever was in the news. It was the friend who worked in the City and was defending the current economic system, and it was the hot but annoying guy holding court in the kitchen at a party, who was winding me up over my earnestness about my work. In the moment when we are speaking, acting or thinking as an activist, it is anyone who is not doing the same as us. So I think that people implicitly recognise a distinction between activist and 'not-activist' even if they don't use those words, and I would like to meet them there. My using the distinction as a tool, then, is not to suggest a realist map of the world in which activists and not-activists can be simply identified. But it is a response to what I have heard and observed, and a way of temporarily teasing apart the deep entanglement of activists with everyone else in order to investigate what is going on as they react to each other.

When I started asking people I know who are not activists how they feel about activism and how they feel when they encounter activists, I found myself collecting a list of allergic reactions. Their list of complaints about activism sounded like a typology of inflammation, with a number of common symptoms. Activism is an identity that I don't share, they said. It looks like a performance. It's emotional and irrational, often angry. It's hypocritical. It's smug and it's hiding in a cloak of moral righteousness. It sounds shrill. It's telling me what to do. Crucially, these encounters make people feel bad. They feel guilty at not acting. They feel unfairly demonised. They feel they are being made responsible for the problem when actually they are trying to do their best too, whether at work or in their own lives. They feel that they are not good enough. They resist being told what to do.

Images of protesters in the streets provoke a negative reaction in the majority of people, concluded a study commissioned by climate campaigners seeking guidance on the most effective images to use in their activism. In focus groups and an online survey in the UK, the US and Germany, and regardless of participants' levels of climate scepticism, such images attracted 'widespread cynicism' and 'only really resonated with the small number of people who already considered themselves as activists and campaigners', the study found.[45] Negative reactions to activism come with stereotypical views of activists, and the stereotypes have an effect: they make people not want to join in, and not want to share the activists' views. A study by Nadia Bashir and her social psychology colleagues at the University of Toronto investigated the effect of negative stereotypes of activists. Drawing on research showing that people desire membership only of groups they view positively, and are less inclined to adopt the opinions of stigmatised groups, they found that participants had negative stereotypes of environmentalists and feminists which reduced their willingness to affiliate with 'typical' activists and, ultimately, to adopt the behaviours that these activists promoted.[46] Being what people perceive as a typical activist, the study suggests, can make people not want to be activists.

Activists could reasonably feel cynical about a list of allergic reactions to activism. Provoking discomfort, guilt and the knowledge that the activist is doing something and maybe they should too, might be a ripe moment – ripe enough for a person to make a decision to match their values with a greater action, to do something differently. Whether the target is recruitment to activism, shifting public opinion or prompting behaviour change, then the whole point, activists might say, is to make people feel uncomfortable. ('It annoys me to see people comfortable when they ought to be uncomfortable,' was George Bernard Shaw's justification to critics of his 'preaching'.)[47] I turned to the scholarly study of activism and that seemed to point in the same direction. These allergies to activism that I collected seemed to converge on issues around identity, performance and emotions. For those who study activism, these are all central to activism being what it is. In the fields of both sociology and political psychology, these three themes are key to understandings of what activism is, how it happens and how it works.

An identity is central to the creation and maintenance of activist movements. People's individual identities need to include some sense of the political in order for them to be personally engaged when those political issues arise in the world outside them.[48] Then individual identities have to join and become collective for there to be a movement at all: for you to see yourself as an environmentalist, and for there to be an environmental movement, for example. There are different views on how this process works. In the outdated view of American sociologists' 'resource mobilisation theory', which relied on a rational-actor model of human behaviour,[49] mobilisation happens when people with pre-existing values (like environmentalism, for example) join together to take action. European scholarship of social movements emerging from neo-Marxist critical theory sees activist identity as dynamic and socially constructed. An individual changes and redefines themselves in interaction with others as they struggle together, so that a movement develops an identity as it goes along, as an emergent process.[50] Critical race theory and feminist theory argue that the ideology of those in power can hide people's real interests from themselves, and that developing an identity – as a feminist, for example – through sharing personal stories and experiences is essential to escaping oppressive ideologies.[51] With both of these last two sets of theories, belief systems are a means of control by the elites in charge, and while people may not have control over other organs of the state, they can take charge of generating new ideologies and redefining their own identities. It is this work of identity generation that happens in activist movements. Once a movement identity is in place, however, it is not only motivational but also gets defended in 'boundary work':[52] the forging of internal cohesion against external opponents, against factions with differing views within the movement, and against its own members who appear to transgress.[53]

The 'performance' was another aspect of activism that seemed to be riling or discomfiting observers. From the view of those who study how activism works, however, it is essential. It is to ensure that they are seen. Making resistance visible is often what makes it resistance at all. This is true of direct resistance against existing problems – the great protesting 'No' that *is* activism, to so many people observing it – and the kind of 'lifestyle activism' in which alternative styles of living and consuming are modelled in a rejection of current norms and an attempt to prefigure something better.[54] Social movements are 'a form of acting in public', narrating, dramatising and framing opposition within a storyline, said the sociologist Ron Eyerman.[55] They are themselves a form of 'new media', who through what they do, as well as how they do it, announce to society that something else is possible, said Alberto Melucci.[56]

Emotions, meanwhile, help to create activists. Linguistically, emotion and movement have the same etymological root. Practically, emotions help to create our own actions by directing our attention and are guiding our behaviour. In campaigning terms, movement organisers put great effort into converting fears and angers into action: 'tapping into the wellspring of emotion', as the veteran trainer George Lakey puts it,[57] although non-violent direct action also encourages putting on a calm face in moments of confrontation. Dismissing emotions because they are irrational is, of course, still commonplace in a culture founded on the primacy of reason. It is done by those who are reacting to activism, and it has been done in the past by those who have studied activism. Sociological study of social movements did this until the last three decades of the 20th century, focusing on collective-behaviour approaches that emphasised the irrationality of crowds. Partly in reaction, the following three decades saw studies of the factors that prompted people to mobilise into social movements in terms that emphasised deliberation and rational decision-making.[58] Since the turn of the century there has been increasing study of the emotions of activism: the emotions that provoke or deter it, that sustain it, that undermine it, that cause it to burn out, and that can be suppressed in a hierarchy of emotions within activist movements.[59]

In turning to the academic literature about activism, I wasn't trying to analyse or rank the many theories about how activism arises and how it works. I saw things I recognised in many of them. But it was interesting to note that almost all study of activism ends up looking at these three aspects that were at the heart of the negative reactions among the people I spoke to who were experiencing activism negatively. Identity, performance, emotion: this is what activism *is*, the literature is suggesting – activism as something that is performed, that has a particular, albeit perhaps unattractive, identity, that contains emotion. Allergies to activism on this basis may therefore be inevitable. We could say that people are reacting to activism simply because they are bound to do so, and indeed, perhaps because they are supposed to do so. But also contained in that list of allergic reactions I was collecting was a set of clues that something else may be going on. People were talking about the righteousness, the hypocrisy and the moral certainty of activists. But they were also talking about how activists made them feel, as someone who is not doing activism. They mentioned their own feelings of guilt, insecurity and resistance to what activists are saying. And there was much less on these topics in the social movement literature that I was reading, focused as it is on what activists *themselves* are doing to generate and maintain the phenomenon of activism.

Regardless of who is experiencing them, guilt, insecurity and resistance are all phenomena that occur when unconscious emotional material is in play. It was this observation that led me to turn from my pile of papers on social movements to the study of depth psychology. This is an umbrella term for approaches to psychology that recognise the role of the unconscious. As a clinical practice, depth psychology includes many forms of talking therapy, each with its different name and tradition. What they have in common is the attempt to bring material that troubles us out of our unconscious mind and into the light of our conscious thought. As a theory rather than a practice, the most widely used general term is psychoanalysis, and when I use this word it is to describe a wider theory of unconscious motivation, not just the specific form of talking therapy that carries the same name.

So much of what makes our inner life 'inner' at all is that we do not have access to it with the thinking tools of rationality in which public discourse is conducted. Our unconscious is not rational and predictable. It is the part of us that makes itself known through feeling, intuition, images and dreams, as well as those moments where we experience that expansive sense of the existence of something larger than our driven, controlling ego. With stillness and attention – some might call this spiritual practice, while artists might call it creative practice – we can learn to cultivate access to it. But the unconscious makes itself known in less welcome ways, too: through emotional pain and trauma and our convoluted attempts to defend ourselves and avoid feeling them. It makes itself known in those moments of reactivity and flare when we do not realise that we are bringing emotional pain from unrelated times, places and people into the moment we are in right now. When people are experiencing negative reactions to activists, they can feel just that they 'disagree' with what the activists are saying, or that they just 'don't like' activists. I have heard both of these many times. Depth psychology suggests that there can be other reasons. And conversely, when activists are full of righteousness for our issue, we feel that we are entirely justified. Attending to our unconscious motivations brings other reasons for our righteousness into the light.

Without a deep account of how we function, we risk seeing activism through the same lens that activists habitually and often unthinkingly use in our attempts to change the world. Rational thinking is an essential part of our human capacity and we cannot hope for a just public realm without it. The way that populist and authoritarian leaders harness fear is evidence enough. William Davies, a sociologist, describes how modernity was founded on the separation of emotion from reason, making space in public and political life for expertise and discussion. His book *Nervous States: How Feeling Took Over the World* is about the recent erosion of that separation, with eruptions of 'nostalgia, resentment, anger and fear' increasingly disturbing the status quo.[60] He suggests that the origins of this eruption of feeling into public life lie not only in the obvious effects of the digital revolution in undermining trust in fact and experts, but also in the divergence between what the facts and experts say – 'the economy is growing, we're better off than ever' – and the real-life pain and economic difficulty that so many people experience under the West's regimes of growing inequality.

Faced with populism, authoritarian appeals to fear, and nationalist, exclusionary sentiment, it is more tempting than ever for progressive campaigners, who want to insulate themselves from such sentiments, to stick with the rational and argue from the facts. So we are in the habit of bringing only the parts of ourselves permitted by a shared, albeit threatened, public culture based on the terms of rationality. Using only this lens to *do* activism is one limitation. It risks missing deeper aspects of the problem we are trying to change, as I explore in later chapters. But using this lens to *think about* activism is another limitation: it risks missing important aspects of what we ourselves are bringing to our attempts to create change. It's not only the problematic people in charge or the people who are voting for authoritarian leaders who are in thrall to their unconscious motivations.

It is all of us – and perhaps the political right has always been better at implicitly acknowledging this.

'The devil has the best lines,' my friend Andrew Simms, an author and campaigner, reminded me when I was starting my research. We were having a long conversation about our campaigning experiences over a veggie fry-up in a south London cafe, dissecting the various forms of unhelpful activist behaviour that we had encountered. 'The political right has understood the contradictions of existence,' he suggested, 'that we're all a mixture of the angel and the beast, and cannot be hermetically sealed good.' He was talking about why the right is perennially more successful at the polls, but these words kept nagging at me. Simms's sense of this is that, as he described it, 'the right is more comfortable with paradox, better at just accepting it, and that liberates them, allowing them more easily to exploit the flow of a human condition which resists moral simplicity, whereas the left is more inclined to tie itself in knots because it is not comfortable with paradox and accepting human complexity.' These are big questions, and they were speaking, I realised, to my instinct that as progressive campaigners we should be looking below the surface, at our shadows (our 'beast') as well as at our high-flown ideals (our 'angel'). The human complexity that I would like us to allow for includes the shadow in ourselves, and in everyone we are talking to and about. The shadow is in us when we are becoming righteous. It is in the people we are talking to, when they are feeling resistant or guilty or uncomfortable. So by proposing that we look at the irrational material that runs below our surfaces, I am not suggesting that we stop thinking or using our rational capacities. I am suggesting, however, that we allow our thinking about activism to include the *effects* of all that cannot clearly be thought about.

That is the problem with the shadow – its very point is that we cannot see it. It contains the emotions and aspects of our personality that we disavow in ourselves and push out of sight. Jung said the shadow 'personifies everything that the subject refuses to acknowledge about himself and yet it is always thrusting itself upon him directly or indirectly'.[61] It's everything our parents, teachers and culture have told us is unacceptable: anger, desire for power, selfishness … and perhaps also our undeveloped talents and gifts.[62]

Acknowledging these hidden aspects of ourselves that we have pushed into our subconscious is painful, and we avoid doing so by projecting: by locating and judging them in others. The advice for identifying our own shadow is simple: work out what we find most irritating in others.[63] The mud-slinging of politics, particularly in adversarial structures that pit one party against another, conceals vast amounts of projection. It's easier to hurl abuse at the other side than to do the hard work of identifying your projections and acknowledging them as part of yourself. On a mass scale, projection can become a demonising of entire groups, or countries, and by turning others into 'enemy' it paves the way, ultimately, to armed conflict – the kind of deadly conflict that activists find themselves trying to prevent, or to solve, or to protect people from.[64] Yet by spending our time looking critically at others, activists have an excellent cover for our own projections. A lens of shadow and projection started to make sense of the reactions I was hearing to activism, as well as the reactivity of activists to everyone else.

What activists project

Anger and righteousness are common observations of activism from the outside; common ingredients of the activist cliché. As with the allergies to activism, which I'll discuss shortly, I've come to see them as clues about what activists are projecting onto others. Indeed, when it comes to anger, it's not even a clue – it often *is* anger that is being projected. The question is: what is the anger about? Sometimes it is anger for the issue in question. But sometimes it is anger about something in our own lives that is not connected to the issue. Righteousness, meanwhile, may offer a clue that something else is being projected; something that the activist does not want to associate themselves with.

Anger is a legitimate catalyst and fuel for campaigning. Many activists will say that anger about the issue they want to change – inequality, violence, destruction of non-human beings – forms part of their motivation. Many movements that have successfully resulted in change were fuelled by anger. It provides spark and recruitment for new movements and is a fuel for difficult tasks that cost activists energy and might make them unpopular. A classic mobilisation strategy by campaign groups across all issues is to provoke anger by providing incensing information, then asking the recipient if they are 'Outraged by this?' before suggesting that they 'Take action now'. And to question activist anger, to suggest that it is too emotional, can be a way of undermining the activist and downplaying the issue. When men tell feminists that they are too angry, or when the 'angry black woman' trope is used, it is a defence that draws on sexist and racist ideas about who has or doesn't have emotionality, rationality and self-control. Questioning the anger of people who are making complaints can be a form of guilt. 'I cannot hide my anger to spare you guilt, nor hurt feelings, nor answering anger; for to do so insults and trivialises all our efforts,' said Audre Lorde in her powerful invocation of the 'uses of anger' in fighting racism.[65]

Anger is undeniably powerful: it is useful, it has validity, it plays a key role as a protective response to trauma. Nobody should question the legitimacy of another's anger nor should they grant permission for it. My motivation in asking questions about anger is not to devalue or dismiss activists' anger. I am driven to complicate anger partly with my own behaviour in mind, as well as that of other activists I have worked with and encountered over the years. Political anger, specifically in those who have not experienced the problem personally, is interesting. So is an urgent desperation to get the problem fixed, an urgency that runs close to the need to be in control. There have been times when my rage about the targets of my activism has been incandescent, when it has been hostile and verbally violent. For many years my understanding of this was clouded. I thought that if someone wasn't as full of rage and urgency as me, they obviously didn't care enough.

But once I started looking more closely, I realised that I have met and worked with many people who are deeply motivated to change the injustices, but who do not carry – nor shed all over other people – this excess rage, this desperate urgency. I started to face the uncomfortable possibility that the reactivity I was noticing in activists, including in myself, might be driven by *more* than the issue at stake and the appropriate and legitimate anger that it generates. If it had been the conditions of my own life that I was fighting for, perhaps my anger would have made more sense. But I can't vouch that my anger was entirely for the people and other species I was advocating for, and I suspect this made my activism hard to hear. Ultimately, there is a difference when someone expresses anger at their own experience of

45

oppression, and when someone is speaking in anger while trying to support others, as I was doing. In the former case, an uncomfortable response on the part of the hearer may be rooted in guilt at their own complicity, which is one of the things that Lorde's 'Uses of Anger' essay is about. In the latter case, perhaps those on the receiving end of the anger are uncomfortable because they sense a dissonance between expression and intention.

It was when I spoke about my work from such high-temperature anger that people would ask: 'Are you ok?', which only aggravated me more. Talking about the issues I cared about even outside of my work on them, including at social events, would be enough. I came to dread being asked 'What do you do?' at parties, because my inevitably heated response felt so exhausting. No wonder that guy in the kitchen at parties, whoever he was each time, would wind me up. He knew that he could get some attention and an entertaining 'show' from me, as I inevitably exploded (thus reinforcing the stereotype of the angry activist). Even now, although I have been taking some time to think about it – and, whisper it, although I am now in my mid-forties, perhaps due for some mellowing – if I choose to allow it, my rage is still white hot. Both for issues that don't affect me personally, and those that do. Campaigning for a liveable planet is a question that brings my own children's lives into the balance, as well as the lives of so many people who are already struggling to live with the effects of ecological destruction, or who will have to do so before I or my children have to. My anger, at the accelerating loss of this gorgeous biosphere that is our human home and the outrageous unfairness to those who are already suffering and the many more who will suffer, is real. But I also know that anger burns me up, burns me out and burns too fast to be a sustainable fuel for my activism, which is why I want to be critical about it.[66]

One of my problems with anger was that I was speaking directly from it, rather than digesting it first in order to use it as a more sustainable fuel. Gail Bradbrook, one of the founders of Extinction Rebellion, spoke of 'compassionate rage', which is rage that has been neither suppressed nor thrown away. 'Anger rises up in your body as energy, then if you spit it out, you've given it away. If you can contain it, not suppress it, it's in your back. That's what I mean by compassionate rage. I'm not going to blame someone, slap them, put all my pain about my childhood on them, but I'm not going to stand for it,' she said.[67] In using those words 'pain about my childhood', Bradbrook is speaking about how the activist's motivational rage about the issue can get caught up in their personal sources of rage that have quite different, often unacknowledged targets.

This is the other risk with anger, that I was beginning to acknowledge in myself: that it is anger about something else entirely. The emotional war zones of our early family life can be carried over into our combative approach to the outside world and then compulsively, repeatedly acted out. This is a dubious campaign strategy when the dynamic that we are re-enacting is our failure to 'win'. A talented campaigner I know stepped back in exhaustion from what he was doing after realising that his whole life had been spent fighting, the first half in his family home and the second half against the companies whose wrongdoing he was trying to expose and prevent. He had at least become aware of it, but it took his exhaustion from fighting for so long to bring the awareness. When the source of the 'something else' that is fuelling our anger is old, we may not even be aware of what is going on. We might not have been able, or allowed, to get angry about the thing that happened to us, but that does not mean the anger is not there. As soon as we encounter an incontrovertible issue that we can get legitimately angry about, it is unleashed. We may be convinced that the anger is about the injustice in front of us – and some of it usually is. I know lifelong campaigners who, while fighting their political battles, may also still be warring with the authority figures of their families or their boarding-school childhoods. I now understand that I was doing the same.

Anger is a 'mask' emotion that many of us feel instead of more painful feelings such as sadness and loss. More specifically, anger is also the habitual cover for other emotions that the majority of men in our culture have been taught from childhood they cannot safely express without compromising their masculinity.[68] (Although conversely, there may be not enough anger from too many women who have been socialised to turn their anger into something else, often tears.) Not everyone is motivated by anger; it is not always going to work as a recruitment tool. Some don't want to be anywhere near it. People may be repelled by it because of early experiences in life, because they are frightened of other people's anger. One activist told me, 'It may be we need the angry voices in the system.

But I don't identify comfortably with the angry voices … for me anger isn't a safe space.' Alternatively, people may veer from activism because they are frightened of their own anger. I was told by a man in his middle years who is not an activist and has never wanted to be one, that fear of his own anger erupting may be behind his reluctance:

> It's not the anger of activists that alienates me: it's the skills of some activists in using their anger that makes me feel powerless by comparison. It's not the world I don't know how to change: it's my own fury. When I look at activists I really admire – Peter Tatchell [the gay rights campaigner] springs to mind – it's their ability to manage, marshal, use anger that impresses me, the capacity to work with it without becoming it. But I don't have those skills. When I get angry, it swamps me, it makes me speak in ways that are self-defeating, ego-driven, hypocritical. It's not a wave I can surf upon; it's a tsunami, and I'm the low-lying island. I don't think most of us are taught or take the time to learn what to do with our anger.

Taking part in activism can itself become a source of trauma and anger, through exposure to upsetting situations and information, experience of police brutality or movement infiltration, and the burnout from repeated, intense efforts that are not met in results. Those who have brought old trauma to their activism, whether consciously or not, can find it re-traumatising to take part in activism. All of this produces distress, grief and anger that needs an outlet. Grief, too, comes from the enormity of what activists feel we are taking on. It can be easier for an activist to express anger at the 'other side' than our own grief at the seeming impossibility of whatever we are trying to do to counter the suffering or death of other people and non-human species. When support is not provided to metabolise grief, as it rarely is in activist circles, or indeed in the culture at large, then activists can attack each other, in toxic movement cultures. We can turn on ourselves, in the form of mental and physical illness. And we can turn on our opponents, in the form of displaced rage. None of this anger is sustainable. It causes burnout, and risks activists' mental health.

The other problematic activist projection that I want to look at is righteousness. The word *righteousness* carries a specific meaning of defining oneself as right against someone else who is wrong. The split within ourselves is at the root of this process. Activists focus on the wrongdoing of others, perhaps the other person's lifestyle choices, or their 'immoral' job in a company or other institution that the activist wants to change. But in focusing only on the wrongdoing of the other person, activists are pushing away awareness of the part of ourselves that can behave – that is behaving, perhaps – the same way. This could be the environmental activist whose consumption, in relative global terms, is not dissimilar from that of the business leaders she blames. I have been that person, leading an urban life in the UK with plenty of international plane travel while complaining about the bastards in charge. It could be the human rights or humanitarian worker who treats his colleagues in imperious, demeaning or abusive ways. I have worked with that person – indeed with more than one of them. And I have tried, too, not to be that person. I can't guarantee I was always successful: at my least awful I still have a sharp tongue and can be horribly impatient. As activists we want to identify with the 'good' and dissociate from the 'bad', as we define them. But the problem with the shadow is its tendency to emerge in unforeseen ways, erupting out at others. The activist and author Alastair McIntosh calls it 'shadowstrike'.[69]

When focusing on the external power structures we want to change, activists deflect attention from ourselves. Activism is inevitably about engaging with power, whether by directly opposing it, or constructing something new as an alternative to it. But as Laurie Michaelis, who coordinates Living Witness, a Quaker organisation, points out: 'The problem is partly about power, but that's putting it "out there" … it's hard with the power frame to really be looking at ourselves and our own role in the problem.' He has found the work of the anthropologist Mary Douglas on cleanliness rituals in her book *Purity and Danger* helpful in recognising the purity thinking that activists are caught up in when we define ourselves against what we would like to change. She was observing how our tendency to impose separations, demarcate what is pure and punish transgressions is a human attempt to impose order on the inherently untidy business of life. It can only ever be an attempt, she said, because 'that which is negated is not thereby removed'.[70] There's a dualism, Michaelis continues, 'in the way we separate ourselves off from stuff that's unclean …. Recognising my own capacity for being there is an important part of learning to live with it in other people.'[71]

The purity thinking extends to activists' views of other activists. There is a rich literature within social movement studies looking at policing of activist identity and opinion, both on the borders of activist groups and within them. This can include ideas of what constitutes a 'good' or 'bad' activist.[72] (It is also a rich subject for comedy, like Monty Python's 'People's Front of Judea' sketch in *Life of Brian*.) Purity thinking can have painful roots in real experience: deep pain and trauma, and years of feeling invisible and angry, can make people uncompromising. It can also be a way of drawing boundaries to make ourselves feel better. Frances Lee's essay, 'Excommunicate me from the church of social justice', went viral in 2017 as they pointed out the fundamentalist religious overtones of activist dogma in the queer, trans and leftist movements they were involved with. They confessed:

> I self-police what I say in activist spaces. … The amount of energy I spend demonstrating purity in order to stay in the good graces of a fast-moving activist community is enormous. Activists are some of the judgiest people I've ever met, myself included. There's so much wrongdoing in the world that we work to expose. And yet, grace and forgiveness are hard to come by in the broader community. At times, I have found myself performing activism more than doing activism. I'm exhausted, and I'm not even doing the real work I am committed to do. The quest for political purity is a treacherous distraction for well-intentioned activists.[73]

It can also prevent participation. The author and activist Jonathan Smucker, who was involved in the New York Occupy camp in 2011, observed how enthusiastic offers of participation and support from 'mainstream' public figures were rejected in case they sully the movement.[74] This is purity thinking in action. The split within each activist, between the good parts that they like and want to identify with, and the bad parts they hide from, is mirrored in the split between an activist group and everyone outside it.

On the other side of purity is disgust. Once activists have projected unwanted aspects of ourselves onto not-activists – or, indeed, other activists who are taking a different approach – we can then view those other people with disgust, which is how humans react to something that is 'unclean'. I started noticing the disgust that would be triggered when people, institutions or even other activists transgress in areas that activists hold sacred. 'That's disgusting' is a response that I've often heard among campaigners when a problem is being discussed. It is rampant on social media, although that may be a social media thing as much as it is an activism thing. But it pre-dates social media. I saw it – and would take part in it until I started noticing it and cringed – during NGO campaign strategy meetings. They would have been convened to plan what we were going to do about a problem, and we did do some planning, but we'd also spend time talking enthusiastically about the awfulness of the people responsible, eventually declaring, 'let's get the bastards!' It sometimes went beyond that, into an obsession with particular characters: arms dealers, timber traders, warlords, tax-haven defenders, kleptocrats. It is not uncommon, in the type of morally infused investigative reporting I was doing, to be consumed with one person or company, not least because it takes such a punishingly long time, on limited resources, to find and stand up the information and sources you need in order to publish without ending up in a libel court. Now, though, I wonder what else we were up to.

What is disgust really about? On an evolutionary basis, it makes sense to recoil from bad smells and things that look unclean. But this adaptive response is also triggered by moral violations. Jonathan Haidt, an academic psychologist who studies morality and politics, suggests that the human mind perceives a vertical scale, with 'God' – or moral perfection – at the top, down through humans, animals, then monsters and evil at the bottom. So people feel moral disgust when they encounter or hear about people whose behaviour puts them low on this dimension. 'If we had no sense of disgust, I believe we would also have no sense of the sacred,' says Haidt. This idea that sanctity and disgust are on the same spectrum helps explain activists' common allergies and infatuations. But as Haidt warns, this 'ethic of divinity' has a dark side. 'Once you allow visceral feelings of disgust to guide your conception of what God wants, then minorities who trigger even a hint of disgust in the majority can be ostracised. The ethic of divinity is sometimes incompatible with compassion, egalitarianism, and basic human rights.'[75] Most obviously, Haidt is describing what happens when populist or authoritarian intolerance takes hold, of which there are currently too many examples. But if we substitute activists' own sense of sacred ideas for 'God' in that sentence, it becomes clear how activists can start to judge our opponents with disgust, in a way that is hard to square with our professed values. It's something of a strategic error, too, to say the least. Do we really expect to win if we treat the people we are trying to influence with disgust? We see how easy it is as activists to lose our compassion for the humanity of the people who are doing things we disapprove of and how easy it is to dehumanise some people in order to humanise others.[76] We can also see how activists end up treating people in our own movements badly.

The philosopher Martha Nussbaum, whose work elegantly unpicks the emotions underlying our supposedly rational thinking, digs deeper into the roots of disgust. In her account, disgust is what keeps us separate from our own animality and mortality, and is easily projected onto other people and groups. All forms of prejudice are different, but running through them, she says, is 'the intolerance of humanity in oneself'. The aspects of our humanity we find hardest to handle are our bodily vulnerability, our ongoing need for interdependence and cooperation with others and, behind these, our certain knowledge that we will die. We find them particularly hard to handle, she says, drawing on John Bowlby, Donald Winnicott and Ronald Fairbairn's foundational work on attachment and child development, if our vulnerability has not been appropriately met when we were infants.

What does this mean? The vulnerable infant doesn't know if its mother will respond to its cries. It wants to be omnipotent, to control her. With steady responsive care, a baby learns it doesn't have to be omnipotent to get its needs met, that others can be relied on, and this is the beginning of understanding that we are cooperative beings. It is the beginning of tolerating vulnerability. But if such care is not available, or if it is too controlling, the infant 'will cling, in later life, to its own omnipotence, demanding perfection in the self and refusing to tolerate imperfection either in [other people] or the inner world'. Nussbaum calls this 'primitive shame', and suggests we all have some form of it – some a lot more than others. 'One might say without exaggeration that the root of disgust is primitive shame, the unwillingness to be a needy animal,' she says. The central challenge for society is therefore to produce people who can live with their humanity: 'surrendering omnipotence is essential to compassion'.[77]

Attachment theory tells us that our capacity to tolerate vulnerability in ourselves and others is shaped by the care we receive as babies. I hadn't even heard of attachment theory until I had my first baby and was baffled at the incompatible advice I received on how to manage this small and awake-all-night human. 'Hold her close, she needs you to soothe her,' on the one hand. 'Put her down, she needs to learn to stop crying by herself,' on the other. I started reading, and learned that the former is the view informed by decades of research into how babies form an 'attachment' with their primary carer that sets their template for being able to relate healthily to themselves – and thus, ultimately, to everyone else.[78] The latter – 'let her cry' – is the advice and practice that has been passed down generations of parents, a cascade of insecurity and reduced capacity to tolerate vulnerability. Larkin said it most simply: 'They fuck you up, your mum and dad'. The psychologist Oliver James used those same words as the title for a book that explains simply, even to the most sleep-addled, how a parent whose own attachment needs were not met in infancy may become triggered by their baby's overwhelming needs and find it challenging to meet them.[79] Now, there is the potential here for loss of nuance. For loss of recognition that exhausted parents who have to go to work or stay sane may, at some point, need to sleep-train their baby by leaving them to cry. For loss of recognition that being isolated on your own in a dwelling-place with a new baby is not how humans evolved to raise their young, and puts appalling mental pressure on that isolated parent.[80] There is great potential, too, for mother-blaming, which is another old story that needs to stop. I've written about this, and its political implications, in more detail elsewhere.[81]

The point is that our culture still does not systematically support parents in a way that recognises the primacy of attachment needs. Indeed, for more than a century it has continued to promote as fashionable, legitimate, morally necessary or economically essential those styles of infant care and childrearing that can work against the formation of healthy attachment.[82] Many of us, then, have insecure attachment styles in the way we relate to others. Even if a 'good-enough mother' creates the holding environment in which healthy attachment bonds are formed, a person's ability to tolerate their own vulnerability, to not split it off and project it onto others, is always going to be contingent.[83] We are formed in the back and forth between our infant feeling of dependency and, with loving help, our slow mastery of ourselves. But our vulnerability is never eliminated.[84] Displacing our horror of this fact into disgust at others is always going to be a risk in the human condition, until each person can find a way to integrate their dependency and vulnerability into their full sense of self.

Nussbaum has used her thinking on disgust to great effect, arguing that disgust plays too great a part in the laws governing family life, sexual conduct, reproductive decisions and same-sex relationships.[85] I find her thinking a helpful reminder that the disgust which activists sometimes feel for people doing the things we don't like is part of a wider human problem. We are all likely to experience discomfort at our own vulnerability, a discomfort that is easily armoured and protected by disgust at others and the comforting hierarchy this creates. I was certainly making myself feel better when I sat in campaign meetings complaining about awful arms dealers or the bankers and lawyers who helped corrupt politicians steal the healthcare budget of their country. Environmental campaigners do it when they gripe about the people whose habits are creating more carbon dioxide emissions than their own.

It is easy to mistake what's going on when a mechanism for making ourselves feel better creates as strong a sensation as disgust does. But the fact that we feel disgust is not, in itself, an indication of our superiority. We are not necessarily better than anyone else just because we have different values, and it is useful to hold this awareness even when we think those values are worth fighting for. Nor is feeling disgust a confirmation that we have successfully differentiated between right and wrong. It is possible, with awareness and practice, to hold the view that someone is wrong and that the alternative to their view is worth fighting for, without being overwhelmed by disgust. Understanding disgust and how it fuels righteousness can help us, too, in starting to distinguish what kind of anger we are hearing – or using. Is it a principled and justified anger, or one which emerges from righteous disgust?

What 'not-activists' project

If splitting and projection are human, then of course activists are not the only ones doing it. The people who see activism and feel uncomfortable are busy projecting back. 'Taking up the identity of feminist has always meant weathering projections,' says the psychologist Jan Haaken in her study of the women's movement through a psychoanalytical lens.[86] What are the people who do not see themselves as activists projecting onto activists? What unacknowledged aspects of self are not-activists defending themselves against feeling or acknowledging?

One projection by not-activists can be their own unwanted emotion. In a culture that has until very recently repressed expression of emotions, particularly in the realms of the public sphere, work and politics, people who do express their feelings induce discomfort because they are doing the thing that we cannot. A parallel dynamic is at the heart of men's regular discomfort with female emotionality. If men receive cultural messages that emotional display (or dependency, or vulnerability) is not compatible with masculinity (and although things are changing, I still regularly see, in playgrounds, small boys being indoctrinated with this message by their parents), they can split it out of their self-image and project it onto the women in their lives.[87]

Activists are expressing the emotion about shared human and environmental problems that many might like to feel, but cannot allow themselves to. This operates strongly at work, where organisational cultures are still based on the principle that dispassionate behaviour and judgements are required in order to be effective, and that emotions will have a disruptive effect.[88] A person in their work role, encountering activists openly expressing feelings about the consequences of that work – and I have many experiences of being the passionate activist in the room – is likely to experience discomfort that can be relieved by projecting those feelings outwards.[89] This discomfort will be heightened if the job requires them to be engaged in activities that are in some way socially or environmentally destructive, as many jobs in a capitalist economy do. You have to switch your emotions off in those circumstances. It can be upsetting for people who have worked hard to avoid experiencing disturbing feelings about environmental destruction to encounter activists who are refusing to do this; it suggests that they may have badly misdirected their own efforts.

Another not-activist projection is guilt at not acting in a way they feel they are being told to. The guilt can be quite direct: feeling bad because 'maybe there's something I should change and I can't be bothered', as one person put it. Or there is guilt that is more aware of itself. Another person said: 'I admire people who have the energy, and feel that I should have it. But I have an inkling in advance that it wouldn't solve the issues. If I take action, it will assuage guilt, but I see futility and exhaustion.' Guilt isn't an inevitable response to awareness of a problem and not acting on it. The not-acting can come from a belief that nothing can be done because nothing will work. Not-acting can come from unconscious psychological coping mechanisms to protect us from despair, as Renée Lertzman's work on people's responses to information about ecological catastrophe shows. The so-called 'value-action gap' between people's values and the action they often do not take is not a gap at all, she argues: it is a space filled with a tangle of anxieties, fears, losses, anticipations and desires.[90] And multiple defence strategies can be employed even to reject the incoming information, as Irene Bruna Seu's research into the strategies that people use to 'do denial' when they receive humanitarian appeals demonstrates.[91]

What I noticed, in my conversations with not-activists in which guilt came up, is that guilt may be tied up with agency, which is our personal feeling that we can be effective in the world. 'I just want somebody to tell me what to do,' said one self-described 'in-activist', who in the same conversation also said: 'Don't give me any more things I have to do. Either I comply, or I don't and I feel guilty.' Wanting somebody to tell you what to do, or resenting somebody telling you what to do – or, indeed, both – sounds like not having agency. Ruth Potts, one of the 'Stansted 15', who were convicted in December 2018 under anti-terrorism laws for lying down in front of a plane being used for deportations to prevent it taking off, defines activism as 'a realised sense of agency'.[92] Feeling agency makes us freer to act. Yet it is also part of the human condition to fear living our agency fully. Existential philosophy recognises this: Sartre's 'bad faith' is the self-deception that we do not have freedom to make choices. Existential psychotherapy recognises it, seeing freedom and the associated responsibility as one of four existential 'givens' that everyone has to grapple with (the others are death, isolation and meaninglessness).[93] We find complex ways to avoid acknowledging that we have freedom, that we could have done things another way.[94]

Tied in with all of these possible reactions to activism, there is also the dawning realisation of complicity in the problem that the activist is talking about. If the subject is ecological breakdown, then anyone in an industrialised consumer nation with an industrialised food system is ultimately complicit, although of course meat-eaters, regular car users or frequent flyers are consuming substantially more than others. Denial of that reality gets thrown back at the activist, as some of the reactions to Extinction Rebellion's protests have shown. Interviewed by local media, members of my local Extinction Rebellion group were repeatedly asked how they travel to protests: a car, even if shared, is jumped on as evidence to take them less seriously. It is easier to focus on the green campaigner's hypocrisy and fossil fuel-powered travel habits than our own, though this tendency has been encouraged by long-standing efforts, from those with most to lose from pro-environmental action, to frame green questions as moral issues of individual consumption rather than structural ones requiring concerted political action.

Then there are problems that specific groups of people can be complicit in: those who are 'in power' in some way. Their reactions here depend on who is confronting them. An activist who could in other respects be just 'like them', who might, if they hadn't reacted against their context to try to change it, be doing the same job as them – this activist, merely by *being* an activist, is making an implicit judgement about what the other person is doing in their work, a judgement that the other person may feel sensitive about. The judgement can be felt even before the activist opens their mouth; it is announced by their very presence, which can be enough to trigger a defensive reaction. The reaction is stronger, of course, if the activist does make their judgement explicitly known. In this light, I now wonder about the bankers, lawyers, oil company executives and IMF functionaries I was beseeching to change their ways, on behalf, so I believed, of the citizens of African countries who were adversely affected by their activities. Those encounters were frequently awkward and defensive, occasionally stunningly so. My view at the time was that these were people who had the same opportunities as me, attended similar universities, but had taken this 'wrong' turn and ended up on the wrong side. My judgement of them was, I now think, palpable. I have heard, since, from people in similar positions of power on different issues that they find the righteous judgement of activists on the 'other side' extremely uncomfortable, and unlikely to make them shift their views.

And then there is the privileged person who is confronted by an activist who is naming their complicity in systems of oppression that the activist is personally suffering. I have observed, in men I know, their discomfort when women are speaking about men's complicity in ongoing systems of male dominance. I have felt, as a white woman, the discomfort that white people can experience when people of colour are speaking about white complicity in ongoing racism, or when I read the work of women of colour such as Reni Eddo-Lodge and Guilaine Kinouani, who write about it.[95] This discomfort can go further than discomfort, than reactivity; it can become resistance, a resistance that is thrown back at the activist's initial work of resistance. The feminist scholar Sara Ahmed, who resigned her post at Goldsmiths, University of London, at its failure to tackle a culture of sexual harassment, sees blaming the messenger – the activist – as a way for nothing to change. Those who describe a problem *become* the problem. Their reactions to the problem become the issue at hand. Writing about feminism, and particularly being a feminist of colour, she describes the multiple patterns of reactivity that the person who protests experiences:

> When you speak of something as being wrong, you end
> up being in the wrong all over again. The sensation
> of being wronged can thus end up magnified: you feel
> wronged by being perceived as in the wrong just for
> pointing out something is wrong. It is frustrating! And
> then your frustration can be taken as evidence of your
> frustration, that you speak this way, about this or that,
> because you are frustrated. It is frustrating to be heard as
> frustrated; it can make you angry that you are heard as
> angry. Or if you are angry about something and you are
> heard as an angry person (an angry black feminist or an
> angry woman of colour) then what you are angry about

> disappears, which can make you feel even angrier …
> We are dismissed as emotional. It is enough to make
> you emotional.[96]

Ahmed is writing here about the experiences of women of colour raising complaints about diversity and equality. These are activists who are fighting for their lives. In her view, a focus on the purported wrongs of the activist is an old story, a way of not listening to uncomfortable truths. There are reasons why people who are not activists are reacting to activists, and they go to the heart of why activism is still needed: we are talking about stories that are not yet over. To those who are reacting to the activist pointing out ongoing problems, this should be 'over': the discriminatory laws have gone. Yet discrimination and prejudice continue; new discriminatory and prejudicial legislation continues to appear. 'You are asked to get over it, as if what stops it being over is that you are not over it,' says Ahmed.[97] Those who react to the people pointing out the problem may still be implicated in the problem, may be helping to constitute the problem as it still stands. Activism may be resistance against power, but there is much resistance to the truths being named by activists.

In the psychological literature on threat and coping, derogation of the messenger is a way to deny responsibility and protect ourselves from the threat being posed to our self-identity as a good person. Both the method and consequence of this defensive mechanism is to deny responsibility, shift blame and reinforce in-group/out-group distinctions.[98] When an activist is fighting for liberation from an oppression, their message can be uncomfortable to those who may be complicit in that oppression by benefiting from it, whether currently or historically. And it is uncomfortable in a very particular way to those who like to think they are not complicit, who think they are part of the solution. Some of the men who are most scratchy when women use the word 'patriarchy' consider themselves supportive of gender equality. White 'progressives', who find so hard the suggestion that they are complicit in racism, believe in racial equality. Men who have benefited from patriarchy often don't enjoy being reminded of it. The defensiveness about race can be 'white fragility': an inability to tolerate the slightest 'racial stress' – even in the form of difficult conversations – in a culture that protects white people from having to think about race.[99] To that inability is added the human tendency to reject vulnerability in ourselves. Difficult conversations can trigger, in white people, uncomfortable feelings about the unacknowledged vulnerability in them, which has been hiding behind a dominant social status and has benefited from continuing to be projected onto others.[100] If your whiteness or your maleness – or both – makes you feel implicitly or unconsciously superior, then it will be hard to be reminded, by conversations about racism or patriarchy, of your real and human vulnerability. The result is defensiveness, denial and a complete inability to listen.

Awareness of privilege, and guilt about it, may have already driven people to activism themselves: there is a truth in the cliché of 'middle-class guilt'. Many activist organisations are trying consciously to help participants become aware of their own privilege. But a broader point here is that even activists can be triggered by activists, though our reactivity may have a different flavour to the reactivity of the 'not-activist' I described earlier. Privileged-activist guilt can then be displaced – projected – onto those activists' 'targets', and so the dance continues. It was terribly convenient for us, white middle-class people working for a well-funded NGO, to demonise as 'the bastards' those arms dealers, oil companies and timber traders who were trashing human rights and the environment so obviously. It was much easier to do this than seriously to question our own consumption patterns, flying habits and cumulative historical benefit from misery elsewhere, let alone the fact that we were still, by having paid NGO jobs, benefiting from global inequality while trying to change it.

Working alongside all these projections is the shared cultural baggage about activists that is in place before an activist even appears on the scene in a current scenario. It can start early in life, and quickly become solidified. Laurence Cox, an activist and scholar of activism, spoke of how people's first encounter with activists will set their view of such people: 'it's their peers in college who were working out their own identity stuff, and in quite destructive ways, it was pretty visible. You decided at that point, no, I'm into sports, or that's such a nerdy loser thing to do, or whatever particular set of clichés are around it at the time.'[101] Strong cultural ideas about activism, whether negative or hero-worshipping, are also spread by the media. The projections help to create an activist.

Valeria Pecorelli, another activist and scholar, notes how these ideas can trap activists in certain ideas of activism if they are not aware of the risk. 'A "shabby" outfit, a radical sentence on a red t-shirt does not transform an individual into an activist,' she writes.[102] But conversely, these ideas and images condition the reactions that not-activists will have each time they encounter an activist. I was told a story from the Occupy camp in Bath in 2011, in which the teller, who was participating in the camp, was shouted at by a young man who yelled 'Get a job!' He was invited to come and sit down and talk, and asked why he shouted those words. He was 16, and he started crying. 'I don't know why,' he confessed. 'It was just what everyone else was saying. You're a nice bloke.' He had been conditioned to assume, from the shabby visuals of the Occupy camp, certain things about the people in it.

The creation of activists and not-activists

Perceptions of how activists are, what activism is like, arise inseparably from these negative feelings that are triggered by activism. Reactivity to hypocrisy, righteousness and emotionality may have an objective-observation component: activists really are doing those things. And at the same time, some of this will be not-activist baggage, projected onto the activist. So not-activists are projecting their discomfort about what activists are saying about the problem, their own sense of implication and guilt, their powerlessness and their insecurity about not knowing enough about the issue (another thing that came up in my conversations) back onto the activists. But meanwhile the activists are projecting our own implication in the problem, our fury, our insecurity and disgust, onto the not-activists. At the centre of this interaction is the creation of two categories: an activist, and a not-activist. They seem ontologically separate categories – two different things.[103] But they are bound together by the way that they create each other, are constituted against each other.

I have found psychoanalytic thinking helpful in understanding what might be happening here. Lynne Layton, a psychoanalyst, describes how:

when splitting occurs, each side of the polarity becomes a monstrous version of whatever it once was: when autonomy and dependence are split (and gendered, or raced, or classed), for example, we find that autonomy is lived as omnipotence and dependence as helplessness, clingy and hostile. We also know that whatever is split off continues to haunt the psyche; although the split polarities may seem independent of one another – and are constituted to seem so – they, in fact, live off each other alternately as host and as parasite. The form taken by the interdependence of the poles is thus as monstrous as each pole itself, monstrous because it is a form built on the repudiation of the actual interdependence of the sets of human attributes that were artificially divided in the first place.[104]

What does this mean in practice? Layton is saying that if we push away the side of ourselves that is dependent, we become excessively identified with our independence. If we push away our autonomy, we will become over-dependent on others. And when we do this, whatever it is that we have pushed out of conscious sight has not in fact gone away. It is hidden in us, and we are drawn to it in other people. The unwanted aspect 'appears' in someone else. Our strong identification with the aspect of ourselves that we can live with works only in relationship – entangled – with what is hidden. This entangled relationship, both with the hidden aspect within ourselves, and the visible manifestation of it in other people we encounter, will be difficult.

I have come to think that something like this, each side holding some characteristics of the other, is what is happening in the creation of activists and not-activists. Each side of the activist/not-activist polarity becomes a 'monstrous' version of what it was. Each needs the other in order to exist: there's a mutual fascination. So the activist is shouty, passionate, righteous, busy and frequently burns out. The not-activist is passive; they don't need to do anything because the activist is so busy doing it. The activist needs the not-activist to blame and shout at, to feel superior against, to define herself against as an activist. The not-activist needs the activist to do the work of speaking up on issues they care about, though they may criticise the way in which the activist does it. Action and inaction have become polarised, and located in different people. We each need the other to receive our own projections. So both the activist and not-activist are entangled with the other, different as they both think they are. There is no activism that is not entangled with the people it is trying to convince or change. And there is no reaction to activism that has not got something of the activist in it.

Meanwhile, each are guarded, by our own defences, against observing what is going on. Activist busyness can be a defence against admitting lack of agency – or, in other words, powerlessness. Joanna Macy observes that we fear admitting powerlessness against the enormity of the problems because it might cause us to collapse.[105] Not-activist passivity and non-engagement can be a defence against the psychological threat of acknowledging the enormity of the problems.[106] But in sending out and receiving these projections, both forget the 'sets of human attributes that were artificially divided in the first place' – the agency and capacity to act, the potential to participate in the shared social space in some way or another, that is possessed by everyone.

One of the apparent paradoxes of 'progressive' activism is how it can appear to preach tolerance of all diversity, except those who do not agree with its view. Viewed through a lens of unconscious motivation, however, the paradox dissolves.[107] Unconscious responses, and unwitting displacement onto others of the parts of ourselves that are uncomfortably close to those we criticise, help to explain activist reactivity towards not-activists. It is hard for us to see what we are up to. But likewise, the reactivity of not-activists towards activists can come from an unacknowledged place in which all manner of denial, defences and guilt might lie.

Any projection is a form of defence. We are defending ourselves against feelings, experiences and parts of ourselves that we cannot bear to acknowledge, whether good or bad. Here is Toni Morrison, whose novels repeatedly explore the link between projection and exploitation; how domination cannot happen without the oppressor splitting off parts of themselves – vulnerability and violence included – and projecting those parts onto others.[108] I have yet to find better words on the phenomenon than hers. Describing how she learned to withdraw the projections she had made onto a beguiling woman she once met briefly, she says that she came 'to understand that I was longing for and missing some aspect of myself, and that there are no strangers. There are only versions of ourselves, many of which we have not embraced, most of which we wish to protect ourselves from.' The alarm we feel at being confronted with unacknowledged parts of ourselves 'makes us reject the figure and the emotions it provokes' and 'makes us want to own, govern, and administrate the Other.' But in doing so, she says, 'we deny her personhood, the specific individuality we insist upon for ourselves'.[109]

'There are only versions of ourselves, many of which we have not embraced.' The activist may not have embraced the side of themselves that is defensive, unsure and terrified of doing nothing in case the feelings that all this activity and noise are keeping at bay begin to surge. The not-activist may not have embraced the side of themselves that can speak out and take action. Both, as is human, may be avoiding acknowledging their own vulnerability in the face of a very uncertain world. Both, perhaps, could be more effective in the world if they were able to acknowledge that they hold some attributes of the other.

5 Common habits of entangled activists

DURING THE few weeks between handing in my notice and leaving Amnesty International's London headquarters where I worked for just over a year in my late twenties, I had a conversation in the windowless room that contained the printers and photocopiers for my floor. It was with a woman senior to me, who had run many teams and campaigns. She had heard I was leaving and asked why. I summarised the difficulties of working for my boss, who was a dedicated campaigner and delightful person but a capricious manager; who generated chaos and anger on a regular basis, and left junior staff, including but not only me, to clear up. 'Well,' she said, not disputing my assessment of this person, 'those of us who really care about human rights, we put up with all that kind of stuff.'

Here was someone almost incapacitated by repetitive strain injuries that may well have had something to do with 'all that stuff'. Her body was stiff and immobile. She took frequent time off and needed someone to type for her as using the keyboard had become too painful. She was operating on a fraction of the energy that might have been available for her to dedicate to human rights, had this way of defending them not made her so ill. As an unarguable physical complaint, repetitive strain injury was one of the only acceptable ways for stress and burnout to manifest itself at Amnesty's headquarters at that time, which is probably why so many people in that building had it. A massage therapist I know offered to come in with his portable massage chair to give stiff-necked workers a 15-minute break, but was informed that they couldn't countenance such indulgence when the people they were trying to get out of prison were suffering so much. An exhausted researcher went to their senior manager in distress, and was told, point blank, 'if you don't like the heat, get out of the fire'. Amnesty has undergone many internal changes, yet a decade and a half later, monstrous workloads and senior staff who ignored the pleas of those struggling under them featured prominently in a report it commissioned into its toxic culture after two staff members committed suicide.[110] A separate investigation found that serious failures at Amnesty had contributed to one of the deaths.[111]

Just as the assumption of superiority over people who are not activists that I examined in the previous chapter is a classic activist habit, so is treating your own people badly while trying to help others. Such habits can seem like the usual quirks and annoyances of activism. That's how activism is, we say: whether critically, from the outside, or resignedly, from the inside. Explanations can focus, in psychoanalytical terms, on the operations of our shadow. In this case, human rights defenders are so intent on being 'good' and helping others, so invested in that version of themselves, that they can't acknowledge the parts of themselves that are not – the parts of themselves that are unsympathetic to colleagues' distress, and capable of bullying – and they split them off. Under stress, these 'not good' parts erupt out at those nearest them.

But while the shadow is certainly part of what's going on here, I do not think it is the only factor. As well as being entangled with those we are trying to influence, as we saw in the previous chapter, activists are entangled, too, in the culture that produces the problems we are trying to change. The actions of a manager at Amnesty who puts a fellow campaigner under intolerable pressure – and, too, the actions of a campaigner who works under such pressure – are guided by stories in our culture about sacrifice, about being a saviour or a hero, and about attaining status from work. They are guided by stories that encourage extraction of every last possible drop of the resource in question (in this case, energy for work and for a cause), and stories about individualism, how we are all alone and separate from everyone else, and so must shoulder our burdens ourselves.

Activists have traits and habits that may be symptoms of our culture. Activists do what the culture does, even – perhaps particularly – when we think we are not doing so. I began the previous chapter with some of the activist traits that are most noticeable or bothersome to people who are not doing activism: the righteousness and the anger. This chapter begins with noticeable and bothersome traits that *activists themselves* identified in our conversations – although these traits are often noticed and criticised from the outside too. They include the kind of sacrificial behaviour raised by the Amnesty story I opened with, and the pressure to shoulder the burden individually. Then there is the saviour complex, and status-chasing.

Carrying the world on our shoulders

A story that repeatedly emerged in my conversations with activists was that they had to do it all themselves, in a way that felt sacrificial. Professor Jem Bendell is a scholar and activist whose career researching sustainable business and alternative currencies and consulting for the UN and NGOs changed direction when he published his 'Deep Adaptation' paper on climate change and likely civilisational collapse in July 2018.[112] It was downloaded hundreds of thousands of times within a few months and he now works on deep adaptation as a 'philosophy, framework and range of initiatives aimed at reducing harm in the face of societal collapse'.[113] When I spoke to him a few months before he published that paper, we talked about the process of becoming an activist. He described how deciding to be an activist in his teens 'subsumed my life into a discourse of sacrifice to a cause', and created a sense of self-worth as someone who helps others.

'Even if I wasn't taking on everything the religion of my culture was saying – I thought I was interpreting it for myself – I still inherited the notion of struggling to be good and needing to be good,' he says. 'You're not already fully worthy as you are …. We have to be unique and self-authored and have huge responsibility, to be good and do good, and because we're so separate, we have to do it all.'

Bendell is picking up, here, on the way that activists can feel that we have to prove ourselves, and the only way to do this is through our work. It is not obvious that we can separate this pressure to prove ourselves from the sense of duty and wanting to help that led us into the job in the first place. For those who are working late into the night to get somebody out of prison, like the people at Amnesty, who will do it if we don't? If an MP has offered us a chance to give input on a piece of forthcoming legislation that will improve lives on the issue we work on, the opportunity will disappear if we don't take it now. And yet, Bendell's description suggests how our striving can also derive from an ambient cultural Protestantism – a faith that is based on its adherents demonstrating they are God's elect by repeated and ongoing good works – as well as from the broader notion of sacrifice which is at the very heart of Christianity. These notions underpin the work of some campaigning groups, and not only the explicitly Christian ones. Stephen Hopgood's anthropological study of the culture at Amnesty's London secretariat, which he was researching when I was there in the early noughties, described the movement's view of itself as a 'secular religion', upholding strict moral values and aspects of a monastic life of difficult toil for its staff.[114] There's a sense in Bendell's description of his younger self, too, of the approach to activism being shaped by the individualism of our culture. To many activists, individualism underlies the problem we are trying to tackle, since we connect it, correctly, with the socially atomising and ecologically disastrous effects of capitalism. Yet here it is, moulding an approach to being an activist, telling the activist that we have to do it all ourselves.

Iris Andrews is a former climate change campaigner, who worked for years at Greenpeace and other environmental organisations. She had long been interested in justice, and by the time she was 18 she was volunteering on peace campaigns while at art school. Her mother had just died, she says, and

'I made the decision that my art practice was pointless and I needed to go and save the world. Campaigning work was more outer-directed, thinking about the outer world and other suffering put my suffering in context of the bigger suffering, and I felt better.' Talking about it in retrospect, her passion for the issue of climate change and grasp of its importance is undimmed. But she can now see how much her own needs were also involved and intertwined. She was 'deriving vast amounts of identity from this story of doing good work' and using campaigning to mitigate anxiety and doubts about her worth. 'The story about how I'm doing good work in the world became very important. The sense that my generation has to tackle climate change, it consumed me. It felt like there was potential to do big stuff, a sense that it was winnable,' she said. This was before the failed Copenhagen climate summit in 2009.[115] She was doing carbon policy work, on the basis that 'we just needed legislation to suck carbon out of the atmosphere', even though she was conscious that it didn't suit her temperament. 'It was a terrible fit for my personality. I was self-flagellating about how I didn't like it, but it was important so I had to do it. I was destroying myself for this story. I also knew I was exhausted, anxious.' The atmosphere at work was unpleasant, too, 'so many people are working themselves to the bone, getting angry'. For a while, this sacrifice of her health and peace of mind seemed justifiable: when set, ostensibly, against the challenge of climate change, and also, less obviously, while it was meeting some of her inner purposes. Eventually, however, she was able to gain some perspective about the limits of the individual contribution she could make on climate change, especially if it was burning her out, and moved into attempts to use art and culture to do environmental consciousness-raising.

Sacrifice can be necessary for activism. It can be a decision to make oneself uncomfortable for the benefit of a wider good, and in this light, it is inherent in attempts to change the world, most of which involve discomfort. It is not comfortable to immerse ourselves in stories about the worst things that people can do to people, as the human rights defenders at Amnesty and other organisations do. When I worked at Amnesty I had frequent nightmares about the material we were dealing with – these horrific things that had been done, by real people, to real people and their children – and I know other people who worked there who were badly affected by it.[116] I have great respect for those who can find a way to live with this, to hear these stories from those who suffered them, tell them to the world as witness, and to keep doing so for the long term. Activism of all kinds is full of people making themselves more uncomfortable than they might have been otherwise: by speaking out in their communities, by using their time outside of work and family responsibilities to organise rather than relax, even by putting their bodies on the line in direct protest. Such actions can reasonably be described as sacrifices of some kind: of time, comfort, sometimes security. Taken to extremes – as they were being taken at Amnesty – they can become martyrdom: a feeling that we must suffer ourselves in order to be alongside the suffering of others. For activists who are martyring themselves, or activist cultures that are encouraging it, empathy – appreciating the gravity of someone's experience or feeling, without having personally experienced it – seems insufficient.

And so there are two things to tease out here: sacrifice, and feeling that you have to do it all yourself. They are not quite the same thing, though they get tangled. Not all of the people making activist sacrifices are driven by a feeling that they have to do it all themselves. It's the individualistic shouldering of the burden that turns necessary sacrifice into something that looks rather like the systems we think we want to change. Having to do everything ourselves is part of the problem that activists are trying to tackle: it's what becomes necessary when the social fabric and shared safety nets are eroded by structuring society around market forces. It can be hard to see the individualism at work here, since activist sacrifices being made by multiple individuals who feel they have to do it all themselves can, paradoxically, bring a feeling of group identity and belonging. A group identity can form around those who are making these sacrifices alongside each other. I have experienced this in both NGOs and community campaigning where everyone is overworking towards a common goal, where the internal discourse is anchored in a shared narrative about how busy and stretched we all are.

This narrative of busyness and overstretch frames the decisions – often poor ones – that are made by individuals and the organisation about how much more work to take on. While these sacrifices are being made by more than one person, they are sacrifices that are being made only alongside others, as toddlers at a playgroup will play alongside their peers but not, yet, truly with them. There is still, in these situations, a strong flavour of each member being that striving individual, toiling away at being a hero. 'Over time it became more about my need to be validated, more than the actual issue of climate change,' says Andrews of her time campaigning in NGOs. Eventually, despite the pressure she was putting on herself to keep going, she says, 'I became less and less able to convince myself that I as a single individual had to do it all on my own'. Indeed, sometimes the sacrifices are not only being made alongside others, but in direct competition with them: look who can sacrifice the most, work the longest hours, cause themselves the most discomfort.

There are several problems with having to do it all ourselves. One problem is that such stories tie our self-worth to our success. But what is success for a campaigner? If the activism we are doing is not succeeding in its goals – which, realistically, is a lot of the time – then we cannot derive a sense of success, nor therefore worth, from results. We feel we must try to obtain it, instead, from the amount of work we put in. This is a sure recipe for burnout. Awareness of burnout is becoming more visible in campaigning organisations than it was 15 years ago and, in some, support structures are in place. But these are better at picking up the pieces when it happens than preventing it through awareness of the root causes; the culture of martyrdom persists.[117]

Another problem with needing to do it all ourselves is that it is a selfish endeavour: in the sense that it keeps the attention focused on the self. It keeps an activist's attention focused on what 'I' am doing to solve the problem, on questions about whether 'I' have been successful. It can be, as Andrews acknowledged above, about '*my* need'. That need might be to shore up a sense of self-worth that feels lacking. It might be to build a sense of identity that is lacking by adopting the powerful and particular identity of 'activist'. Doing-it-all-ourselves can be a lifelong survival technique against feelings of scarcity, that something is lacking. Having to figure it all out on our own, to have our own backs, not trusting that we will be supported by others if we allow ourselves to lean on them: these can all be practices we learned in childhood because we had to. We perhaps needed them because we were not sufficiently nurtured, or because we were raised by parents who prioritised their child's independence over their sense of security. By the time we reach adulthood such go-it-alone practices are ingrained habits that would require support to change. It may not even feel safe to do so. These practices are entirely normalised, too, by the culture of individualism in which we live. In trying to do it all ourselves in our activism, therefore, we are sacrificing some of our basic needs – perhaps for a healthy balance of work, rest and play – in order to meet these other deep needs. But whatever need of our own we are fulfilling by carrying the world on our shoulders, the result is that we can make our activism about ourselves, not about those human or non-human others we think we're trying to help. The beam of our attention is focused, busily and noisily, outwards. This can be a good way to avoid noticing what we're up to; to avoid noticing that we are, in some way, feeding ourselves. It also makes us less likely to notice when our campaigning strategies are constructed with ourselves at some imaginary centre, with our intended effects rippling outwards. And it's a convenient way of avoiding thinking about whether we are actually being effective. Jim Coe, who supports campaigning groups in planning and evaluating their strategies, calls it the Ptolemaic worldview. This is the tendency of campaigners to put their own campaign at the centre of their mental model and to think in terms of how its effects will ripple outwards, rather than beginning with their target and working out what it would take to create the necessary change. He warns that this habit creates a distorted and solipsistic view for campaigners of their place and importance in the world.[118]

Jem Bendell points out that climate change poses the ultimate challenge to the activist's sense that we, personally, have to solve the problem. In his view we are no longer in a time of prevention, but of 'deep adaptation' to what is already happening. In these terms, nobody is going to be 'solving' the problem, least of all us personally. In a list of suggestions for 'living beyond collapse-denial', he notes that resistance to information about catastrophe 'may come from what you have been consciously or subconsciously telling yourself about your own self-worth, purpose and meaning …. If you are a mission-driven professional in fields related to environment or social justice then expect that you may be driven to rebuild a sense of self-worth and that this need of the ego, while natural and potentially useful, could become a frantic distraction.' If trying to save the world has been meeting our own needs, in other words, then the grief that comes with understanding that the world cannot be saved in its current form is not just grief about what is happening to the world and its ability to support humans and other species. It is grief about the loss of what we thought was our purpose.[119]

Doing it all ourselves is also a form of extraction. When we do this as activists we are treating ourselves as bottomless resources, in the same way as the economic systems we are criticising, which relentlessly extract wealth from the lives and lands of other people. We are not running a healthy economy of the self.[120] We are expecting our physical and mental resources to remain available even though we are failing to replenish them through a balanced cycle of activity, rest and nourishment. This increases the chance that we will burn out, as I know too well from my own experience as a young journalist. But it becomes a problem for others too. By keeping the tempo of the work at a constantly frantic pace, we treat our colleagues and collaborators as bottomless resources too. We spread the burnout culture, the extraction culture. Furthermore, having to do it all ourselves can become our organisation or team having to do it all, which means having to grab turf – tasks, airtime, funding – from others. So activists who try to do it all ourselves risk excluding the voices and agency of others, including, sometimes, the voices and agency of those we are trying to help. By doing so, we are perpetuating the colonial dynamics that have given rise to the global inequality that we are working to alleviate.[121]

Being the saviour

An appealing aspect of doing it all yourself is that you get to be the hero. The hero's journey is a very old story, as old as culture, as old as humanity. It is as attractive to activists as it is to everyone else. If activism is ultimately a performance, both in the sense that it is in being seen that it has its effect, and in that it is creating a storyline out of opposition, then it will often feel like it needs a hero. And what do heroes do? They save the day. It is very easy for a hero story to become a saviour story, especially if our ears are tuned to the idea of a saviour by ambient cultural Christianity. Saviour stories can run deep in our personal lives, too. Stephen Karpman's 'Drama Triangle' is a model of interpersonal roles derived from transactional analysis.[122] This is a psychoanalytic theory and practice developed by Eric

Berne in the 1950s that focuses on how people relate to each other. It soon escaped the consulting room into the workplace and management training courses, which is where some people may have come across it. Karpman's triangle explains the interdependence of the commonly adopted roles of 'victim', 'rescuer' and 'persecutor', which for many people are learned in childhood through the workings of their family dynamics. The model is not static and the people involved can 'switch' positions: a victim can become a persecutor and a rescuer can become a victim. Karpman used fairy stories in his original paper, which is available on his website, to illustrate how this can happen.[123] The drama triangle does not map directly onto activist dynamics since the position of 'victim' in particular was intended to suggest someone who is, in psychological terms, choosing to take the victim position in an interaction, even if that 'choice' is made subconsciously. This is obviously not the same as being the actual victim of an oppression or marginalisation, one that is the subject of activism. And nor is it inevitable that experiencing oppression or marginalisation necessarily turns us into a victim; one of the problems with rescuers is their tendency to push people into a victim role they do not wish to occupy.

Karpman's model is, however, suggestive for activism that is being done on behalf of others. It can help us to see what can happen if the activist is not conscious about their own need to occupy the saviour role, perhaps if they are occupying this role to avoid feeling like a victim themselves. If activists are adopting a 'rescuer' position for unconscious reasons connected to their own needs and their own interpersonal history, they may ultimately need the person or groups they are rescuing to remain 'victim', as they will need someone to keep rescuing. Tangled together with the ongoing colonial assumptions of agency and voice that I described above, this would create a powerful incentive for saviour behaviour. Karpman's triangle also shows the inextricable role of the 'persecutor' figure in rescuer dynamics: the existence of someone onto whom the rescuer can project all the blame for the victim's situation. These are the 'bastards' who I wanted to 'get' with my investigations: the bankers, mining executives and tax haven lawyers. As the discussion of activist projections in the previous chapter showed, it is much easier and more satisfying for somebody who likes being a 'rescuer' to apportion blame in this way – much easier, that is, than acknowledging their own complicity and entanglement in the problem.

Psychotherapists must routinely handle the 'transference' that happens when a patient is working through the traumas of their past. It is part of the process that the person in therapy may cast their therapist in a role of saviour, persecutor or victim. Judith Herman, an American psychiatrist and trauma specialist, describes the risk that the therapist, unable to bear the sense of helplessness in the face of what she is hearing, assumes the role of rescuer. 'By so doing, she implies that the patient is not capable of acting for herself. The more the therapist accepts the idea the patient is helpless, the more she perpetuates the traumatic transference and disempowers the patient.' At its extreme, this behaviour can lead to 'a stance of grandiose specialness or omnipotence'. She quotes another therapist, Henry Krystal, observing that the therapist's 'impulse to play God is as ubiquitous as it is pathogenic'. Therapists are trained to handle these 'narcissistic snares'.[124] But activists who do 'development', humanitarian work and any form of campaigning in support of others are not. My intention is not to draw a simplistic analogy here between a 'patient' and 'therapist' relationship and a 'helped' and 'helper' activist relationship. But the juxtaposition of activism with therapy – with its training, ongoing supervision and explicit recognition of the risk of narcissistic positioning – does highlight the potential unawareness with which those who think they want to 'save' others can dive into their chosen task. It highlights too, the dearth of meaningful support and supervision around these issues for activists.

For activists from rich countries, there can be guilt and horror at how an economic system that has benefited them has hurt people elsewhere. These feelings send many people into 'international development' work, or into campaigning to reduce global inequalities – as they did me. Yet the same mental structure that created those economic systems is still at work. The idea that the activist is the one with agency, the one who knows the answers, the one who speaks publicly, who is acting on behalf of others, persists.[125] 'If you have come here to help me, you are wasting your time. But if you have come because your liberation is bound up with mine, then let us work together', goes a line attributed to the Aboriginal activist and scholar Lilla Watson. I wrote in Chapter 3 about the differences in perspective between activists who are fighting for their own lives, and activists who are fighting in support of others. Many activists observe that the most effective campaigning is done when both types of activists are working together in solidarity. But the tensions of saviourhood may also emerge.

What are those tensions? One is that the helpers may not have the best perspective on what is needed, and that becomes a problem if their self-image as saviour makes them think they don't need to ask. Activists who are intervening to support others rather than fighting for their own lives get described as 'do-gooders', who are fuelled by 'middle-class guilt'. That pejorative term 'do-gooding' has implications of 'well-meaning but misguided', and there may be a truth here, since those fighting for their own liberation – who do not get called 'do-gooders' – tend to have a stronger sense of what is needed than those trying to help them. The international development industry, long a bastion of white-saviourism, is riddled with stories of inappropriate interventions and projects over many decades, but this tension is also built into the structures and procedures of aid agencies and development charities and the 'technical assistance' that they provide to governments. The scholar, author and activist Robtel Neajai Pailey's dissection of the 'white gaze' of development describes how, when she was a young Liberian staffer in Ellen Johnson Sirleaf's administration, white American colleagues, also in their twenties, were permitted to promote themselves past her. White British early- and mid-career bureaucrats were serving as 'governance advisors' to senior Liberian managers with decades more experience. 'I began to understand slowly,' she writes, 'that the … "advisors" only assumed these titles because Western whiteness remains a signifier of expertise, whether real or perceived.'[126]

Emilia Roig, who now runs the Center for Intersectional Justice in Berlin, began her career working on women's rights in Cambodia, Kenya and Ecuador. 'There were things I found completely disturbing in the international development complex, especially the colonial structures that were in place, not even disguised,' she says. 'I could see it in the very way expats and experts related to the national workforce. Local staff expertise was completely devalued, this could be seen in salaries, decision-making, what language you used, status and recognition. I found this extremely disturbing.'[127] Attempts are underway within many of these organisations to shift power and change their culture. Yet, as some staff working within them have observed in our conversations, the dynamics continue to play out even as campaigning organisations consciously try not to let the priorities and voices of the people in 'headquarters' override those of their partners, staff or beneficiaries 'on the ground' or 'in the field'.

Saviourhood also carries the risk that the do-gooders can choose the terms of their engagement. They can shift focus when they think it's not working, when they think there's a different place to put their energy and attention. At the start of 2019, as Sudanese citizens faced their government's teargas and bullets in an uprising (which, later in the year, was brutally crushed), a comment piece in *The Guardian* enquired into the whereabouts of celebrity advocates for the Sudanese people, such as the actor George Clooney who had been so vociferous in defence of human rights in Sudan only a few years before.[128] Clooney responded defensively in a follow-up piece that he was still working behind the scenes, but had turned his attention to investigating the financial structures that were supporting the regime.[129] This is a relevant angle that I am familiar with because I have worked on it myself. Brutal regimes cannot survive without the banking services extended to them. But the fact remained that at this moment of evident crisis, violence and suffering in the place that he had publicly invested himself in, Clooney's voice now *appeared* to be missing. Less publicly and all too commonly, NGOs will engage for a few years in a campaigning project in a particular country, raising funds for it, relying on the expertise of local collaborators, diverting local NGO partners from their other projects, before casually re-allocating funds to something else when their 'organisational priorities' shift.

The very frame of international 'development' has long been criticised for labelling some countries 'developed' when they have in fact dispossessed, annihilated and impoverished entire populations.[130] In this sense, to focus on the alleged pathologies of other countries is a turning away from your own culture's problems (as well as, perhaps, your own problems: some of my encounters in Sierra Leone suggested there is some truth in the 'missionaries, mercenaries, misfits' cliché of the humanitarian worker). This structure resonates with the pattern of narcissism. Those who are 'saving' for their own purposes are performing the narcissist's double move of taking the gaze off what is uncomfortable about themselves while at the same time elevating themselves. Contrary to popular opinion, narcissism is not about someone wanting attention because they think they are so damn fantastic. It is about the paradox of someone not being able to love themselves and thus needing attention to compensate for the lack of a healthy and stable inner sense of themselves. A narcissist is someone who seeks to hide their vulnerability from others by distracting them with grandiose outward shows that serve to obtain validating praise. This is tiring for those who must live with it at the best of times, but the form of narcissism that is so utterly rattling to those who receive it comes in the form of 'I was only trying to help you'.

The deep tension of the saviour complex is that being the one who is helping others – who has time and resources to help others, who thinks it is their task and that they have the ability to help others – is a result of privilege. This word refers to the suite of often unacknowledged advantages that come from accidents of birth, accidents that can deposit a person into a life where their path is smoothed. It is smoothed not because they are 'lucky' or have done anything special, but because of painful histories that have been inflicted on someone else. It is not only about the accident of who you are: that you are middle or upper class, or that you live in a 'developed' or peaceful country, or that you live in a body that has not been racialised. It is that through land enclosures, industrial exploitation, colonialism, enslavement, unfair global trade and debt regimes, and ongoing racism and other forms of discrimination, terrible things have been done, by people like you, to secure the comfortable life of people like you.

Saviourhood, then, is a form of entanglement in the histories of abuse, pain and oppression that activists are trying to confront. Activists are positioned in relation to these histories. We have experienced them, or we are benefiting from them, or both; as the theory of intersectionality so illuminatingly demonstrates, any one person can live in multiple positions in relation to multiple different histories.[131] And our ancestors experienced them, or were complicit in them – or perhaps, as in my case, both. My paternal grandfather was the child of Jewish refugees who arrived in the UK having fled pogroms in Russia and Poland; my paternal grandmother was the child of a colonial railway engineer in India. All activists working to reduce global inequalities are likely to be aware of the histories of abuse and theft that have led to the current situation. But for white activists, acknowledging our own place in these histories, which is what a reckoning with whiteness calls for, brings painful truths – including the recognition that any success we have had does not come only from hard work or our own smarts. Dedicating our life to helping others does not prevent us being complicit in the ongoing suffering of those others. And the surfacing and realisation of privilege, as we saw in the previous chapter, brings awkwardness, discomfort and defensiveness that can get in the way of being alongside the activists who are experiencing the problem that is being tackled. 'The hardest people to facilitate in this work are the people who think they are saving the world already,' says Vanessa Faloye, a facilitator who runs equity and inclusion training for both NGOs and the private sector.[132]

It takes a lot of inner work and ruthless self-honesty – digging over sometimes difficult and painful ground – for an activist to examine this complicity, to uncover their own paternalistic attitudes and hidden assumptions, to be able to work, without awkwardness, in solidarity with people who are fighting for their lives. For activists to liberate ourselves from these attitudes and assumptions might be the kind of liberation that Lilla Watson is talking about. It takes a lot of work to be able to come truly alongside someone, to be as aware as we can of the agendas we are carrying, and say: 'I don't know how it is for you. What do you need?' and to be able to receive the same question in return. In the absence of this work, the awkwardness-avoidance strategies – the awkwardness being the self-consciousness that can come with half-suppressed awareness of the privilege gap – kick in. These strategies include being the expert, knowing best, talking noisily about solutions, maintaining hierarchy and, sometimes, just maintaining the kind of blithe unawareness that lets us think we're doing our bit by hogging the limelight. All of them widen the gap between those doing the work and the people they are supposedly doing it for. I heard the words 'imperious' and 'Victorian' used to describe the 'us and them' approach of staff to beneficiaries in some UK homelessness charities. Ruth Hunt, who was until 2019 the chief executive of Stonewall, had noticed the bluffing that occurred when inexperienced campaigners in the UK found themselves dealing with questions about issues faced by LGBT people in low-income countries. These were strategies, she said, 'made up by people who've not experienced the issues to demonstrate that they're awake to the issues'.[133]

Some of the results of this gap, this unwillingness to be alongside and to listen, became clear when I contacted some of the people running NGOs in Uganda with whom I had worked on resource-revenue transparency campaigns a few years earlier. They were open, and very critical, and I realised that I had not heard them making these points in this way before, because I had not asked in a truly open way. And would I even have wanted to hear it? We had turned up, even under the rubric of 'consultation' – which we thought we were being careful about – with our own underlying ideas about what was important. This tended to be the subject of the global-level campaign that we were working on in London. In conversation with Winfred Ngabiirwe, the executive director of Global Rights Alert, a human rights organisation focused on the impact of natural resource extraction in Uganda, I asked about how her interactions went with funders and NGOs in the global North. It was clear that she sometimes had to make pragmatic decisions because of the power dynamic of where the money was coming from. 'They write proposals from where they are, and say they have this money to do a, b, c. They already have their country-specific plan, and they will only come and tell you this is the money we have to do certain things,' she said. 'You would not say, our interest is supporting women investors in the mining sector; it's our mining sector. They are interested in a certain aspect, even if it's not your priority as a country, and you end up working on that issue and not on the issue that has more value for the lives of people, because the chances of you convincing them to switch to that important aspect are 1 per cent.'[134]

Another tension of saviourhood is that those who are stepping in to help save others do not have to take the situation as urgently as those who are fighting for their lives. Nor do they have to look for sufficiently deep solutions. Imani Robinson, a writer, curator and prison abolitionist, worked for a time in NGO policy advocacy to try to change the police's approach to stop-and-search in the UK. This experience strengthened her view of the profound limitations of policy change when the attitudes that underlie the policies – in this case, racism – go unchanged. She saw, in the policy change world:

> this commitment to incremental change that only the
> privileged cling to. It's really something that's quite

depressing and upsetting for people who are at the brunt
of that incremental change, doing us a disservice. There's
a reliance on this 'we can't do everything in one day' that
allows people to believe that actually, policy is the way
forward, or these things are worth our time or our lives.
And this is not to say that policies changing can't make
change. There are a set of policies that we could put
into place tomorrow that would ensure better livelihoods
and higher well-being for a lot of people, but they're not
radical changes, they're not changes that allow us to be
seen as full human beings and to bring our full selves,
they're changes that are only ever in isolation, they can
only ever work with every other policy working with them.

Those who are not living the problem, cannot see the extent to which it
needs to be changed.[135]

Activists who try to help don't know enough and are too scared to
acknowledge that they don't know; they can choose to disappear; they can
afford to assume that certain types of incremental change will be enough.
These are all examples of the privileged continuing to enact that privilege,
continuing to play it out in activist relationships. A classic assumption of
the privileged activist who is trying to help is that they are the one with
agency: the space to speak and the voice. Organisations are created around
this assumption – like some of the ones I have worked for. I've been
thinking, while writing this book, about what I was doing in those jobs.
NGOs in wealthy countries try to use their geographical proximity to the
global institutions of power to advocate on behalf of those whose lives,
far away, are affected by the operations of that power. There is a logic to
this. Not all of those affected can leave their work and families and travel
across the world to have a go at the IMF or the European Commission. It
makes a practical kind of sense for those who are on the doorstep of these
institutions to do some of the advocacy with their representatives. And
those who are closer to that power know how to speak to it. They share
cultural assumptions with those who are in power. Sometimes, as taxpayers
or voters or shareholders, they have some form of democratic or financial
leverage over that power.

This was what I wanted to do, what I was doing: making the voices of those affected by the problem heard in the institutions that potentially had the power to fix the problem. Working for a small aid agency in Sierra Leone after the civil war ended, I understood that I could do nothing there that wouldn't be better done by a Sierra Leonean. I turned down a job offer with UNDP, the UN's development agency, in Freetown. It felt awful to do so because I wanted to just *be* in the country; I loved being there from the moment I arrived. People's ways of being with each other, their sincere warmth, felt new and refreshing to me. Yet I couldn't justify staying in Sierra Leone professionally; I couldn't find a post that would be both right for me to be occupying and that would fulfil my sense of purpose and search for justice. But I could run round the UN corridors in New York pursuing meetings with diplomats who were voting on an international agreement to control the second-hand gun trade that had fuelled the war in Sierra Leone, which had deprived so many of my friends there of family, land or limbs. And it seemed more useful to face up to the institutions, such as the regulators of banks and mining companies which operate in my own country and continent, rather than trying to 'help' in the countries whose economies were being hollowed out by the banks and mining companies that those regulators were failing to control. I was becoming impatient with the illogic of the 'development' industry: surely it was better to make global economic distribution fairer in the first place, rather than causing the problem and then drip feeding 'aid'.

Trying to tackle power at home, then, in the City of London and other financial centres, I did make the voices of those affected heard. But I did so through my voice. I did so while also elevating me, as the person doing this important work. I enjoyed the kick of being the disruptive person in a big international meeting. A typical location might be a heavily air-conditioned, thick-carpeted, zero-daylight basement conference room at the headquarters of the OECD (an international organisation where the world's richest countries pursue economic cooperation) in Paris. The subject: banking regulations that were supposed to prevent money-laundering, regulations which in practice were failing to prevent banks from helping grand corruption to happen. Banks were continuing to accept and house dictators' loot with impunity. Present at the meeting: scores of banks and law firms who were 'consulted' on – in practice, offered a chance to water down – the regulations that were supposed to bind them. Not present at the meeting: anyone from the most impoverished countries, those most affected by illicit capital flight. I had lobbied the bureaucrats in charge for two years, and finally talked myself and a colleague from another NGO into the room.

As the introductions proceeded around the table, the job titles a litany of banks and corporate law firms and their lobbying associations, I liked hearing the uncomfortable murmur when I said who I was, that I investigated the deadly impact of banks' behaviour on some of the most impoverished people in the world. As the discussion began, I repeatedly interjected to try to widen the frame of what they were talking about. I explicitly defamed the institutions they worked for by describing what I found in my investigations – the real impact of their actions. I tried to force them away from bland technicalities and into talking about reality. The 'corruption' these regulations were failing to prevent was not just a technical term. It was women dying in childbirth and children dying for lack of clean water. I enjoyed feeling righteous in those meetings. I liked being able to make those people uncomfortable, and I liked the effect we sometimes had when we prevented the rules being rolled back. I liked the tacit approval from the small number of bureaucrats running the meeting, who were secretly delighted that I was being a pain for the bankers and lawyers.

But that kick I felt was not only about the feeling-rightness of the work I was doing, or about the people I knew in Sierra Leone and my sense of doing right by them. It was also about me, my image, my status, what I experienced as my moral superiority to the other people in that room. I enjoyed being disgusted by these people, and having an opportunity to feel superior. I liked being able to say, I'm off to Paris or Geneva next week to give a bunch of bankers a piece of my mind. (In the terms of Karpman's drama triangle, I was casting them as the perpetrators.) In fact, I so enjoyed the saviour-ish feeling that I was helping others who were less able to be there, that I didn't consider, when I was doing it, the extent to which I was making it all about me and my performance of uprightness and righteousness. It was only after I stopped going into such rooms, buoyed up by my sense of difference from those people who habitually occupied them, that I started to notice that the only reason I had been there at all was that, while I did not have the same job title or employer as the people I was making temporarily uncomfortable, I shared their privileges. I was white, middle class and able-bodied like them; I had the same university education. It was only after I stopped going into those rooms that I realised that by being so keen to get myself into them, I might have been preventing somebody else being there. Because actually, why shouldn't an international organisation with a big budget, like the OECD, ask someone to speak who is truly affected by the failure of the rules that are under discussion, rather than someone who is claiming to speak for them? It was me doing the work of making the case for NGOs to be in the room, but I made the follow-on assumption that it also had to be me who actually turned up and spoke. The overwhelming feeling of righteous adrenaline that I was cruising on, as I enjoyed my performance of giving the bankers a kicking, made it less likely I would question whether it was right for me to be the one doing it.

Status-seeking

Another tendency that activists turn away from recognising is our competition for status. While activists are not typically pursuing status in the ways that it is commonly conceived, through financial and material success, we can still chase its other manifestations: prestige, recognition and position. Activists might ostensibly have put the goal of material advancement to one side in order to critique the economic system we want to change. But we often retain our underlying need for status, even when we are criticising the competitive capitalism that tells us market methods are the best way to meet those needs. We seek status through our achievements in activism, or through our hierarchical advancement within it. Counting 'media hits' and speaking appearances was built in to many campaigning methods even before we had to start counting social media 'likes'. Being a certain kind of campaigner requires that you 'build your profile' and network with a wide range of contacts. This means being out there, being 'on', being seen: all useful for those needing status reassurance. The title of a book published in the US, *How to Become a Nonprofit Rockstar*, seems to say it all.[136]

It can be hard to separate the demands of the job from our own desire for status. Campaigning usually requires us to make ourselves publicly seen and heard, and public visibility is also an obvious way to meet status needs. Of course there are forms of quiet activism, of helping on a one-to-one or community scale. And there are forms of noisy activism that don't need a big audience to be effective: the direct action of putting bodies in the way to resist an eviction, or to prevent a habitat being lost to a construction project. But campaigners know that even these discrete events will have much wider impact if footage and reports are shared widely. And we know that whatever we are doing, getting our argument into mainstream media debates makes it more likely we can change things, and that getting our organisation more widely recognised and quoted makes it more likely that funders will support our work. So this isn't as simple as saying we shouldn't be jockeying for public recognition. But even if public recognition is indeed part of the job, there is still the matter of our own personal desire for status.

Psychologists have been split on whether status is a fundamental human need. The idea that it is core to our health and well-being was popularised by Abraham Maslow who placed it on his famous hierarchy of human needs in the 1940s (where it comes after physiological, safety and belonging needs), and has been supported by scholars of evolution who saw the reproductive benefits of status. It is one of the core needs or 'givens' of the Human Givens model of therapy, which places our emotional needs equal in importance to our physical needs.[137] Others have downplayed it. The psychologist Viktor Frankl, a concentration camp survivor, saw the search for meaning as the key to psychological survival;[138] more recently Edward Deci and Richard Ryan, whose influential self-determination theory of human motivation is constructed around three core human needs of competence, autonomy and relatedness, are among the psychology researchers who have not included status in their categorisations of fundamental motives.[139]

One way of looking at status is to view it as tied up with materialism. Tim Kasser, a psychologist, and his colleagues have studied the negative consequences of materialism on mental health. They place status in the same category of damaging 'extrinsic' goals (those based on the esteem of other people) as wealth, possessions and image, and in opposition to self-generated 'intrinsic' goals such as personal and spiritual growth and caring for the well-being of others through connection and community.[140] Capitalism, by appealing to materialistic aims and organising society around them, encourages the adoption of these extrinsic goals that are associated with poorer mental health and well-being.[141] They are saying that seeking status, based on how others might see us, is not good for our well-being. The Common Cause project in the UK has extended this thinking to activism. Common Cause was set up by Tom Crompton, a former campaigner from WWF who was inspired by Kasser's work, as well as the models drawn up by another researcher, Shalom Schwartz, that suggest how the values that we can hold relate to each other.

Common Cause has spent the last decade using this research to persuade activists that if we try to reach our campaign goals through activating 'extrinsic' motivations, we will ultimately be strengthening the unconsciously held values that are at the heart of the problem. For example, if an environmental group tries to persuade people to install solar panels on their houses using the argument that it will make the neighbours jealous, then the underlying message is that material wealth, status and image still matter. Overconsumption, which is a deep cause of environmental problems, is not only untouched but reinforced. The language that activists use is not only a matter of effective messaging or tactics, Common Cause is saying: it is about the deep questions of what, exactly, we are trying to shift.[142] And this insight doesn't just apply to how as activists we frame our appeals. It applies to how we motivate ourselves. On this basis, activists who are seeking status while trying to overturn other damaging values may not succeed.

The author and filmmaker Nora Bateson observes the following deep-framing failure:

> I was sent an entry for a contest to win a prize of several
> million dollars awarded to the person that provided the
> winning project for developing social collaboration. The
> irony was too much. Competing for ideas on collaboration
> is a perfect illustration of why so much change-making
> today is riddled with toxic fumes of the last century's
> hero-envy. The rush-for-the-gold and step-over-the-next-
> guy approach is the thinking that got us into this mess.

> Surely, it won't get us out. This sort of contest will divide
> people who could be working together. They will need to
> keep secrets about their work, lest their ideas be stolen;
> they will claim credit instead of giving it. The hunger for
> the keynote gig, the bestseller, the viral meme about how
> to save the world is better suited for Wall Street than for
> change-makers. Watch out. The future lies in the capacity
> to understand and respond to interdependency. When you
> see collaboration with a promise of fame or awards, you
> are seeing lingering ideologies of capitalism.[143]

She is suggesting that competition for status is not a helpful frame for change-makers who are seeking to remedy the effects of an economic system that is already powerfully skewed towards competition at the expense of collaboration. (A campaigner I spoke to observed how social entrepreneurs, too, are taught that collaboration is important for impact, 'and yet baked into social business models is the requirement to identify "competitors"'.)

I am including Bateson's observation somewhat uncomfortably here, since I conceived a campaign that brought in a \$1 million prize from TED for my campaigning organisation.[144] At the time, my discomfort was that while our campaign was proposing to outlaw secret ownership of companies, a change that would limit people's ability to accumulate such vast hoards of wealth in tax havens, TED was an organisation quite comfortable in the company of the very wealthy. My colleague Robert Palmer, with whom I'd launched the campaign, travelled with one of Global Witness's founders to the announcement of the prize, and returned home to describe the delicious awkwardness of being in the 'billionaires' bullpen' at the front of the audience as they realised the implications of the 'transparency' we were talking about. But still, we took the money. And the money was certainly useful in resourcing us to turn up the volume on our campaigning noise. Ironically, it was from a communications specialist, whom we paid from those prize funds to sharpen up our campaign messaging on this tricky subject that we'd taken on, that I learned about Common Cause's research on framing and values, which I later realised was applicable to the optics of the prize itself.

In Common Cause's terms, our campaign for transparent information about company ownership, which if successful – and together with other radical changes to the tax system – would hinder the possibility of extreme wealth hoarding, was ultimately working towards bigger-than-self values like 'universality' and 'benevolence'. It was working for the greater good, in other words, of people well beyond our own personal or community circles of concern. Yet competition for the status of such a prize would subconsciously reinforce, in the mind of anyone hearing about it (let alone those of us working on it), the opposing and hard-to-reconcile values of individual financial success. I think this is what Bateson is getting at in the example above. This uncomfortable recognition became part of my growing awareness that what needed to change was so much greater than the levels of intervention that we were arguing for, and contributed to my doubts about whether we were going deep enough in our analysis of the problem.

The 'values and framing' view promoted by Common Cause suggests that individualist status-seeking is something that always exists as a potential human motivation, but that we can choose to downplay. It suggests that the environment we are in can reinforce or diminish status-seeking, and that we can choose as a society to alter that environment, including by choosing carefully the language that we use to frame the issues. (Kasser's work has plenty of practical policy suggestions for how to do this.) Other researchers are more emphatic. Status *is* a fundamental human need, according to a 2015 meta-study of research across the social sciences. Of course, any such finding depends on how status is defined, and this result was based on disaggregating the desire for status from other needs. One of the criteria for any study to be included in the review was that the need for status must not be seen as derivative of other needs, such as a need for social belonging or for power.[145]

In this view, the inevitability of our desire for status, and the fact that we need it and seek it, is not the same issue as the question of *how* we obtain it. The need for status can promote sacrifice, generosity, hard work … or competitiveness, consumption, aggression and violence. It can prompt the creation of a social enterprise that ploughs its profits back into the community where it operates, or the creation of a predatory enterprise that tries to circumvent even minimum wage standards while funnelling its profits into a tax haven where careful arrangements are made for quiet disbursements to its owners. The things that we must do to gain a sense of belonging and esteem from our peers are culturally specific, and in individualistic capitalist culture, status based on extrinsic measures of wealth, achievement and position in a hierarchy is the goal that societal messages instruct us to chase. Many activists ditch the wealth requirement, while happily maintaining these other socially sanctioned methods of obtaining status.

Activists' search for status takes particular forms in NGOs, which are workplaces as well as places where activism happens. Work is a key arena for the hierarchical manoeuvrings that can indicate status, and turning activism into a job by working for an NGO can turn up the volume on status-chasing. A colleague who was about to bail out of the London NGO rat race once told me, 'I've realised I don't want to become one of those Conference People, the ones who progress from participating on panels to moderating discussions to giving keynotes as they become more important.' There are justification-to-funder reasons why NGOs often try to carve out turf for themselves, why they battle with their peers for media space, but it's also because the individuals involved want recognition and status as experts, as being senior; indeed, these two phenomena often interact. The research on the fundamental nature of our status needs suggests that this might be inevitable.

The problem is that our recognition of what we are up to as activists is uneven, at best. When we start to recognise that status needs have been co-opted by the damaging emphasis on consumption that fuels capitalism, we can turn against all forms of competitive status questing, including those that obviously fuel activism. And to a certain extent, that is a healthy thing to do. Competition *is* over-valued in our culture, and cooperation *is* under-valued. We do want to change this balance. Nora Bateson is right: to focus on competition for status as a way to motivate campaigners removes from sight the possibility of engaging our other equally powerful human potential, for cooperation and solidarity. But the risk, when we recognise the problematic side of status-chasing, is that we push the inevitable status need within ourselves into shadow. We become able to see it only in those we are criticising. It is easier to criticise flagrant status manoeuvres in the people obsessed with consumption whose behaviour we wish we could change, or in our campaigner peers who are overly fond of talking in meetings or putting themselves in front of the camera, than it is to acknowledge it in ourselves.

In my experience, there is very little acknowledgement of any of this – at least, not in a healthy way, that supports activists to reflect consciously on our own needs that we are bringing to the task. The only time individual status needs got talked about, that I saw, was the mostly good-humoured ribbing of those who hog the camera and the lectern, with some occasional behind-the-scenes snark. I wasn't an outrageous media tart but I did quite like doing TV and radio, although I never reached a point where it stopped scaring the hell out of me (in the early days I once froze up entirely on the lunchtime news). I quite like speaking in public and at meetings, and I know I can do it effectively. So my enjoyment in the use of a practised skill has been tied up with my desire to improve the problem at hand, as well as with my desire for recognition for its own sake. And goodness, I have had some of that too. I became a professional campaigner after walking away from my job on a newspaper when my career as a journalist had barely begun, and I still had a scorching desire to prove myself, to do something I could point to and say, 'I did that'.

My extrinsic values – the part of me that cared what other people thought of me – wanted to see me have a recognised impact. My intrinsic values wanted me to have an *actual* impact on the real problems, an impact that benefited others because it was necessary. These two motivations ran so closely together it was hard to separate them. I suspect they do in many campaigners, although of course it is also possible to want to be seen and heard simply because you want to be effective, and not because you have an inner need to promote yourself. The kinds of status that are a reward for doings and achievements, even those that are obtained from mere visibility, can be a proxy for our simple need for recognition: being seen and acknowledged for who we are, for our being-ness and not for our outputs. 'If I'm not doing what I'm known for, what am I?' one campaigner wondered, when we spoke about this. In these terms, chasing status is an entanglement in capitalism, which measures and values us by our outputs.

But status obtained from doings and achievements can also be a proxy for a self-worth that is missing. It can substitute for that inner-generated sense of being utterly accepted in the world, that sense that your very being-ness is enough, which a few lucky people don't have to strive for because it was gifted to them in childhood. Everyone else, irrespective of varying material privilege, is slogging for it, encouraged by our culture's focus, which starts early in children's education, on extrinsic motivation and the rewards of status. And social media, of course, *really* doesn't help.

With these all-too-human sources, status-chasing is not limited to the professionalised NGO sphere. Studies of 'lifestyle activism', in which people reject – and demonstrate their rejection of – societal norms through their clothing, living arrangements and consumption choices, are full of observations of the status hierarchies that form around these very visible decisions.[146] The status-seeking in NGOs, however, has the potential for wider-reaching consequences than the status-seeking in grassroots campaigning. This is because the NGOs often have more access to power than grassroots movements. This access gives them the potential to cause more damage to what is seen as necessary or possible. The author Andrew Simms, who has worked in several NGOs in the UK, suggested that the status needs of professional NGO campaigners can constrain what their organisations even try to tackle, by making them want to be acceptable to those in power. 'It's an acute risk aversion … they're hungry for a kind of establishment acceptability in Whitehall corridors, that leads to the kind of compromises that are indistinguishable from being co-opted,' he observed. This has consequences for what their organisations will say publicly. 'Let's take the environmental and development sector. If they embraced the challenge of describing their mission in terms of a world not dependent on growth, it would require a leap of imagination that they've not been willing to do. In the long term, it's to concede defeat. It speaks of a deep lack of self-confidence. It feels like excommunicating yourself from polite company.'[147]

Unacknowledged status needs can lead to the tactical error of mistaking access to power for real power. Access to power feels good and exciting because it is meeting our own need to feel important as well as being a potentially useful way to achieve campaign goals. There are campaigners, in my experience, who will not miss an opportunity to tell you which senior officials they have met, where they have been travelling for high-level meetings and which important functions they have been speaking at. I have been one of those campaigners too. For as long as it brings with it the power to obtain changes, it can feel like real power. But this is power granted on power's terms. Those who wield it are choosing to engage with you. This is why the high-level influencing that NGOs do is not the same as the bottom-up people-power of a social movement. In reality, you have only got the power that those in power are offering you, and that is always limited to the matters that they are willing to meet you to talk about. They control it effortlessly because you don't even ask for the big stuff in case you lose your access and credibility.

If Nora Bateson was describing the reinforcement of the existing competition-and-hero *frame* through appeals to status, then Simms is hinting here at the reinforcement of existing power *structures*. Activists seeking status recognition from those in power might deliberately limit the scope of what is on the agenda for change. Off the table, in his example, would be the profits of those who continue to benefit from an economy organised around endless growth. Off the table would be the grip on power of those whose politics are funded by donations from such profits. And this is not the only problem. Activists seeking status through their proximity to power will also guard their access to that power, as we saw with the 'saviours' (indeed, they may be the same people as the saviours). This keeps activists with marginalised identities away from opportunities to grapple with the power-holders for more radical changes; changes whose urgency is not comprehended by those without the same life experience and who are not listening because they're busy trying to change the world on their own terms. Off the table, then, would be reparations for the histories of enslavement and colonial plunder, or indeed any other policy change that the most marginalised can ill-afford to wait for.[148] This dynamic interacts comfortably with the desire of many of the wealthy people who engage in philanthropy to obtain the status of 'philanthropist' while actually helping to keep things as they are, as outlined in Anand Giridharadas's book *Winners Take All*.[149] So here we have activists who are deeply entangled in current power through their own privileged position in working for an NGO, or a foundation that funds NGOs, helping to set the terms of what kind of change is possible. Helping, in effect, to keep things as they are.

If we could acknowledge that we are as driven by status needs as the people we criticise, we would stand a chance of facing up to their impact on our strategies and our ways of being a campaigner. Of course, we should examine and seek to change our internal narratives in order to calm our grasping need for status, so we don't have to struggle so hard for it in the outer world. This might leave more of our energy available to put where we most want to apply it, according to our intrinsic values. And we could usefully infuse our campaigning with a deeper understanding of how the framing of values works, and how important it is to emphasise our human potential for collaboration as well as competition. We can try, in short, to minimise the negative impact of competition for status. But wishing our status needs away almost certainly isn't going to work.

Part 2

What activists are entangled in

6 Some words as tools to think with

I BEGAN MY enquiry with questions about why activists so often treat each other, as well as our opponents, in ways that are incompatible with the values we are arguing for. I had questions about why we burn out, and why we think we have to save the world ourselves, and why we are as caught up in our status-quests as any self-respecting hedge fund manager. I was finding some possible explanations, as the last two chapters have explored. But the questions were not going away. Why did we *continue* doing these things? Why was it so hard to switch course? I was hardly the first campaigner to realise that we were often engaged in self-defeating behaviours. Gary Lachman, a prolific chronicler of 20th-century counter-cultures, was keen to warn me that every generation realises its version of these problems, but integrating that realisation remains hard. Every generation has people who start to see that political change requires us to attend to our inner lives, while others want to stay focused on the politics and the economics.

Why is it so hard, then, for activists to see what we are doing when we are caught up in righteousness, sacrifice, individual shouldering of the burden, saviourhood and status-chasing? As we have already seen, some of it is about the workings of our own shadow, our splitting-off of what we don't want to see in ourselves. And some of it involves culturally learned patterns, too. The effect of our culture upon us is like the water that fish swim in and cannot see. It is hard to see how our context shapes our perception. It is hard, then, to see how deeply the problems run – including through us and our activism.

If we could start to perceive how deeply the problems run, we might start to see the extent of what needs to change. But it is hard to talk about, because we don't really have the words. Language can constrain the extent of what we can imagine, and English is short on well-understood and popular words that adequately describe how, simultaneously, we are a product of the world and yet we produce the world. That we live in 'a world partly constituted by human consciousness', to use the psychiatrist Iain McGilchrist's description, is simultaneously a straightforward observation and a complex one.[150] It is true in a simple constitutive sense: together we constitute the world, and so if the world changes we change, and if we change the world changes. But it is also true in deeper ways, which recognise not only how we make the world through our actions but also how the world creates us at – almost – the very core of our being. Our development varies from its shared and evolved pathway according to the influences and environments that we encounter. And the way that we perceive everything and everyone who is not us profoundly affects all that we do. Yet we persist in thinking, as our culture instructs us, that we are separate from everything that is not us.

If we are going to talk about the ways that activists are entangled in what we are trying to change, then we need a suitable language for this overarching shared context of thought and perception that needs to change, if the changes are to be lasting. There are a few candidates, which I have borrowed from philosophy and sociology. Activists sometimes talk about the 'paradigm' that we want to change. We tend to do this when we are trying to think big, beyond the laws and policies that can be simplest to get changed; towards culture shifts, perception shifts. The term was coined in 1962 by the physicist and philosopher of science Thomas Kuhn. For Kuhn, a 'paradigm shift' is what happens when a scientific framework of understanding starts to buckle and break down under the impact of new research and then, suddenly, shifts – like the move from Newtonian to quantum physics. While he was thinking specifically about the natural sciences, where uncontested paradigms can exist in a way that they cannot in the social sciences, the idea of a 'paradigm' quickly escaped into more general use, to mean a worldview or intellectual framework.

As the systems thinker Donella Meadows put it:

> The shared idea in the minds of society, the great big
> unstated assumptions, constitute that society's paradigm,
> or deepest set of beliefs about how the world works.
> These beliefs are unstated because it is unnecessary
> to state them – everyone already knows them. Money
> measures something real and has real meaning; therefore,
> people who are paid less are literally worth less. Growth
> is good. Nature is a stock of resources to be converted to
> human purposes.[151]

In campaigning terms, then, a paradigm shapes the terms of all of the 'systems' that activists want to change. For example, feminist campaigners might be trying to change the *laws* to recognise the ways that domestic violence works, with its insidious forms of undermining and control, as well as direct physical aggression. The *system* that we really want to change, though, is patriarchy, the control of society by men, together with the sexism that props it up and the violent misogyny that polices it.[152] But behind the system of patriarchy is a *paradigm* of thought, feeling and relating, based on assumptions of superiority and dominance, that makes sexist assumptions and misogynist violence even possible. Meadows' point is that paradigms get changed when we can step outside of the 'system' and see it whole, see how it sits in its paradigm. The term 'paradigm', then, is a useful indicator of the scale on which activists need to operate.

It's not a bad word, and I do find myself using it. But it is not quite rich enough. It only hints at what is going on. It does not help us to understand how the unthought-about ideas, assumptions and practices that constitute a paradigm become part of our inner worlds, or, conversely, how we generate them.

There are two other words that do seem to say a bit more about how we are held in the world while generating it: the 'lifeworld' and the 'imaginary'. The 'lifeworld' is an idea that takes account of our inner lives and the way they can be connected to the inner lives of others. It was suggested in the early 20th century by Edmund Husserl, a philosopher who studied our experience of consciousness (a field called phenomenology) and was built upon, later in the century, by the philosopher and sociologist Jürgen Habermas. The latter saw the lifeworld as the shared background understandings to the lived experience of people, communities and the social sphere. 'This stock of knowledge supplies members with unproblematic, common, background convictions that are assumed to be guaranteed,' Habermas wrote.[153] It is shared, a form of collective consciousness that we take for granted. Any social grouping has its lifeworld of shared meanings and understandings. Activists, for example, will have a lifeworld that is mutually intelligible – of values, priorities, lifestyles and understandings that underpin their ways of thinking, interacting and communicating with each other. Groups that differ in their outlooks, however, will share a wider-scale lifeworld that allows their different 'languages' to be, more or less, translatable. So activists will share, with everyone else, the lifeworld of the society of which we are part: the assumptions, social norms and ways of thinking that come with shared language and culture.

For Habermas, the 'lifeworld' is in contrast to the 'system': the commercial imperatives of the economic market and the administrative bureaucracies of the state, with their instrumental rationality that treats individuals as means to their own end.[154] In traditional and premodern societies, lifeworld and system were tightly interwoven. But as societies become more structured, with stratified division of labour, increasingly complex states and legal processes, and economic activity separated from the family and home, lifeworld and system become more differentiated. The personal and interpersonal are removed from the public realm, in which the market and the state now set the terms. (As illustration of the concept, the extreme state that Orwell speculated in his fiction is one where everything has become system and there is no lifeworld left.)[155] It was precisely this separation of the personal and social from the politics, science and bureaucracy that allowed the 'system' to become so complex in modernity. But the irony, Habermas argued, is that while this complexity could not have happened without the shrinking of the lifeworld, the complex bureaucracies and markets that result then start to intrude upon – to 'colonise' – the lifeworld.[156]

What does this look like in reality? It's what market-driven society does to people's ways of relating to each other in communities and as citizens, by monetising transactions that were previously done through mutual support, or by changing the relations between extended family members when the working-age adults have to spend more time at work. The system starts to predate more and more upon the lifeworld. Habermas saw the 'new social movements' – the activist uprisings of the sixties and seventies for civil rights, women's rights, peace and the environment, which were 'new' because they no longer followed the lines of class and labour agitation for redistribution – as emerging forms of resistance against various colonisations of the lifeworld.[157] Activist movements take place along the 'seams' between lifeworld and system. When I talked my way into that OECD meeting to confront those bankers, lawyers and government employees about a set of laws that I wanted enforced, as I described in the previous chapter, I was facing up to a 'system' of finance as well as legislative and regulatory power. I was doing so in defence of a 'lifeworld' that was under threat in countries whose people were being exposed to the destabilising forces of footloose global capital.

Habermas's rich concept has set the agenda for at least a generation of sociologists, and is useful when thinking about what goes on in activism. It suggests a way of understanding what activists are trying to do: to restore a lifeworld that we sense has been profoundly deformed. It also suggests what may be happening when activists speak and are not understood, as we saw in Chapter 4. We are speaking, from our own lifeworld, with its assumptions and values, to a 'system' which speaks a language that works in different terms. But is it a way to describe all of what we are shaped by? On its own it is insufficient for the task, because, by definition, it does not encompass the 'system'. And as we have been seeing, activists are as shaped by the intrusions of the 'system' as much as anyone else. When the system demands, for example, that we see ourselves only as individual consumers, and leads us to do so through its structuring of government, public services and education, then this is a powerful influence on how we do activism that we need to be able to take account of.

This brings us to the concept of the 'imaginary', which is another term I am borrowing from sociology and philosophy. At first glance it appears to have some things in common with the 'lifeworld'. It is a way of describing the shared background assumptions to what we think and do. But by being a bit less specific, it can hold a bit more. For the Canadian philosopher Charles Taylor, the social imaginary is the 'common understanding that makes possible common practices and a widely shared sense of legitimacy'.[158] It's the unconsciously held – or at least, rarely thought about – set of ideas that govern how we relate to each other, and what we think is normal or ought to be. 'Imaginary' seems a tricky word when we meet this idea for the first time. We are used to hearing it as an adjective rather than a noun, an adjective that means 'not real' and that is used pejoratively to suggest we have made something up that is in contrast to what is real and true. Encountering the word as a noun that names a phenomenon, it is hard, at first, to get past this feeling that we are being asked to think about something that is 'not real'. The 'imagine' in 'imaginary', though, is being used in the generative meaning of the word: it is what we generate with our imaginations. This is what makes it very useful for thinking about activism. Activists are living in the shared imaginary of our culture – and, as we have been seeing, are ourselves affected by it – while simultaneously perceiving that it could be different and that changing it could be worth the effort.

'All of us make the imaginary, it is how we imagine things to be,' says Sam Earle, who is studying the philosophy and practical application of thinking in terms of imaginaries. We are all, constantly, creating the imaginary we live in, and it shapes us. 'The imaginary is intimately connected to the imagination,' she says. It holds 'the capacity to reproduce existing tropes that help to cement collective identity, and, conversely, the capacity to conceive of radically new ways of being in, and relating to, the world.' For Earle, the imaginary of each society has a unique constellation of ideas that are either reinforced, or shifted, by our actions – by 'words, gestures, behaviours, politics, institutions' as well as by our thoughts. 'Our actions are the backbone of the social imaginary: they are our imagination made visible,' she says.[159]

So the imaginary is a capacious description of what activists are trying to change, as well as what we are enmeshed in. It is a way of describing the world and our place in it that takes account of what activism is trying to do. Taylor's description of 'common practices' and 'legitimacy' is precisely the stuff that activism concerns itself with when it is trying to alter norms and laws. If activism is a work of imagination which can see that something could be different – and all activism must start with such seeing – then the imaginary starts to shift as soon as some people start to see differently and to act differently in response to their new sight. The idea of the imaginary contains a recognition, then, that activism can begin with an act of imagination. It also, however, contains an implicit recognition that this 'seeing' can fail. We can fail to see the terms of the dominant imaginary we are living in. We can fail to see how its terms hide from us the nature of our relationship with the world. We can keep on trying to change a 'system' without seeing the assumptions that lie behind it. The dominant imaginary frames our thinking and our acting, while hiding, in plain sight, the fact that it is doing so.

What both of these ideas – the lifeworld and the imaginary – help to illuminate is that everyone, activists included, has been created by the forces that activists are trying to unpick. The activist's job is complicated because we are trying to change a system we are implicated in. In the next three chapters I'm going to look at some of the ways this is happening, by examining some of the contents of the dominant imaginary that activists find ourselves caught in. But if imaginaries contain 'words, gestures, behaviour, politics, institutions' as Earle suggests, then where on earth do we start? That sounds like everything under the sun. It contains ideas as well as matters made concrete, stories as well as structures. It might seem, at first glance, that stories affect our inner worlds, while structures and systems – in the forms of institutions of power – affect our material life. But as Taylor points out, the very nature of the imaginary means that it's no good trying to separate what is 'inner' to us and what is material in the world: we would be creating a 'false dichotomy between ideas and material factors as rival causal agencies'. It is hard to separate ideas and human practices, he warns: 'one cannot distinguish the two in order to ask the question, Which causes which?'[160] The ideas and the systems we create, he is saying, are themselves entangled. And of course, there is no description that can set out the complexity of human experience in a linear way.

Still, that ideas and human practices are entangled is precisely what activists are dealing with. My intention for the next three chapters, then, is a temporary untangling, so we can get a glimpse, a feel for what activists are caught in. I am going to start with stories, then move on to the institutions of power – the systems – that are created by the stories, and that shape people, activists included. I'd then like to bring the circle round, and back to how these *stories* and *systems* affect our inner lives – which of course then plays out in our behaviour. The concept of the 'psychosocial' – a word to describe psychological processes interacting with social contextual forces to shape behaviour – contains a recognition that psychic and social processes are always implicated in each other and cannot be understood separately in a meaningful way.[161] To even separate 'what is arriving' in our inner world from 'what is already there' can only be a narrative trick, as we have been shaped by our environment since before we were born.

So activists are entangled in stories; entangled in power; entangled in the ways that stories and power shape our inner worlds and our experiences of being an embodied human. Once we start to think about it in this way, the very idea that we can change the world without even acknowledging this complexity comes to seem rather extraordinary. Whichever of these aspects of our entanglement we look at, there is much to observe about how far we are from being able to change the world if we perceive it as something 'over there', separate to us.

7 Entangled in stories

FOR ANY activists who had not realised the strategic importance of stories by 2016, the votes for Trump and Brexit made it impossible to ignore. These were votes for the stories that their campaigns were telling, not for the facts about what the practical impacts might be. Alex Evans, a campaigner who had spent his career as a development expert working for NGOs and writing policy reports for UN committees, woke up to the limitations of such activity and wrote a book called *The Myth Gap*, exhorting progressive activists to wield emotionally activating stories as effectively as conservatives do. Andrew Simms, who has authored several books on climate change and the need for a new approach to economics, began, alongside his campaigning, editing books of 'modern folk tales for troubled times' that would invite readers to 'engage a different brain'. (I took the opportunity to turn 'Bluebeard' into an offshore tax lawyer in the second collection.)[162] There has been a proliferation of projects, trainings, consultancies and exhortations encouraging activists to think about storytelling and to find stories that will engage the hearts and minds of those we are trying to influence. 'Narrative' and 'storytelling' have become campaigning buzzwords and are useful for attracting the attention of potential funders. This emphasis operates at a superficial, tactical level: what is the story we can tell about this issue we are working on that will reach the people we want to influence? It is happening at a strategic level, too, on issues where campaigners have recognised that the policies they want to change are based on an underlying story that needs shifting, and 'changing the narrative' becomes the aim and not just the method of their intervention.

Whether storytelling is adopted as a tactic or the crowning of a 'new story' is the goal, we assume as activists that we are in a position to manipulate the stories we use. We assume we can send them out into the world at our command. It has a whiff of paternalism as well as exceptionalism. Those people out there are being influenced by stories; we, the activists, need to tell some new stories; and we have got sufficient perspective on the stories that already exist to create some new stories that will work for our purposes. But is that true? It's a succumbing to a particular story, as the fantasy author Terry Pratchett observed: 'people think that stories are shaped by people. In fact it's the other way around.'[163] Or, perhaps, it is both. Ben Okri describes what novelists perhaps understand more instinctively than most campaigners: 'One way or another we are living the stories planted in us early or along the way, or we are also living the stories we planted – knowingly or unknowingly – in ourselves. We live stories that either give our lives meaning or negate it with meaninglessness. If we change the stories we live by, quite possibly we change our lives.'[164] But in order truly to change narratives and stories, activists need a sufficiently deep understanding of the stories that are already in place – and that we might be embedded in ourselves. Martin Shaw, a mythologist, storyteller and wilderness guide, complains about the story-illiteracy of the young 'eco set' with their 'premature intelligence and even strident wisdoms. Your insights, though brilliant,' he warns, 'cannot yet carry the chthonic weight of images that have trawled countless thousands of years to lay their treasure at your door.'[165] His point is that we have plenty of stories already; the problem is that we don't know them or don't understand what they are telling us.

Stories don't just underpin the institutions and rules that activists say we want to change. They hold the invisible aspects of the imaginary that frame what we think is normal. Narratives become normative. They tell us what should be common sense. They form the unseen structure of tangible institutions that wield tangible power. Stories with ancient roots in the religious cultural bedrock, with their injunctions about sacrifice and hard work and proving worth, later came to the fore in the Protestant Reformation and were built into the structures of capitalism, outliving the widespread abandonment of formal religious observance.[166] Stories that were made up about the existence of race as a scientific category, told to justify the exploitation of colonialism and the trade in people who had been enslaved, have outlived the previous manifestations of those practices. Stories with their roots in the earliest agricultural societies about human freedom from the web of life, gained through technological mastery, have gained strength over millennia through incorporation in religions, social structures such as patriarchy, and more recently mainstream economics, which still do not recognise ecological limits, even as we face ecological collapse. Activists may develop a critical stance on some aspects of the story and want to do something about it: that is why we became activists. But other aspects hold us firmly. Progressive activists might have separated themselves from the moral prescriptions regulating personal life and behaviour that came with old religious stories, but we are still caught up in ideas about the work ethic, proving our worth and having to be good. Stories about freedom from the web of life can lead activists to advocate for technocratic or technological changes to 'save' nature, but from within a frame that still fails to challenge the faulty positioning of 'nature' as only an input to 'economy', and as separate to 'human'.[167]

A thread running through many of these stories, and one responsible for ensnaring many activists, is individualism, an ancient story with its roots in the Axial Age in which the monotheistic religions emerged. As the author and broadcaster Mark Vernon points out, you needed some sense of yourself as an individual to be able to comprehend the great monotheistic 'I am'.[168] At the dawn of the modern era the individual became the locus of resistance to previous manifestations of power. Protestantism overthrew the rules about who had access to God, and liberalism overthrew the rules of deference to monarchical absolutism. Some new heroes emerged from these revolutionary new stories. One was the individual, whose freedom and – so the theory went – equality are protected by prioritising the individual over the collective. Another was the rational actor, 'homo economicus', of classical and neoclassical economics, who – so the theory went – will weigh economic opportunity and behave logically to maximise his benefit.

The capitalism that current activists often want to modify (or, depending on the activist, overthrow) has, they argue, taken individualism down a destructive path by elevating the rights of individuals as consumers and the rights of some individuals to profit at the expense of others. Neoliberalism – which, to use the political economist William Davies' description, has been the state-led attempt to remake society more firmly in the image of the market over the past generation – has added fuel to the stories of liberalism. It has done so by further emphasising the role of the competitive individual and, as the state increasingly legislated itself out of the job, by de-emphasising the role of the collective. Yet the human rights that activists defend and want to extend are also founded on the primacy of the individual that is at the heart of the Eurocentric liberal imaginary. These are rights that each person holds, as an individual. In individualism, too, is rooted the very possibility of the activist as a thinking self who can express the views held by that self. When we think that we have to save the world ourselves, as Chapter 5 described, we are acting out the individualist script even if our campaigning is condemning the effects of individualism.

So we are deeply entangled *in particular stories* that underpin the problems we are trying to change. We think we are changing them, and perhaps we are changing some aspects, but we remain held by others. We are also entangled, however, *in our habitual ways of relating to stories*: in how we respond and react to them. To be more precise, we are entangled in our habitual ways of relating to particular types of story, the ones that can be called ideology. What does it mean to say we are entangled in how we relate to ideology?

When activists criticise the stories that have been most absorbed into mainstream common sense (which is how the imaginary is often disguised), we are often accused of being 'ideological'. When do stories become ideology? An ideology is a set of political ideas, so one answer to that question is when, taken together, stories about what humans are like and what we need are used to create a political or economic theory. An ideology is a set of ideas with a practical intention; ideas that somebody wants to put into practice, rather than ideas that are going to help us transparently see reality.[169] The other answer to that question of 'when do stories become ideology?' however, is 'when we don't like them'. It can be an accusation of *wrong thinking*. The way that the other side's thinking is 'ideological', while 'our' thinking, naturally, is rational and logical. Ideology has a way of disguising itself as common sense when applied to the doctrines that we do agree with, or – for those who like the status quo – when they support the status quo. People who support 'neoliberal' policies without describing them with that word, for example, can feel uncomfortable when confronted with the suggestion that neoliberalism is not just 'common sense' but a deliberate doctrine that was developed, researched and implanted in university economics departments over decades before it emerged into policy under Thatcher and Reagan.[170] Marxists would call this unawareness 'false consciousness', a failure to acknowledge the reality of dominant economic and class interests.

But ideology as an accusation is also an accusation of *not enough* thinking; and that is where many people's allergies to it – and, by extension, to activists – come from. The history of the 20th century reminds us that ideology can be the road to concentration camps and gulags. Some people's horror at the mere prospect of progressive activism arises because its ideas sound, to their ear, too much like socialism, and that sounds like a very obvious version of 20th-century ideology gone wrong. As Hannah Arendt observed, ideology was central to the operations of totalitarianism. But in her view, this wasn't because the ideologies that underpinned Nazism and Stalinism – racism and communism, respectively – were themselves inherently totalitarian. It was because ideologies of any kind contain elements that make them, as she put it, 'disturbingly useful for totalitarian rule'.[171] These elements include ideologies' claim to total explanation, their promotion of thinking that can proceed without any reference to reality or experience, and the vulnerability of such thinking to being extended into an endless logic with deadly consequences (such as that those people deemed inferior must be killed). These tendencies, she argued, all operate in direct opposition to free thinking.[172]

For the political theorist George Kateb, what ideology has in common with all other kinds of stories – personal, historical, fictional, myths, legends, religion, theology – is that it is an attempt to confer meaning and structure on the raw material of reality.[173] Stories satisfy our longing for clarity, structure and meaning. Any teller of any kind of story is leaving out some of the details of life as it is lived, moment to moment, in order to create a compelling narrative. The problem, then, is any kind of story or idea that is taken literally. In this view, the ideology-fuelled totalitarianism that Arendt anatomised was the ultimate attempt to impose structure on reality, by controlling the everyday reality of everyone. Our fear, when we fear fanaticism, is, in Kateb's words, of the 'story that the ideology tells about reality'.

But it can also be the mere prospect of activism that is troubling to observers. The mere prospect of people who are sufficiently convinced by a story to be acting on it can feel, to those who do not feel the same, like over-conviction. For someone who is not doing activism, anybody acting on stories and ideas holds the potential to appear a bit suspect, rather like the way that anyone who holds more anger about politics than we do ourselves can seem a bit incomprehensible.

Activists of all kinds are telling stories all the time: about what is wrong with the world, about what will make it better, about how to get there. Someone's reactivity to activists who are telling 'stories' – or ideology – about reality is grounded in a fear that those stories and ideologies will become weaponised against certain people, certain beneficiaries of the status quo … perhaps against themselves. Such opposition to ideologies can even become ideological in itself; and I am saying 'ideological', there, in the pejorative sense of 'something that is done without thinking'. Somebody 'just knows', for example, that they distrust conservatives. Or, that they distrust activists. Or that they distrust anyone who talks about 'white men' or 'privilege'. They observe what looks like lack of thinking in activist ideology. They do not always observe the possibility of their own defensiveness about the problems that the activists are trying to talk about, a defensiveness that may be rooted in the stories that they like to tell about the world, or about themselves as good people.

The thing is, activists *are* often ideological. We *are* often working according to a set of ideas about human needs and how to meet them with particular political and economic actions. We are acting towards the adoption of one set of ideologies, while trying to unwrap the tentacles of the old ones from around our ankles – and perhaps failing to see quite how many tentacles there are. And we are, too, often busy promoting our chosen ideology without being aware of what we have invested in it.

I encountered this idea that we might relate differently to ideology as *a way of thinking* in the work of developmental psychologists like Robert Kegan, Jane Loevinger, Bill Torbert and Susanne Cook-Greuter, who study how we develop throughout our lifespan. The lens through which they see 'adult development' varies: values, worldviews, cognitive capacities.[174] Whatever the focus of the model, they are describing the same thing: that humans develop in stages, potentially throughout our whole lives, and that we remain at each stage for some time, before a transformation to the next. These stages of development happen to individuals, and also to the evolutionary history of culture. As the theorist of consciousness Ken Wilber puts it, 'each of these stages of development occurred to humanity as a whole, and repeats itself in essentially basic ways in individuals today, with everybody starting at stage one and proceeding essentially up to the average level of development in his or her culture (with some individuals lower, some higher).'[175] I found these theories interesting because they describe the process by which people can both change their ideology, and their relationship with ideology. While the models are not focused specifically on activists, their findings are applicable to what happens when people become activists, as well as to what happens when we change our perspective on activism. They helped me to think about the ways in which activists are entangled in stories.

As a brief diversion before I continue with unpicking our entanglement in stories and ideology, I should add that the developmental models also helped me to think about some of the questions that were troubling me as I emerged from the form of activism that I had been doing. Reading Ken Wilber and Frederic Laloux, who frame the developmental stages in terms of 'values' and 'evolution of consciousness,' helped to explain my sense of bafflement that people with whom I otherwise had plenty in common, including my own family, could hold such different values to mine. In the terms of the Spiral Dynamics model, which both these authors build on, and which are fairly straightforward to grasp with their colour labels, I had perhaps made the classic becoming-activist transition from 'Orange' to 'Green', and was now disdainful of my family's largely Orange values. Orange, in societal terms, is modernity: rational, materialist, scientific, entrepreneurial, expertise, achievement, meritocracy. It fuelled the scientific and industrial revolutions, brought liberation from monarchical and religious authority and outlawed slavery, and it is still the beating heart of leaders in business and government. Green, which emerges from Orange, is pluralism, equality, fairness, cooperation. It was appearing in artists and radical campaigners in the 19th and 20th centuries and emerged into full flowering in the 1960s, driving the new social movements for civil rights, feminism and the environment, and then the NGO scene that they birthed towards the end of the century. It has been at the centre, too, of postmodern culture in academia. Green is troubled by the shadow side of Orange: exploitation, corporate greed and its focus on profit above relationships and ecology.[176]

I was excited to read about this. Here, it seemed, was the invisible architecture of my arguments with my Dad. His centre of gravity was Orange, and mine was now Green. Here, too, was some context for my despair that the senior people in the companies I was targeting as a campaigner could seemingly care so little about what lay beyond the profit motive. It felt reassuring. My turning against some of Dad's values wasn't only my rebellion against his personal authority and identity; it was a cultural move, too, something that happened more widely. But Green also has its shadow side, and it manifests in the phenomena that had been troubling me about activism. In its reactivity to Orange, Green becomes the only outlook that is right. It leads to the paradox that the people espousing tolerance for all are themselves profoundly intolerant of those who disagree; as indeed I was of my Dad's views. Wilber named this shadow side the 'mean Green meme'.

I had, and still have, qualms about these models. One is that they seem insufficiently political. To people who are deeply involved in campaigning for social justice and ecological sanity, they seem to skate over the extent of the oppression, environmental damage and corporate excess created by the Orange cultural value stage, and to see oppression primarily as something that came with the earlier 'Red' and 'Amber' stages. In describing the stages that emerge after Green and that seem to remedy Green's activist intolerance of wrong thinking, they seem to skate over the extent of the work that still needs doing, the work that the people who are operating from the Green mindset are at least trying to do. My second qualm about these models is that they emerge from the dominant imaginary and, insofar as I have seen, contain insufficient reflection on the extent to which the dominant culture has shaped their view. They can sound at times like the worst kind of old anthropology, with its talk of 'primitive' cultures. Capacities and mindsets which we only develop, according to these models, in advanced stages of development, such as interdependence, are central to non-European worldviews that place interdependence of humans, both among humans and between humans and non-human nature, at the core of their philosophy and way of life.

My third concern is that they are prone to misuse. The models propose a 'developmental hierarchy' in which higher stages are not 'better' than lower ones; they are merely a description of how things are. But to readers who are inevitably shaped by the kinds of 'dominator hierarchy' that we see and experience all around us, in which anyone 'higher' on most scales is not only seen as 'better' but is able to wield more power, it is extremely hard to resist the temptation to rank ourselves and everyone we know. It is also tempting, when ranking ourselves, to situate ourselves further 'up' any of these models than we actually are. If 'spiritual bypass' is pretending to a high level of spiritual enlightenment without having done the consistent work and practice to truly attain it, then 'developmental bypass' is, in my view, what these models can encourage in intelligent people who have the cognitive processing and abstracting capacities to appreciate intellectually what the higher stages consist of, but who have not fully absorbed the lessons of each stage along the way in order to encompass and then transcend them. And I am including myself in this observation; I have been as tempted to try to rank myself as anyone else who has studied these models.

That the developmental models are misused, however, does not mean they are without value. Let's return to ideology and storytelling, and specifically to Robert Kegan's model, which focuses on what happens in individuals rather than what happens in the culture at large. In his view, we grow in maturity when we can take as 'object' those phenomena to which we were formerly 'subject'.[177] What does this mean? The developmentalists' insight builds on Jean Piaget's pioneering observations of children's development from infancy to adulthood. Piaget was interested in how children construct the mental models that they use to understand the world. A two-year-old *is* his needs and desires; he wants that toy now and he cannot conceive of a self that is separate from its desire for the toy. The only thing that will work, if the toy cannot be in his grasp, is distraction. His eight-year-old sister is able to do something different. She also wants the toy, but she can comprehend that her desire for it is not the same as 'her'. She *is* someone who *wants* the toy. Her desires have become 'object' to her. She 'has' her desires, rather than them 'having' her. It is well recognised that transitions to a more complex developmental stage occur throughout childhood and adolescence, but less recognised that they continue, with the right conditions, throughout adulthood.[178]

A key adult transition, although not one that all adults make, is from the stage Kegan calls 'socialised' (which most adults do reach) to the one he calls 'self-authoring'. We go from defining our perspective and values according to the norms of the people and society around us (socialised), to being able to form and hold our own values and perspectives (self-authoring). This shift can mirror what in other models looks like the transition from the values of Orange to Green, although there is no direct or easy translation between the cultural value models and Kegan's model. (And there are arguably plenty of activists with an Orange centre of gravity, or a mindset that is socialised within their activist community.)

In Kegan's view, minority groups find both challenge and support for the transition to 'self-authoring' when they work to develop their identities in order to fight for them. 'Any "community of ideology", whether it is a culturally embedded community, and thus less visible (such as the induction of those favoured by the culture into the professions), or a community of counter-dominant ideology and thus necessarily visible (such as induction into feminism or Afrocentrism), can serve as a support or a holding environment for evolving [the self-authoring stage],' he writes. 'They call on their members to construct a theory of their own oppression and an internalised system or procedure for subjecting all their values and loyalties to reanalysis.'[179] This is the consciousness-raising and development of agency that activists who are fighting for their lives know very well, and it results in a person who has consciously chosen their stance towards the world.

The shift to self-authoring can also be the classic move performed by someone reacting against the dominant culture in which they have been raised to become an activist. They start, as I did, to criticise the values that were previously invisible to them, and to adopt a different stance. They now 'have' the dominant ideology – let's say, because this is a common occurrence, 'neoliberalism'. It is no longer invisible, nor common sense: they can see its effects in the world around them, and they can critique it. And they have adopted and identified with, as the foundation of their self-authoring identity, a new and different ideology. It might be 'socialism'. It might be 'deep ecology'. Or it might be 'climate emergency'. The activist has dropped one story and is now in another. For people turning to activism via either of these routes, the ideology of the dominant culture is now 'object' to them. But ideology *in itself, as a way of thinking*, is still invisible. They are still in its grip: thinking ideologically.

Kegan suggests that we can develop further, to a point where we 'have' ideology as a way of thinking, and can see its effect on us. This happens at the stage beyond 'self-authoring', which he calls 'self-transforming'.[180] That there is even a possibility of relating differently to ideology raised questions for me, and I struggled with this idea when I first came across it. I became immediately defensive. Is it even a problem that activists *are* thinking ideologically? Surely that is the motor of activism? And what would happen to activism if we were less held by ideology? When I read Kegan's suggestion that there is a mindset in which we can develop beyond ideology's hold on us, it sounded like he is valorising a detachment from ideology by associating it with greater maturity. To my activist ear, that sounded dangerously close to valorising a detachment from commitment, since the ideology – or story – which guides us can seem inextricable from the vision to which we are committed. To my activist ear, it sounded like an implication that we can 'grow' out of activism, and that, in turn, can sound uncomfortably like our parents telling us that we will become more conservative when we get older.

I have slowly started to hear something else in what he is saying, though. It's that we may still be ideological – committed to a particular story and the alternative picture of the world that it paints – but we can also take a perspective on *how* we are being ideological. In abstract terms, we can 'have', or take as 'object' to us, *the very idea of being ideological*, rather than remaining 'subject' to it by ... well, by thinking that our ideology *is* us. What does this look like in practical terms? We may still be committed to working for the story of our chosen ideology, but we are no longer attached to it *as a way of thinking about who we are*. We understand that our ideology is not us; it's a frame for thinking and seeing and acting in the world that we have chosen to adopt. Its boundaries are not necessarily our boundaries. This means we are more likely to be able to hear what people with other ideologies are saying, even if we disagree, without instantly being activated to defend what we had hitherto thought of as *our* boundaries. We are more likely to be able to stand up for the issue calmly.

To be clear, Kegan is not talking explicitly about activism in his description of the 'self-authoring' mind. I am applying his thinking to my own questions about activism. In Kegan's terms, then, when we 'wake up' to being an activist and use this waking up to develop from the 'socialised' stage to 'self-authored', we are disembedding ourselves from some of the commonly held stories of our culture and adopting new ones that give us a sense of agency and identity. We are a boundaried self, we know who we are because we have chosen who to be, and activism is a key part of our identity. It is more than that: our identity as activist-for-our-chosen-ideology is what has helped us to attain that powerful sense of self. So we get attached to our new and chosen ideology because it feels part of us. It feels part of our identity as a self-authoring adult that we are fighting for our ideology's vision of the world. What this strong sense of self-direction and identity obscures from us is how attached we have become to this view of ourselves, and how attached we might have therefore become to the story that has helped us to develop this boundaried sense of ourselves.

And what I have gradually started to see is that it is possible to retain the depth and strength of commitment to an alternative vision that we need in order to fight for that vision, while not identifying *ourselves* so completely with it. I started to see it in long conversations with activists who are intuiting and experiencing that it is possible to be very committed to the work without being quite so attached to the importance of your own place in it. When they speak from this awareness, they are finding they sound different. Their activism sounds different. They come across differently. To my ear, tuned to Kegan's observations, what these activists are describing is possible because they are relating to ideology – to the *story* of what they are trying to shift in the world – differently. They are identifying with it differently, and the crucial difference is that they can see *that the story is not them*. They are reaching this intuition through different routes. But whether we are fighting for our own identity, or our chosen identity as activist as part of our own evolution – or, indeed, both – this is a hard-won, difficult and utterly counter-cultural insight. The insight is counter-cultural because it seems to go against the culture of so much activism: the 'hero-ness' of it, the sense of me being at the centre of it all, whoever I am and whatever I am fighting for, sword and shield raised against the world. That is why it was hard for me to hear: because I am still disentangling myself from the understanding of activism I had created, with myself at the centre of the story, driving the action. If the vision I'm working for helps me to feel like me, then it can feel hard to hold that vision more lightly. It can be hard to see that it is not all about me. It can be hard to hold myself back from going in for the kill whenever somebody disagrees with me.

So it is hard to gain this stance on our entanglement in ideology. It is hard because, as a developmental move, it cannot simply be done through a willed shift of perspective. Any developmental transition, as Kegan reminds us, requires support as well as challenge and, of course, time. Gaining perspective on our entanglement in ideology is also hard for another reason, however, one that these models, in their lack of focus on politics, pay less attention to. It is hard because the dominant ideologies, the ones that activists are seeking to extract ourselves from and then overturn, have taken concrete form in the world. The dominant ideologies have been made tangible in the institutions of power that shape our lives. To 'see' ideologies from the outside is hard when, applied in practice by those in power, ideologies can alter our embodied experience of the world. They can alter our epistemologies, our ways of understanding what we encounter. Ideologies combined with systems of power develop heft in the world, which is what I turn to in the next chapter.

8 Entangled in power

I F ONE kind of activist entanglement is in stories, another kind of entanglement is in the tangible results of those stories. The stories – whether they are about individualism, or neoliberalism, or human separation from nature – have helped to create political structures and institutions that enforce power. We are entangled in the effect of those systems on our lives and our behaviour. The institutions and rules of the state, with repressive power at their disposal, are usually the first form of 'power' that we think of, but more fundamentally we are in thrall to capital, towards whose endless increase and protection the state is oriented. The institutions and rules that govern the state and the market are the ostensible target of most activism. Let's change them, activists say: let's change how the police operate; let's change landlords' powers, and fracking rules, and how banks create money, and let's shut down the arms trade while we're at it.

It is hard to perceive our entanglement in stories and ideologies when they have been turned into concrete reality, in the form of the systems we want to change. Being surrounded by, living in a world governed by all of the institutions created under the terms of the dominant imaginary starts to change how we think. It has changed our very perception of what we encounter; it has changed what we think is reality. For example, people in the most individualistic cultures, which psychologists call WEIRD (Western, Educated, Industrialised, Rich, Democratic) are more likely to perceive a world of separate objects, rather than relationships.[181] It is hard to see that we are doing this when it is the air we breathe. Even if we do see it, there's the immense practical difficulty of finding a way to do things differently. As the cultural and political theorist Jeremy Gilbert puts it, 'It's one thing to know all this in theory. It's another thing to undo all of our individualist conditioning and to negotiate a wholly individualist set of social institutions, without finding ourselves being forced to behave like competitive individualists despite ourselves, or without simply going crazy.'[182]

There are at least two ways that activists are entangled in the political and economic institutions that turn ideas into power. One is that our perceptions, behaviour and choice of strategies are influenced by the practical workings of these systems, as well as by the ideas behind them. The other – and it is not separate from the first – is that we are entangled by our positions in relation to the histories of pain and oppression caused by those institutions.

When I first started acknowledging rather than repressing my uncomfortable questions about whether my campaigning was effective, one of those questions was about why we were mimicking aspects of the economic system that we were trying to fix. I was keeping a quiet list of examples I was seeing around me in NGO-land, such as battles with unfair pay, a seemingly inexorable move towards more controlling and creativity-sapping management structures as the organisations I worked for grew, and fierce competition for funding. They seemed like problems from the commercial world: surely if we were trying to change aspects of that world, we should be avoiding them? There I was with my list, and it was a good starting place, but I found other activists who had been digging deeper to understand what might be going on. One of them was Ayeisha Thomas-Smith, a broadcaster and Director of Movement Building with the New Economy Organisers Network, a training and support coalition for activists working on alternatives to neoliberalism. She had studied for an MA and was now working on a PhD about the effect of neoliberalism on activism. She was looking at what happens when activist organisations are not vigilant about the possibility of being influenced by neoliberal ideology, and how they can resist it. Her research was initially prompted by questions about why activists were getting so burnt out, and she was concluding that trying to do the 'anti-work' of disrupting a system by using that system's methods led to 'cognitive breakdown'.

Her research into activism in the neoliberal era uses Michel Foucault's theory of 'governmentality', which describes the way that governments try to produce the citizens best suited to fulfil those governments' policies. Foucault, a French philosopher who was writing in the 1960s and 1970s, is helpful for thinking about activist entanglements in stories that have turned into power, because his work describes how knowledge (he used the term 'discourses', but we could also say 'stories' or 'ideology') shapes power through the functioning of institutions, especially those of the state. He described how power is wielded over people whose lives are shaped by those institutions – particularly those whose lives are made marginal by them, including the mentally ill and criminals. When Foucault was speaking about 'governmentality' in his celebrated public lectures in the late 1970s, the neoliberal project had not yet been launched into practical action with the privatisations of the Thatcher and Reagan years.[183] While he discussed neoliberal theory as it stood at that point, he didn't see governmentality as a specifically neoliberal activity; he saw its roots 300 years earlier in the emergence of modernity.[184] But as an idea that describes how the citizen is shaped by the state to the state's own convenience, governmentality is a useful analytical tool for thinking about what neoliberalism, specifically, has done to our activism.

Neoliberalism is characterised not only by the fact that it is the *state* that is leading the reshaping of society in the image of the market, but that, by undermining community, removing social safety nets and turning everyone into an entrepreneur of themselves, it is intruding into the subjective experience of citizens. 'The aim of governmentality becomes not forcing the individual to act in a certain way, but creating the conditions within which he will want to act in that way, believing that he is exercising free choice in his own interest,' writes Thomas-Smith.[185] And this is exactly what neoliberalism has done. 'It's not just a way of thinking,' she says. 'Neoliberalism is a specific political programme that targets a way of being and feeling.' This was the famous Margaret Thatcher quote: 'Economics are the method; the object is to change the soul.'[186] I knew that quote, but I hadn't thought about it in the context of activism.

I was starting to make more sense of my troubled instinct that a modus operandi of providing facts and expecting power-holders to make rational decisions in response to them was gravely inadequate. Not only did this method not take account of our unconscious psychology, as I explored in Chapter 4, but it didn't take account of the fact that we were up against a system that had already been altering our perceptions at levels deeper than rational processing for nearly four decades! The people we were trying to influence in this manner might have had what they thought of as their 'choices' shaped in ways that were not visible to them. And so, of course, had we. I could now see, too, how activists could end up doing things that felt like the outcomes of our good rational choices, but that were actually fundamentally shaped by the environment we were now in. Neoliberalism's greater emphasis on the individual in their personal relationship with the market had made the seeking of achievement and status more of a practical survival necessity than they were a generation or two ago. People must compete more fiercely for jobs in order to live, must market ourselves as a brand both online and off, and this is the environment in which activists, who need to eat and pay the bills like everyone else, are operating. Like everyone else, activists must market ourselves and compete for status. 'If we're trying to destroy the capitalist system but we need enough security and income to be actors within it, it's really tough,' says Thomas-Smith.

What activists can learn from the idea of governmentality, then, is that unless we are very careful, the structures of a neoliberal system can end up producing the *activists* best suited to maintaining the status quo. This is the silent and invisible working of power. Foucault called it 'governmentality', and Antonio Gramsci, the Italian Marxist who was imprisoned by

Mussolini, called it 'hegemony'. Written from prison, his theory of hegemony describes how power is wielded not just by the force of the state, but invisibly by stories wielded in the culture by the dominant class.[187] There I had been at my NGO desk, using a few minutes of my lunch break to add to my list of ways that we were unwittingly reinforcing the system we were trying to change, and of course there was nothing new under the sun. (There rarely is, of course.) But now I could start to see it more clearly. The distinction between visible and invisible forms of power can help us to see how activists who are attempting to change the visible forms of power can still be reinforcing the invisible ways that power is manifested.

Activists maintaining the status quo is perhaps most obvious in professionalised campaigning NGOs. In a world where time has become money, the upside of NGOs is that, by raising money from the public, philanthropic sources or government grants to pay their staff, they offer a way for activists to commit proper time to the job of bringing change. They offer a means for activists to work together, to raise funds, to earn a living, to gain some status. Yet what often happens in these circumstances is that activists adopt approaches, attitudes and methods that look like those prevalent in the economic system they want to change, and in consequence limit the extent of the change they are asking for. Pressure from funders to demonstrate results cascades through campaigning organisations, requiring more managerial control, more planning, more reporting, less creativity and less time spent on activism.[188]

As we saw in the discussion of status needs in Chapter 5, activists internalise the unspoken rules about what is acceptable, and police them when colleagues propose something too radical: 'we're not dealing with that at the moment.' (This reminds me, having spent time in a Murdoch-owned newsroom at the beginning of my career, of observing how people who went into journalism to tell the truth may self-censor what they even try to write about when they end up working for a newspaper whose proprietor has known views.) Meanwhile, companies that are the target of activism like to improve their reputations by being able to point to 'NGO engagement', while simultaneously tying those NGOs up in endless consultation processes to prevent them causing actual damage to business-as-usual. It is well documented that in such circumstances, NGOs can end up supporting free-market capitalism and the interests of the wealthy. INCITE!, a grassroots activist collective in the US, describes such phenomena as the 'non-profit industrial complex'.[189]

If campaigning is funded, transactions are involved, and in the context of a market society, activism can start to look like a market. This can happen in at least two ways. One is that NGOs are selling success stories to the foundations that fund them, and competing with their peers to have the best stories to sell in order to win funding. 'The products sold include the organising accomplishments, models and successes that one can put on display to prove competency and legitimacy,' said Amara H. Perez in *The Revolution Will Not be Funded*.[190] Another is that citizens who support NGOs with a subscription or donation are able to purchase a good conscience. They are making themselves feel better with a market transaction. 'You are somebody who is finding it hard to navigate between your soul, and the ecological destruction you see around you or the human rights situation you see in the media,' says James Marriott, an artist who works with the campaign group Platform in the UK. 'Consumption is when you purchase other people's labour for your pleasure. You're not going to go and stop any fucking whalers, how the hell are you going to get out there? So you buy, off the shelf, somebody who's going to do it for you.'[191]

'The language the corporates want you to talk, that some funders want you to talk, is of deliverables and outcomes,' complains Anders Lustgarten, a playwright who has worked in NGOs as well as taken part in direct-action protests. 'This is the infestation of the attitudes of the private sector into the public. The language they don't want you to talk is of the ruckus … Activism has become a crappy corporatised form of careerism for liberals. Most of the money goes on middle management and expensive offices. Why do you need an office that looks like a firm of Miami architects? A generation ago these people would have been in the public sector. The current system of professional activism is corporate soft power.'[192]

'Liberals' can mean lots of things, often depending on the point of comparison or which side of the Atlantic you are on. In America it can mean you are progressive rather than conservative; here in the UK it can mean you support a welfare state but are not a socialist calling for transformed economic power relations. More broadly, 'liberal' describes the foundation of Western democracies in ideas about freedom and equality of the individual, and freedom of the market. Lustgarten is using the word critically to suggest people who want a bit of change but not too much. I hear a suggestion in his words that 'real' activism would perhaps not be performed by such people; that these might be mutually exclusive categories. I'm not sure I agree that liberals – in whichever use of the term – can't do activism. And there are types of activism, such as protecting human rights, which can sit squarely in the realm of assuring the rights for all that liberalism has long promised. His point, though, which I came to see for myself as I reached the limits of my NGO job, is that if people working for NGOs are not vigilant, they are in danger of succumbing to corporate priorities.

The unwitting submission of NGOs to neoliberal market logic and the symbiotic relationship between NGOs, neoliberal states and corporations have been extensively investigated and written up by social researchers, but the resulting papers tend to hide, as academic papers do, behind the expensive paywalls of academic journals.[193] As an aside, I was struck, researching this book, by the chasm between the experience of the people working for NGOs, who are becoming conscious of the limitations of their approach but wonder if it is they who are going mad, and the wealth of research that makes some sense of this instinct about their entanglement in the dominant system, but which is largely inaccessible to them. (Although clearly, campaigners' preference for action over reflection is also part of the problem; I spent many years not wanting to think about these questions.) Here I am writing a book arguing for us to look into our own inner lives to improve our activism, but our work would benefit, too, from easier access to the research that is done on our struggles and the risks of being co-opted, as well as the plentiful research evidence on what facilitates behaviour change and how to communicate difficult subjects.

The literature on neoliberal manifestations in activism is not restricted to study of the NGO world. Practices of the market occur, too, in the kind of 'lifestyle activism' where lifestyle choices are used to make a point. The cultural scholars Sarah Banet-Weiser and Roopali Mukherjee coined the term 'commodity activism' to describe how people find a way to participate in social activism through the purchase of a commodity that is in some way connected, whether through supply chains or branding, to a good cause.[194] These are submissions to the market, but they are also submissions to individualism. The term 'the personal is political' was originally coined to suggest that seemingly personal problems *are actually structural*; that the problems experienced by individuals in their private lives are shared, are caused by institutions and rules, and need tackling at the level of systems and the collective. These days, this overused catchphrase can mean that what works is a personalised, individual intervention.[195]

Becoming aware of neoliberal entanglements does not require us to assume, however, that an activist is adopting neoliberal or individualistic ways simply because they appear to be doing something 'individual', like acting on their own, speaking of their personal experience, or naming the behaviour of another person who has exerted power wrongly. The feminist scholar Sara Ahmed is insightful here, discussing Audre Lorde's often-quoted statement that 'caring for myself is not self-indulgence, it is self-preservation, and that is an act of political warfare'. Ahmed notes, 'As feminism teaches us: talking about personal feelings is not necessarily about deflecting attention from structures … Are you suddenly concerned with structures because you do not want to hear how you as an individual might be implicated in the power relations we critique? … how interesting: *the individual disappears at the very moment he is called to account* [my emphasis].' As Ahmed is saying, it is a valid argument that structural inequalities can be deflected by being made the responsibility of individuals. 'But we can go too far with this critique,' she says. 'Neoliberalism sweeps up too much when all forms of self-care become symptoms of neoliberalism.'[196]

Another way that activists are entangled with systems of power is through our positions in relation to them. No one is immune. For starters, everyone living in a modern consumer society is involved, to a greater or lesser extent, in the systemic injustice of the supply chains that provide much of our food, clothing and other commodities at great cost to those involved in their production. The injustices, historical and current, that are baked into our material existence in long-industrialised countries are extensive and difficult to avoid without retreating from shared society. The philosopher Timothy Morton suggests we are now in a world of 'hyperobjects': phenomena that are vast, hugely distributed over space and time, and 'that can be thought and computed, but not directly touched or seen', which makes it hard for us to reckon with them. He includes global warming and nuclear waste as hyperobjects and, using his criteria, the injustice behind modern lifeways is arguably another.[197]

One response, commonly seen among activists, is the attempt at purity: trying to source all the necessities of life in a way that causes no pain or hardship to anyone. But this is hard; avoiding abuses in one supply chain may put you in the web of another. For Hilary Prentice, who took part in the women's anti-nuclear blockade in the early eighties at Greenham Common before training as a psychotherapist, this version of the quest for purity leads to what she calls the 'but you're wearing leather boots!' syndrome. She describes a friend of hers, who, 'despite his life teaching permaculture, living all year round in a yurt, growing his own garden and his own tree nursery, planting trees, and running deep ecology workshops', was attacked for his choice of footwear. 'The mistake lies, I think, in believing we can somehow separate ourselves from the global situation,' she writes. 'We are not separate, we are all part of the global situation, and so we are all either very isolated, or we are implicated in any number of ways.'[198]

Another response to awareness of the injustices behind every aspect of our material lives is to try to live 'purely' outside the system. But that can end up reinforcing other aspects of the system. The choices of 'lifestyle' activism, for example, include producing or consuming ethical products, or not working in the mainstream economy. I've made brief forays into this kind of activism, volunteering over several summers 20 years ago on a back-to-the-land, self-sufficiency type project. But these options can be more available, observe critics, to those with the privilege and financial resources to make such choices. 'There are hipster-ish ways of doing politics of life,' said an interviewee in Laura Naegler's study of 'prefigurative' attempts to create alternatives outside of dominant power structures.[199] 'Cooperatives, chickens, whatever, that whole shit can sort of be resistance in a certain frame, but also is totally complicit with the lifestyle idea of gentrifying white people, or not even white, whoever, it's also about class privilege.' The activism of alternative lifestyles, in short, can reinforce existing class, gender and race dynamics. Laura Portwood-Stacer's research into 'lifestyle politics' in the US and the UK concluded that such activity was liable to 'reproduce white, male, heterosexual, middle-class privilege, leading to increased visibility and status for individuals who bring these kinds of privileges with them to activist scenes'. The irony, she observed, is that 'those radicals who are able to freely make "choices" about how to live their lives might, in fact, be seen as the greatest beneficiaries of the policies and ideologies to which they are so strongly opposed'.[200] Without attention to where we are starting from, the same old problems arise.

So activists are not just entangled in the systems we are trying to change; we are also entangled in them differently, depending on how we have benefited from them, or struggled under them, or both. We are not in identical relation to what we want to change. Where we start from makes a difference. And our position within the systems we want to change does not only affect our *relations* with those who are positioned differently, and our *understanding of what it is that needs to change*, both of which we saw in the discussion of saviour and status-seeking behaviours in Chapter 5. It affects our perception of *what kind of tools we think are going to work*.

People who have largely benefited from existing systems of economic and political power can afford to assume that the ideas behind them will work to change them. They can afford to assume that a 'rational actor' approach, borrowed unthinkingly from classical economics, will work to change policies. They can afford to assume that policy change will be sufficient. They can afford to assume that putting facts in front of somebody will induce them to effect the changes they are asking for – and that those changed policies will be enough to change minds and behaviour. These were the assumptions that I made for a long time. And then I began my conversations with activists who had been starting from a different place. 'I was taught that liberalism was workable,' said Imani Robinson, the writer, curator and prison abolitionist we met in Chapter 5. 'And what we've seen in recent times, on a global scale, but also what Black and queer people and people organising from the margins who didn't have the privilege of being middle class and having that access to power and access to privilege, have always seen, is that liberalism doesn't work to fix the things that we are trying to organise around.'

'It's much more a way of life, to be interrogating this problem on a daily basis, that doesn't always look like a theory of change, that doesn't always look like a kind of message,' she said. 'But it's more a practice of surviving. We are led to believe that we can change the whole system, or change parts of the system in isolation, effectively, and – this is a key bit – sustainably, because policies have changed, and changes have been made. But within a system they can always be reversed or augmented or changed again. And so the level of impact that we can have is almost fleeting.' She finds it hard to speak about policy change as activism,

> because it's not an active role, it's a complicit role. It's the kinds of changes we're allowed to make, or rather, allowed to try to make. It's what most people in policy spend their lives doing, trying to make these changes, trying to get this one person to agree to put some pressure on this and on that. And it's really, actually, the level of the stake that we have to change and to transform the world that we live in, is much higher than anyone in the policy world, in my experience and from my perspective, has any idea of.[201]

Robinson has long known a version of this, albeit her experiences of trying out policy campaigning in her work on police stop-and-search powers, made its limitations even clearer to her. The tools of liberalism are necessary but not sufficient to deliver on liberalism's long and unmet promises of freedom and equality for all. Democratically agreed changes to the rules are necessary, but insufficient because structural injustice persists even after formal equality under the law has been achieved. Reasoned argument is necessary, but insufficient when the roots of the problem are buried deep in the implicit and unconscious assumptions that shape the behaviour of those with privilege and power; buried deep in the ways that people relate to each other interpersonally.

But it took me – working for an NGO using these tools, unthinkingly assuming that we could make progress through technocratic policy fixes

– a decade to realise that what I was doing was insufficient. To truly understand, through painful experience, that some new rules for corporate behaviour requiring companies to disclose what they pay to governments to extract oil, rules that hundreds of us grafted for years to achieve, could be turned over in the time it takes for a new president to sign his name on an executive order. That those new rules had left underlying abusive and extractive economic systems in place anyway. Why did it take me so long to realise this? The simple answer is that I had entered activism from a place of privilege and in the course of doing a certain type of activism – a kind of policy change that appeared easiest to achieve, and therefore was least threatening to the system – my assumptions had not been challenged. It felt new to realise that what I was doing was not sufficient, but it was only new to me because I had been protected from having to think about it.

I had, certainly, absorbed the 'rational actor' assumptions that underpin economics and run through the liberal imaginary of modernity, founded as it was on ideas about the separation of emotion from reason. (I'd absorbed them while growing up, too. 'You're not being rational,' Dad would observe if any of us were expressing emotion about any issue.) During the two decades that I've been doing campaigning, these assumptions, that we make our decisions based on rational processing of cost and benefit, have been dealt multiple blows. They came from behavioural economics researchers who, in focusing on our less rational motivations, have been undermining the ideas that hold up the mythical 'homo economicus'.[202] They came from Trump's election and the Brexit referendum result in 2016, with their votes for lies packaged in effective emotional messaging. But I had absorbed, too, an unconscious way of relating to the people whom I thought I was helping when I was trying to alter the economic power structures that had such an impact on their lives. I had absorbed a way of relating in which I was attached, without realising it, to the idea of being the one with agency; the one who can help; the one who can make things happen. To some, these two sets of assumptions underpinning modernity – about our rational capacities, and about who has agency – might seem unrelated. But something connects them, and it is a form of thinking that lies at the heart of the liberal imaginary, inseparable from the violence and theft of colonisation.

When I became a campaigner nearly 20 years ago, I thought I knew a lot about how colonisation worked. Specifically, I thought I understood how the colonisers used knowledge as part of their project of domination; how the knowledge of colonised people was degraded and dismissed to justify the theft of their land and labour. But I hadn't applied this understanding to me, and to my approach to campaigning in the present. I had understood it as something historical. When I studied history at Cambridge in the mid-nineties, I felt drawn to learn about processes of colonisation and decolonisation. I became interested in postcolonial studies, read Edward Said's *Orientalism* and the literature it generated, learned about the epistemic domination at work behind the realities of political and economic dominion. I wrote my undergraduate dissertation on the clashing thought-systems of Hindu pandits and Christian missionaries in the decades that the British were tightening their political and economic grip on India. I had an offer to publish it in a peer-reviewed journal which I turned down because – I thought, rather arrogantly – I was too busy trying to 'get out into the world' and become a journalist to do the work of revising it for publication.

The point is, I probably knew about as much on the subject as any other white British person who was not a scholar of it might. (Descendants of those who were colonised would know rather better, of course.) I had learned how knowledge and culture get caught up in power-projects. I could see how the thinking of those historical figures I had studied was affected by their position in the colonial entanglement. And I could see that the economic structures of colonialism – the flows of money so much vaster from poor to rich than the other way round – were, long after formal political aspects of colonialism ended, now being perpetuated through financialised global capitalism and the use of tax havens to re-route and sequester the loot. I knew, in short, that economic imperialism was still the order of the day and, as a campaigner, I was fighting the tax havens that facilitated it through my campaigning for more financial transparency. I really thought I got it. Yet what I couldn't see, as I turned to activism to try to undo these legacies, was how the thinking behind them might still suffuse my own. Nothing in the teaching I received pointed out the ways that I might have internalised some of the colonial system's assumptions, and I certainly hadn't figured it out for myself. (Indeed, the teaching itself was suffused with those assumptions, starting with the name of one of the courses I took: 'The West and the Third World'.)

In intellectual terms, what I missed, studying in the mid-nineties, was the then only just-emerging idea of *decoloniality*. If political decolonisation is sending the settlers home, and postcolonialism is the recognition that knowledge and forms of knowing have been displaced – an 'epistemic violence'[203] – then decoloniality is *reclaiming* the forms of knowing, conceptualisation and representation that the colonisers replaced with their own. It is the unravelling of coloniality, a mode of thinking that outlasted the end of political colonisation. Decoloniality, then, is the epistemological stage of decolonisation. It is the decolonisation of how we think.

Decoloniality builds on the foundational understanding that the creation of modernity was inseparable from the colonial project, and that there is no modernity without a way of thinking called 'coloniality'. Two of the field's key thinkers have been Aníbal Quijano, a Peruvian sociologist, and Walter Mignolo, an Argentine semiotician.[204] In their account, the new scientific worldview of modernity could see the world from a supposedly objective viewpoint, a viewpoint that permitted knowledge of whatever it viewed, and an ability to manipulate it. This capacity for knowing and manipulation was simultaneously put into practice, in the Americas, in European domination of the people and cultures who had lived there.[205] Paul Gilroy, a British historian, had described the same relationship in his 1992 book *The Black Atlantic*, linking the 'foundational moves' of philosophical modernity with the terror and brutality of enslavement.[206] The political colonies might have gone, but coloniality, in the form of ongoing racism and ways of viewing the world hierarchically, has not.

At the heart of this understanding is that colonialism, enslavement and patriarchy create hierarchies of ways of knowing. The way of knowing and understanding the world of the colonised people is, in the view of the coloniser, not worth knowing; it is inferior, less than fully human, and is suppressed. The way of knowing particular to the coloniser tries to take its place; tries to become 'knowledge' itself, rather than just being one form of knowledge among many. But that is not all. The way of knowing of the coloniser, the one that gets elevated, *is itself the tool for this process to take place*.

The way of knowing that becomes dominant is based on the very possibility of an individual who *can* know, objectively, things about the 'other'. This duality of subject and object, 'doer and done-to',[207] which is at the heart of the modern imaginary, helps to make possible the knowledge displacement, the epistemic violence as well as the physical violence. It is individualism, in this view, that creates the duality of a knowing individual subject who can have knowledge of an 'other', a one-way kind of knowledge that, in practice – and in opposition to the lofty egalitarian ideals of liberalism – was indivisible from the politics of colonial domination.

Decoloniality acknowledges the impact of the idea at the heart of liberalism. The primacy of the individual, the hallmark of modernity, was a powerful anti-authoritarian idea that helped to rescue Europeans from their premodern thrall to theocracy and monarchical terror.[208] But it got caught up – entangled – in what was happening across the seas, where the project of creating modern Western rationality was indivisible from the project of coloniality; as Europeans slaughtered, stole, enslaved and imposed their culture on the people of other lands. This, for Quijano, is what 'spoiled the liberating promises of modernity'.[209] Individualism, in this view, is inextricable from the duality of subject and object, and the seeming inevitability of our placing ourselves in the subject position. Missing from European thought about the individual, he argues, and what existed in some of the ways of knowing that it crushed, is 'intersubjectivity:' our mutual co-creation of each other through our relationality.[210] In this view, Enlightenment thought and liberalism not only brought rationality and the possibility of conducting politics (and, indeed, activism) based on reason and debate over facts; it also brought a fundamental re-orientation of how we understand our relationship to everything and everyone that is not us.

Activists are entangled, then, in liberalism's paradoxical legacy. We wield the powerful and effective tool of individual rights to try to free people from oppression, while not always seeing that behind the very idea of the 'individual' is also a pattern of thinking that works in the opposite direction. It does so by excluding both the possibility of intersubjectivity (that we are created by our relations with each other) and of real equality (that we meet each other not as subject and object, but as two equal subjects). This pattern of thinking can exclude the possibility of solidarity with any 'other' who may be different to the activist, but is still in equal relation to them. It can exclude the chance of our seeing the other as equal in their capacity to know as well as to act. This pattern of thinking sees the people who are being 'helped' through modernity's subject-and-object-creating lens, a lens that identifies the activist – the person who is trying to help – as the subject, a subject who has the necessary knowledge.

You could say that this is a story, a mental construct rather than reality, but it is a story that has been made concrete through the workings of power, over several centuries of violence and oppression. This normalised pattern of thinking has infiltrated the perception and thinking of those who continue to benefit from those histories; those who have been shielded, by privilege and the daily reality of being able to move through the world relatively unimpeded, from having to think about them. It's why I had no idea about the paradoxes of what I was trying to do as an activist, despite and perhaps because of my elite education, until I followed the thread of my curiosity to educate myself further. This pattern of thinking is built into the operational structure of many NGOs and most of the 'development' industry, and is at the heart of the saviour complex I looked at in Chapter 5. And the activist is prevented from seeing this pattern of thinking by the very way that it works: by the way that it centres us, the activist, as the individual who subsequently moves into a relationship with everyone and everything else.

What this means, for activists who have not questioned the underpinnings of the liberal imaginary, is that while we are ostensibly focusing on the problem and those suffering from it, we are still implicitly constructing our response to the problem, with ourselves in the middle. We think that we know what is needed. And we so want the intervention that we are pushing for – the one that we *think* is the right one – to work, that it becomes very hard to acknowledge, even in the face of mounting evidence, that it is not. I used to think it was just our fervour to end injustice that made us so resistant to acknowledging failure or a lack of constructive impact in the NGOs I worked in. The insights of decoloniality, however, suggest that this resistance runs deeper. To acknowledge that we don't actually know what to do, or, following our intervention, that what we thought would work has not worked, feels existentially undermining. It would mean that we are not, in fact, the 'knower' that we have been told we are.

For activists shaped by the modern imaginary, the challenge of decoloniality is to admit that perhaps we don't know best. The stickiness of an imaginary that says 'you and whatever you know are at the centre' is what allows campaigners to put ourselves through endless strategic analyses to unpack our assumptions about the political, strategic and tactical aspects of our campaigning for change, while never seeing the need to grapple with our foundational assumptions about the nature of our interaction with the world. It is also what allows us to think that we are free of constraints – that we can, indeed, try to solve a problem that is 'over there', rather than right in here, entangling us. The very assumption of activism as something that is free of entanglements is a function of the dominant imaginary. The activist who is shaped by it – just as the politics and economics they are trying to change have been shaped – has a view of the world that not only puts us at the centre but also sees us as free from any influence, able to see objectively and to go out into the world to have an impact upon it. As liberation psychologists, who are drawing on traditions outside the European imaginary, suggest, 'that we are completely free of constraints may be the most widely shared fantasy of those who have been educated in Western Enlightenment thought'.[211] Activists who are trying to 'change the world' without acknowledging our own worldview and starting point are participating in that fantasy.

I see a resonance here with Iain McGilchrist's study of the cultural consequences in the West of the creation of a worldview, and thus a world, in the image of the left-brain hemisphere's disposition towards what it experiences. McGilchrist is a psychiatrist and humanities scholar whose profound and extraordinary book *The Master and his Emissary* describes the differences in *how* the left and right hemispheres of our brains perceive the world and the consequences for the culture and society that we have created. This is different, he says, from the discredited neuro-myths of the last few decades about *what* the hemispheres do. Both hemispheres are needed for all of what we do, whether it is logic or creativity. The difference is that the left hemisphere, with its narrow focus of attention, breaks our experiences and observations down into pieces to understand them, while the right, with its broader form of vigilance and attention, perceives them as a whole. The left hemisphere should 'pass' its atomised analysis to the right, for reassembling as a whole. But our creation, particularly and increasingly in modernity, of a world in the image of the left hemisphere's disposition, is making it harder for us to access the perceptions of the right hemisphere. The right hemisphere's reality-checking function is undermined when all it can perceive 'out there' is the concrete world of institutions and rules that has been created (metaphorically and literally) by narrowly materialist left-hemisphere approaches that cannot see nor count all that matters.[212]

There is much of interest in McGilchrist's work for anyone troubled by the deep consequences of technocratic and homo-economicus thinking and what they leave out. Specifically, however, in terms of how we relate to each other, he uses the lovely term 'betweenness', which, in my view, describes the same phenomenon as intersubjectivity. He calls betweenness 'a reverberative, "re-sonant", "respons-ible" relationship, in which each party is altered by the other and by the relationship between the two'.[213] In his account, this characteristically right-hemisphere way of relating to each other is under threat in a left-hemisphere dominated world, where the social and intellectual structures that condition our thinking make it increasingly hard to perceive 'betweenness' at all. I was very taken by McGilchrist's book, by its compelling explanatory power and precise description of so many of the jarring features of life in a world increasingly constructed around what he is suggesting are left-hemisphere perceptions. I wrote him a long letter of appreciation, describing some of my personal experiences that now seemed to make more sense; we met and had an energising conversation. Still, I can also see how his work is an account of the problem that is rooted in describing the problem. He is describing – brilliantly – what has gone missing in the dominant imaginary, and how that is affecting us. What I have also found helpful in grasping the radical possibility of 'betweenness' is understanding that there are worldviews and philosophies that *begin* with it, and from whose perspective many aspects of Eurocentric individualism start to look like a rather odd deformation. Ubuntu, for example, the African philosophy that has been explicitly adopted in post-apartheid South Africa, describes how 'each individual's humanity is ideally expressed through his or her relationship with others and theirs in turn through a recognition of the individual's humanity. Ubuntu means that people are people through other people.'[214] For the South African philosopher Mogobe Ramose, we are 'only and truly human in the context of actual relations with other human beings'.[215]

I have come to see that intersubjectivity or 'betweenness', a sense that we exist only in our relation to each other, is what is so often missing in 'helping-others' activism. Being the subject and the doer, the one with agency, who knows something about the objectified other and can do things to them: this can be a description of how power is invisibly exerted; how some countries exploit others; how the classes in power exploit those who are not; how men seek to control women. Exchange the 'domination' frame for a 'saving' or even just a 'helping' frame, however, and it can also be a description of the dynamics involved in activism. I am not suggesting we abandon wholesale the tools of modernity. The point is not to turn away from human rights, least of all at a time when authoritarian politics are seeking to roll them back. It is not to turn away from the possibility of rational thought, least of all at a time when demagogues are appealing to fear and anxiety. Nor are other ways of knowing always necessarily egalitarian or otherwise laudable simply because they are not European in origin. And there are other processes at play in the world than coloniality.[216] But while acknowledging modernity's achievements, we can also begin to transcend its limitations, by learning the lessons of decoloniality. For some activists it will be about reclaiming knowledge and agency. For others, it will be about taking ourselves out of the centre, recognising other ways of being, doing and thinking, relinquishing the certainty that we alone know, and re-engaging with a new disposition towards our task.

9 Entangled in trauma patterns

WHERE HAD I got to in understanding my entanglements? Looking at stories, I had tracked some of the narratives I am caught in, and was creeping slowly towards a felt and not just intellectually grasped appreciation that it is possible to stand up for the stories and ideologies of the changes that I want, without making them such a part of my identity that I have to go to war with everyone who disagrees with me. Looking at structures of power, I'd made some sense of my list of neoliberal manifestations in the organisations I'd worked in, organisations that often supposedly worked against the damage caused by neoliberalism. I'd realised that it was possible – indeed, many might say, probable – to obtain a first class history degree from Cambridge that covered topics including postcolonial thought, and still have failed to decolonise my own thinking about what needs to change, how, and who has the agency to make it happen. Something was still missing, however. These were still observations from the 'outside'. I was missing the interior view. I still hadn't grasped quite *how* the stories and structures of power are woven into us, and what this means for how we go about trying to change how power works in the world.[217] It was time to return to psychotherapeutic ways of thinking, which I'd earlier found useful in seeing what was going on when people react to activists and activists react to everyone else.

Foucault had been helpful in looking at power structures, in illuminating the risks of being an activist who helps keep the system as it is. His body of work and the scholarship it has provoked is key to understanding how invisible forms of power can entangle us. But he left two big realities out of his thinking. One of them was the 500-year history of colonial domination, and the other was our inner life.[218] Both of these realities, I was coming to see – and as people in different positions to me have been able to see much more clearly – are at the heart of our activist entanglements and how we internalise aspects of the world that we want to change. And the two kinds of thinking that I had been using to cast light on them, so far, were decolonial theory and psychoanalysis. Neither can quite account for activist entanglements on its own. Decolonial theory, as far as I have seen, does not provide a full account of the effect of coloniality on the inner life of oppressed and oppressor. And psychological theories about the unconscious have been notoriously unpolitical. Critical psychology notes how psychoanalysis has been too likely to say it's all in our heads and our projections, and to disavow social and structural reasons for our discomfort. Psychoanalytic theory has missed, too, an analysis of coloniality and racism; has operated, itself, from racist assumptions,[219] with only emerging attempts at awareness.[220] Eco-psychologists would add that psychoanalysis places the human indoors in a room, unable to account for the distress that arises when we are cut off from our roots in the rest of the non-human world.[221] In all these ways, psychoanalysis stands accused of emerging directly from the dominant culture. Does it even make sense to use it to cast light on our entanglements in that culture?

And yet, while emerging from the dominant imaginary, psychoanalysis still offers a key insight into how it works: it understands that we are split. Taking threads of decolonial and psychoanalytic thinking together, I was starting to see the extent of the tangle that activists are in. By attending to what lies beneath our utterances and behaviour, psychoanalysis sees that we split off aspects of ourselves and knowledge of ourselves that we cannot bear or that are not permitted, and we suppress them. This insight is mirrored in decolonial theory's understanding that the dominant imaginary is also split: in its conceptualising of the world as subject and object, a split that was made manifest in the politics of coloniality. This epistemological dualism at the heart of modernity – a binary way of thinking – has been made manifest in ideas, put into practice for too long, that falsely suggest an ontological – materially real – division between some types of human and other types of human.

In short, if psychoanalytic theory sees the split on the inside, then decolonial thought sees the split on the outside. Psychoanalysis sees the split within each of us, as individuals. Decoloniality, while seeing that the individual has to decolonise their mind and heart, also sees the split within a larger 'us' – as communities, as nations, as a global society of humans. These dynamics are not mirroring each other by coincidence. They help to create each other. Coloniality, the idea that some people are 'object', to be extracted from, was and is put into practice by people who have disavowed the violence and inhumanity in themselves and projected it onto the people who are colonised and extracted-from. In this light, activists who cannot see these splits, both in themselves and in the shared imaginary, are trying to heal the world without understanding the hurt at the heart of it. What might activists need to do to heal these splits, in ourselves and in the shared culture? And what obstacles are in our way?

One aspect of the split that needs healing is our splitting-off of either agency or vulnerability to unbearable feelings. In Chapter 4 I used psychoanalysis's insight that we split ourselves to explore what happens in the interaction between those who identify as activists and those who do not. But splitting and projection is key, too, to understanding how oppression works. Those who have suffered histories of oppression, of whatever kind, may have had to split off and hide their agency and power in order to survive. Reclaiming that agency and power has often been a necessary aspect of activism for those fighting for their lives; a necessary step to be able to engage in activism at all. It is a pushing back against the negative projections that have been part of the oppression, and an owning of the positive attributes that may have been pushed away in order to survive. This reclamation has been done by those with racialised identities since the beginning of colonialism and enslavement and it is still being done now.[222] It went on in the consciousness-raising groups that women held in their living rooms during the second wave of feminism in the 1970s, as women learned not only that the conditions of their lives were shared and attributable to patriarchal structures, but also that they could speak up about them. It is still going on now, as people from marginalised groups of all kinds step into leadership and activism and start organising and training others.

Those who have benefited from histories of oppression, meanwhile (and there is no neat division, as one person may be in different positions with respect to different aspects of their identity), have been able to hide their split-off vulnerability and dependency in projections onto the 'others' who have suffered under the domination of the mainstream culture.[223] Their great difficulty in acknowledging that these histories are ongoing is, in part, because it raises for them the possibility of having to face their own vulnerability to unbearable feelings, which has long – perhaps intergenerationally – been put out of sight. This may feel, internally, intolerable, even if materially their lives appear comfortable. Politicians and commentators defending Britain's imperial past act out this difficulty on news discussion programmes; men defending patriarchy act out this difficulty at dinner tables up and down the land. Activists with various forms of privilege may increasingly be able to acknowledge their privilege in words, but reclaiming – which means actually *feeling* – the vulnerabilities that they have been more accustomed to 'seeing' in others, including the people they have been trying to 'help', can be much more uncomfortable.

So, for those with privilege who have been engaging in activism to try to 'help', work towards dismantling projections has rarely been seen as a necessary step. It has not been so obvious to those who assume they have agency, answers and access to power, that there is anything split off from themselves – and I can say 'ourselves' here, as this is true for me – that needs to be reclaimed. Nor, conversely, has it been obvious that there is anything assumed that we should relinquish. It has not been so obvious that what we have thought of as agency and knowledge and power has been experienced that way because another aspect of our self – our not-knowing, and vulnerability to experiencing unbearable feelings – has been pushed away. It has been hiding behind the shield of privilege, or has been projected onto others, including others whom we are trying to help, or are working alongside in our attempts to change the world, or even those whom we are vilifying as the perpetrators of the problem. This is why the lessons of decoloniality, with which the previous chapter finished, can seem so hard. We have been keeping our vulnerability to unbearable feelings at bay by assuming that we know and that we are right, and by keeping ourselves in the centre of the picture.

Another manifestation of the split at the heart of liberal modernity that needs healing is the subject–object thinking that we also saw in the previous chapter. This habit unthinkingly places the activist who is trying to help as 'subject', and the situation they are trying to change, or the person they are trying to help, as 'object'. Those placed as 'object' are faced with the task of epistemic resistance: reclaiming their status as a knower, whatever form their knowledge takes. Epistemic resistance is practised by formerly colonised peoples whose cultural and knowledge practices have been suppressed, and by women everywhere who have internalised men's needs, desires and ways of thinking, speaking and acting as their own. It is part of the process of claiming the necessary agency to engage in activism.

But what those doing this reclamation of agency can encounter in activism is people trying to help who think *they* are the only ones who are the subject with agency, people who are engaged in that particularly activist form of epistemic violence: assuming they know better. I have experienced this in the form of male activists 'mansplaining' things to me, and I have done it myself, as I described in Chapter 5, when approaching NGOs in Nigeria and Uganda as potential partners while holding my own or my organisation's fixed ideas about what sort of policy changes or interventions are going to help, even when we were asking what we thought were open questions. For activists, and indeed anyone, who has been assuming they are the subject and everyone else is object, the very idea that we are all subjects, all entangled to the point of being co-created with everyone else, can feel both cognitively and emotionally challenging.

I found a helpful description of this challenge in the work on 'doer and done-to' dynamics and 'mutual recognition' by the celebrated relational psychoanalyst Jessica Benjamin. Her writing shines light on how our habits of relating to others as if they are object and we are subject can be deeply buried in our psyche. Our routine mode of relating to each other is too often what Benjamin calls 'two-ness': two individuals relating to each other *as individuals*, rather than as people made up in part by the relation between them. Inherent in 'two-ness', Benjamin suggests, is a relation in which both parties are trying to be the subject and place the other as object. This process invariably turns to power dynamics, to the constant push-me-pull-you of what she calls 'doer and done-to'. The 'power of actual psychic experience,' she writes, 'all too often is that of the one-way street – in which we feel as if one person is the doer, the other done-to .... To recognise that the object of our feelings, needs, actions and thoughts is actually another subject, an equivalent centre of being, is the real difficulty.'[224] Once again, the novelists perhaps have it best. Love, the philosopher and novelist Iris Murdoch reminded us, 'is the extremely difficult realisation that something other than oneself is real'.[225] Benjamin is suggesting that this realisation is always difficult, whoever we are relating to. She is talking about the difficulty in allowing others to have – to return to Toni Morrison's words that I used at the end of Chapter 4 – 'the specific individuality we insist upon for ourselves'.[226]

Why is it so hard to relate to other people as 'subjects' in themselves? One answer lies in infancy. In Chapter 4 we saw Martha Nussbaum building on Donald Winnicott's developmental models to explore the roots of disgust in our intolerance of our own vulnerability. Benjamin builds on the same body of work on infant attachment to describe how easily a person can retain, from childhood dynamics with their primary carer, the desire to assimilate others to their centre, rather than allow them to exist, however differently, at their own centre. Another answer, of course, is that we are living in an imaginary that is constructed around subject–object polarisation. The individualistic structures of modernity created individuals and set us up against each other, and then, more recently, turned up the volume on that competition with neoliberal ideology and practice. So mutual recognition requires constant work. 'Recognition continually breaks down,' Benjamin observes. 'We are always losing and recovering the intersubjective view,' she says, and this may be at the root of many of our difficulties in living peacefully with each other, whether in intimate relationships or as communities or nations.[227]

I have found Benjamin's approach, which emerged from her thinking about what happens in the therapeutic encounter between an analyst and patient, a useful diagnosis of some of activism's difficulties.[228] I was sensing that activism is missing something when it goes into saviour mode or shout-down mode, and was starting to see, as I wrote at the end of Chapter 8, that the missing something might be intersubjectivity, a way of relating to each other as interdependent beings with our own centre of gravity. Her writing helped me to see what gets in the way and what could potentially be different. It helped me to see how that motto of ubuntu philosophy and relating, 'I am human because you are human; we can only be human when we recognise each other as human', is, as she puts it, 'not a banal slogan but a representation of a complex psychological process within and between individuals'.[229] Her suggestion of a 'mental space' in which mutual recognition can occur feels like something potentially valuable to activists who are struggling to avoid 'doer and done-to' dynamics in our own actions.

While recognising that absence of mutual recognition can be an illuminating diagnosis, Benjamin's critics question, however, whether the application of mutual recognition as a reparative tool is sufficient in situations where profound inequalities of power are already entrenched.[230] For activists who are willing to start in a different place, mutual recognition may be a helpful lodestar and aspiration, but it may not be enough. And in addition to the limitations of good-intentioned efforts to create mutuality in profoundly 'un-mutual' situations, there is also the limitation in its framing of 'mental space'. We are not just mental creatures; we are also bodily creatures. The ways that we respond to others when we are doing activism are shaped by the workings of our nervous systems, and our nervous systems have been conditioned by the effects of (yes, it's an entanglement) the very problems that we are trying to change in the world.

Trauma thinking

The perspective we need to understand the tensions of mutuality in the context of asymmetric power, I have come to think, is trauma, which is held in the body, mind and emotional memory through the workings of our nervous systems. Rooted in our physiology, a trauma perspective can bring us down to earth in our search to understand how systems of power work within us. Trauma is not just the bad event that happens; it is the long-term dysregulation it causes in the nervous system, a physiological set of changes that can alter how we experience, perceive and respond to the world and everyone we encounter. Thinking in the terms of trauma can help us to understand our challenges as activists to achieve intersubjectivity and mutual recognition, as well as our human tendencies to project onto others what we may not be able to bear in ourselves. Thinking in the terms of trauma can help activists to understand the depth of the impact of the stories and structures that we are trying to change: on ourselves, on everyone else, and on the shared culture and its habits, which can so easily become our own. With a trauma lens, we start to see the ways in which the splits in the imaginary and the splits in ourselves are held at the level of our nervous systems.

For Judith Herman, an American psychiatrist who has devoted her career to the treatment and study of trauma, traumatic events 'overwhelm the ordinary human adaptations to life'.[231] Being traumatised, says Bessel van der Kolk, another trauma expert, 'means continuing to organise your life as if the trauma were still going on – unchanged and immutable – as every new encounter or event is contaminated by the past'. The last two decades have seen a revolution in the understanding of trauma, through new knowledge in areas including neuroscience, developmental psychopathology (what can go wrong with the development of mind and brain) and interpersonal neurobiology (the way that we affect the workings of each other's brains).[232] This new knowledge has changed the way that trauma is recognised and treated, and will continue to do so. Trauma healing is a growing field; there are summits, trainings, online trainings, grief circles and a growing number of practitioners developing ways to resource individual and collective healing. It opens up deeper possibilities for understanding the problems of our collective psychology.

What has this got to do with activism? For those who feel that nothing really awful has ever happened to them, it can seem hard at first to see the relevance of 'trauma' to the question of how we perceive and relate to everyone who is not us. However, I have come to see that trauma is centrally important to how we understand the world and I will try to set out how. Trauma, to the uninitiated, sounds like bad things that happen to other people. It is accidents, violence and the horrors that soldiers experience in combat, or that frontline emergency workers witness on the job. These horrors, we may be aware, can revisit survivors in the form of post-traumatic stress disorder (PTSD): the heightened reactivity and hyper-vigilance, or the locked-down numbness of a nervous system that is stuck in its emergency states of 'fight', or 'flight', or 'freeze'. If we know a bit more, we might be aware that people with trauma can be treated. They need a holding that allows them to establish a sense of safety from which they can, with help, grow the resources needed to tolerate the unbearable feelings. They need a holding that maps a return path for their nervous system to revert more consistently to its healthy cycle of action and rest. We might know, too, that our body's regular cycle of action and rest is led by the two branches of the autonomic nervous system. One is the sympathetic nervous system, which is our 'accelerator'; it enables us to get up in the morning and do our normal activities, to enjoy physical activity as well as, in extreme situations, to fight or run away. The other is the parasympathetic system, our 'brake', which enables us to rest and digest and, in extreme situations when fight or flight is not an option, to freeze and play dead.[233]

That we know this much about trauma, that it is recognised at all, is because of activism. 'The study of war trauma becomes legitimate only in a context that challenges the sacrifice of young men in war. The study of trauma in sexual and domestic life becomes legitimate only in a context that challenges the subordination of women and children,' says Herman. It was the anti-war movements after the First World War and later during the Vietnam War that made possible the developments in trauma understanding that, in 1980, resulted in complex PTSD being recognised as a specific psychiatric condition. The feminist movement of the 1970s was the context that helped to legitimise research into the trauma caused by rape, domestic violence and childhood abuse. It was ground-breaking to be able to show that the suffering of women who had been raped and abused in the home had strong parallels with that of men who had experienced the battlefield. Herman observes that 'the study of psychological trauma is an inherently political enterprise because it calls attention to the experience of oppressed people'.[234] She is right, though it is also not that straightforward. There has been an immense and warranted effort to understand the traumatic intergenerational and ongoing consequences of the Holocaust, for example. But there has been – so far – less focus on the equally warranted matter of the traumatic intergenerational consequences of colonialism and enslavement. And the conversation about the trauma that people experience as a result of ongoing racism and other forms of marginalisation is only beginning.[235] As with every other field of enquiry that is now seeking to decolonise itself, the study of trauma has been shaped by the assumptions, priorities and unconscious motivations of those who have been in positions to do the research.[236]

What we might not know about trauma is quite how widespread it is, quite how unrecognised the extent of it is, and – manifesting as it does in other symptoms – quite how shockingly normalised it is. One cause of trauma is distressing experiences in childhood. Reading Bessel van der Kolk's book, *The Body Keeps the Score*, it became startlingly clear to me, to give just one example, what a high proportion of adult distress has its roots in childhood trauma. A landmark study in the US in the late nineties identified 'adverse childhood experiences' including physical, sexual and psychological abuse, neglect, witnessing domestic abuse and having a family member with addictions or mental health problems. It showed that these 'ACEs' cumulatively increased the likelihood of multiple problems later in life: mental and physical health, addictions, obesity, violence and being in abusive relationships.[237] Eradicating child abuse in the US, one of the researchers concluded, would reduce depression rates by more than half, alcoholism by two thirds, and suicide and domestic violence by three quarters.[238] Studies in the US and other countries continue to back these findings up. Yet trauma researchers are still battling for formal recognition of what they call 'developmental trauma disorder' for children whose symptoms do not meet the adult PTSD criteria, yet who display pervasive emotional and physical dysregulation. Children may be diagnosed with multiple different psychiatric syndromes, none of which recognises the systemic abuse and neglect that is at the heart of their problems.[239] What looks like mental illness, behavioural disorders, educational problems, then, is actually trauma: in this case, children who have been gravely hurt by the adults they live with, and who are likely to go on living with the consequences.

'Trauma decontextualised in a person looks like personality; trauma decontextualised in a family looks like family traits; trauma in a people looks like culture,' says Resmaa Menakem, an American trauma therapist.[240] His point is that trauma disguises itself. Unattended to, it remains at the heart of a person, a family, a culture, manifesting in a wide variety of symptoms, behaviour and habits, which are either pathologised – seen as ill, criminal or deviant and treated as such – or are normalised and become invisible. The reason, then, that I am talking about trauma in a book about how we do activism is that I have started to see the trauma 'habits' that run, normalised and invisible, through the heart of the culture that we live in. That have been running, normalised and invisible, through my own behaviour. Trauma patterns help to shape the tone of public life – and family life – as well as shaping how activists go about our task of changing things.

I was introduced to this perspective by Sophy Banks, a psychotherapist and co-founder of the Transition movement, who is now researching the way that trauma patterns create a 'deep frame' for how we relate to each other.[241] I wasn't thinking about trauma when I went to talk to her. It was early in my enquiry and I'd seen her writing about her observations and experiences of burnout in Transition, a community-scale initiative that has spread around the world, where people work together to restore and increase local resilience to climate change and ecological breakdown. After my own experience of burnout and chronic fatigue as a young journalist, and my intuition that my illness was about something more than 'me' and 'my' behaviour, something in what she was saying had touched me, and I wanted to hear more. But our first conversation went far beyond burnout, which she takes as just the starting point: a feedback mechanism from a system that is not functioning healthily. I left her kitchen table, reeling at the implications of what she was saying, and after two years of conversations, reading and exploration, I find that her account, rooted in emerging trauma research, offers a deep and valuable perspective on how our inner lives are entangled with the world we live in and that we are trying to change.[242] Activist behaviour is entangled in trauma patterns, because the culture we live in – and that we want to change – is shaped by them too.

In what ways is trauma at the heart of the dominant culture? There is a bit of unpacking to do here before looking at how activism is shaped by the terms of trauma. The first point is that this country is full of traumatised people. That the UK *produces* trauma is perhaps more obvious than that it is itself traumatised. Historically it has colonised and enslaved other nations and peoples. Now it makes and sells weapons to other governments who use them against civilians; creates and maintains poverty in other countries through economic, trade and tax policies and the power of its financial markets; and then employs racialised immigration policies to turn away, detain and deport people who arrive here seeking safety from the impacts of all those actions. But such behaviour has never solely been inflicted on people elsewhere. The ruling classes have long produced trauma for people here in the UK. They (and might I say 'we' if I knew more about my family history? Two of my ancestral lines that I know about were working-class people, but there are other lines whose origins I do not know) have done this historically through colonisation within these islands, enclosures, factory conditions and forced migration, a brutally violent criminal justice system and the savagery of the witch hunts. They (and again, should I say we?) continue it currently through systematic inequality and the oppression of the poorest, via austerity and the dismantling of public services.

It is tempting, here – activists do it all the time – to point to particular groups and say, 'those people over there are the oppressors, and they have oppressed these people over here, who experience trauma as a result'. It's not that this isn't true. And the trauma that results from oppression is grave. But, in looking at cultural trauma patterns as I am here, a binary opposition of oppressed and oppressor is not the focus. The concept of intersectionality fragments such polarisation, allowing as it does for some people to experience particular forms of oppression and not others. Nor is the point to generate a false equivalence between the trauma experienced by those who have been oppressed, and the trauma experienced by those who have benefited from the oppression of other people. There is no equivalence. The point here, is that a culture which produces people who oppress others and cause them trauma, is a disturbed and unhealthy culture. This holds whether the oppression in question is racism, violence against women and children by the men they live with, or the devising of economic policies that punish people for being poor or having a disability.

Another factor that embeds trauma at the heart of the dominant culture is that, by and large, we don't have healthy ways of dealing with it. Sophy Banks observes that the 'missing link' in traumatised cultures is the 'return path' from the fight/flight or freeze states to regular nervous system functioning. The return path should be a social one. People who have experienced trauma need the soothing of others. They need holding, and they need practices that create safety and that support them to 'shake out' the emotional and physical residue of the event.[243] Rituals, spiritual practices, community: all of these can serve that function. These social pathways are a 'holding' that can return individuals from the overwhelm of the traumatised state, in a resonance of the way a parent holds a baby to soothe them when their immature nervous system is overwhelmed. But these social pathways can be broken. They can be broken by colonial violence: invasion, dispossession, forced migration, enslavement, the forceful imposition of alien culture … horrors experienced within these islands, and that the UK has exported to other lands. They can also be broken by war, the terrorising of healers by torturing and drowning or burning them as 'witches', enclosures and land grabs, industrialisation, migration to cities, secularisation, individualism … all things that have happened here in these islands, as elsewhere in Europe.[244] C. Fred Alford, an American scholar who writes about the political aspects of trauma, suggests that despite its limitations as a clinical diagnosis, 'PTSD is a pretty good political diagnosis', revealing 'something about the emptiness of modern life, at least in Western industrial societies. PTSD is a diagnosis that fits someone who is cut off from traditional sources of support that people have relied on for millennia.'[245] The violent processes that helped to cut off those sources of support were doubly traumatising: both as events in themselves, and also because they destroyed the social means of recovering equilibrium. When the lines of knowledge of holding trauma are broken, there are few people modelling how to do it well. These capacities to 'hold' are rarely available, because we need to have received it to know how to offer it to others, and many of us have not received it. There are few people who can meet trauma with the presence, empathy, co-regulating touch and 'being with' that it needs. Many of us opt instead to offer a cup of tea or an alcoholic drink, or to talk over it, or we just shuffle nervously because we don't know what to say.[246] So we learn to suppress unbearable feelings in ourselves or turn them into addictive behaviours, for they have nowhere safe and social to go.

Trauma remains at the heart of the dominant culture, too, because of the well-documented fact that it is passed on intergenerationally. It is not just the people who suffer trauma personally who are exposed to it; trauma is passed on, through time. Evidence is building for epigenetic changes that alter how DNA responds to our environment.[247] And then there is social transmission, through the intimate personal relation between parent and child. Alford, who has studied Holocaust testimonies and the relations between survivors and their children, observes that one generation transmitting its experiences on to the next generation is more likely to happen when the older generation is 'unable to speak its trauma, or when the way it speaks and the way it acts are at odds'.[248] Traumas that occur 'inside', in the privacy of the home, are passed on too: the children of abusers are more likely as adults to be in abusive relationships;[249] a minority of those men who have been sexually abused will go on to abuse their own children;[250] boys who witness domestic violence are seven times more likely to abuse their own partners.[251]

Abusive and other adverse childhood events are not the only kinds of trauma that occur in the home. Developmental trauma occurs when children's needs for loving responsiveness are not met, usually despite best intentions, or at the instruction of socially sanctioned childrearing advice. And this, too, is passed on, as we saw in Chapter 4. Mothers who were not sufficiently held as babies are more likely to fail to attune to and meet their own children's attachment needs, especially when they are isolated and insufficiently supported, as so many are.[252] This can result, in turn, in another generation of children with insecure attachment who have not learned to regulate their own emotions; who can grow up to be adults who are unable to cope with their own strong feelings, including or especially rage, guilt, shame and sadness. If rage, guilt, shame and sadness feel unbearable, it can be easier to project them onto other people. People who have power – in relationships, or in their job – are at risk of misusing their power in this way. They are at risk of using it to make other people more vulnerable, to make themselves feel stronger. The damage can be compounded, for the upper classes, when young children are separated from parents by sending them away to school and teaching them to put away their emotional selves, an abusive tradition long practised by the British ruling classes and those who aspire for their children to join it.[253] 'A peculiarly British form of abuse,' the journalist George Monbiot called boarding school, in an article about the prevalence of politicians 'drawn from this damaged caste'.[254] 'Having forsworn all forms of vulnerability since they were seven or eight, they can't imagine that humans might depend on one another,' writes the psychotherapist Nick Duffell, author of *Wounded Leaders* and himself a boarding school survivor.[255]

So there are arguably many people who are traumatised, and trauma is continuing to pass down the generations, without sufficient cultural and social forms of trauma support. These are things that are happening to individuals. Before we start looking at what this all means for activism, what does it mean for the culture at large? Is it even true to say that if lots of individuals are traumatised, then the culture is too? Links between the individual and the collective can never be as simple as saying that if lots of people are doing or feeling 'x', then that adds up to the culture doing 'y'. The limitations of drawing such causative lines are debated across the social sciences. Sociologists and psychologists often view each other's work with mutual suspicion, because their methods do not reach across the gap between what the individual experiences, feels and thinks, which can be described subjectively, and what happens in that large group of individuals constituted as society, which has to be described objectively. The growing discipline of 'psychosocial studies', which aims to be in critical conversation with both sociology and psychology and is motivated 'by the belief that the division between ... sociological and psychological understandings of the human world is a mistake', only fledged and started publishing its journal with an academic publisher in 2019.[256] Trauma thinking, in my view, can be another solid bridge across the gap between the individual and the collective.

Studies of 'cultural trauma', told from a sociological perspective to widen out the medical or psychological focus on the individual, tell the story of how collective identity can be disrupted, forged or transformed when an entire group experiences an event, or events, that leave 'indelible marks upon their group consciousness, marking their memories forever and changing their future identity in fundamental and irrevocable ways'.[257] Collective trauma events are felt in individual bodies and minds, and also in the shared identities and narratives, as well as the shared taboos and avoidances, of the collective. The emergent field and practice of 'cultural somatics', meanwhile, which is being led by therapists seeking to heal racial trauma, works with the link between individual bodies and their reactivities to racial difference, and cultural 'bodies' of people of colour or white people whose members react in culturally conditioned ways.

'Only a small fraction of white supremacy lives in our conscious mind,' says Resmaa Menakem, the American trauma therapist who coined the term 'cultural somatics'.[258] He describes the 'constriction' in white bodies when conversations about race arise, and teaches practical tools for white people to begin noticing the constriction – which is a fight or flight response – and to learn to stay present. White people's nervous systems have been culturally primed, he argues, to register even mention of race as a threat, which is why they so often become defensive or turn away from the conversation. With their grounding, then, in the operations of our nervous systems and the ways that we affect each other when they are activated, trauma thinking and therapeutic practice legitimise the drawing of deep connections between individual bodies and psychology, and the wider culture. Trauma is an embodied link between what happens in individuals, and what happens in the collective.

Trauma patterns in the culture and in activism

Sophy Banks, like the cultural somatics practitioners, sees patterns in the shared culture as a mirror and a result of the widespread trauma that has been and continues to be experienced by so many individuals. In the cultural landscape of the collective, she suggests, we can see reflected the patterns that occur in the landscapes of the nervous system, physical body, emotions and mind. Her observation is that, over time, defensive behaviours and states that we use to cope with traumatic events have become self-replicating cultural patterns. And once they have become cultural patterns, individuals have to mirror the collective patterns in order to fit in, and so the patterns are perpetuated. They become an invisible deep frame that guides what we think is normal, that guides how we respond to each other, as parents, workers, lovers and friends. If enough people behave in traumatised ways, it starts to become normalised: invisible. And if people in positions of power behave in traumatised ways, it is legitimised.

What happens to the culture at large that activists are grappling with, in a country like the UK, when the underlying social rules are defined by the logic of coping with trauma? What happens when a significant number of people are permanently attuned to a form of 'fight or flight'; when many people are driven by the need to feel safe and not experience unbearable feelings; when those in charge cannot admit their vulnerability? The question of power, Banks argues, becomes primary. When the sympathetic nervous system is aroused in this way, the result is a form of altered perception, in which the question that matters is this: do I need to fight or do I need to run? To make that choice we need to know: can I win? Who has more power here? The *frame* through which we see the world, the frame that structures our questions about it, becomes power and dominance.

In a culture structured by invisible and normalised trauma, people seek power over others, see everything as a competition that must be won, and need at all times to be in the dominant position in order to feel safe at all. It's another way to describe the jockeying for the 'subject' position that Jessica Benjamin calls 'doer and done-to'. The consequence of 'fight' mode is not just a mental frame that elevates the importance of power, however. The power gets used, whether in the home or in politics. The dominant person, or group, behaves in such a way that the shame, worthlessness and vulnerability they can't bear to feel themselves are experienced in and by the more vulnerable person or group.[259] Activism is trying to fix the problems that are caused by this dynamic, but activism too is structured by this same deep frame. What does this power frame arising from 'fight' mode look like in activism? It is the framing of activism as conflict, and the arising of and failure to manage conflict between activist groups, and I will return to what this looks like in practice in a moment.

In 'flight' mode, meanwhile, we have to keep running: this aspect of trauma logic is about speed. As Resmaa Menakem points out, speed is at the heart of trauma. Everything is sped up by the hyper-vigilance of a nervous system on red alert, which is why healing involves slowing down enough to notice what is going on in our bodies.[260] In flight mode, what feels safe is relentlessly driven activity: and those three words are a good description of modern life. In this altered perception, the logic of an economy built on endless growth makes a perverse kind of sense: at least we are still running. A rapid-fire reactivity has come to be seen as normal. We see commentators doing it on the news every day. It rarely feels safe to pause – really pause – before speaking, because we will be seen as not knowing, and in practical terms somebody else will just jump in. For activists, the tangible result of 'flight' mode is reactivity, hurry and burnout. Activists' habit of valuing speedy action over reflection is partly because of our awareness of the urgency of our task, but it is also culturally conditioned. Conflict, speed and burnout are endemic, then, in our homes, workplaces, activist movements and the wider culture. An underpinning feeling of scarcity feels normal. There isn't enough power, so we have to fight for it. There isn't enough time, so we have to move quicker. We haven't achieved enough, so we need to keep going. Almost every activist I have spoken to, regardless of background, has acknowledged this internally felt pressure to keep going, no matter the cost.

My personal experience is of the fight and flight version of activism. This is what I would be doing when people asked, 'are you all right?' because I was speaking so aggressively and so fast. If there was a chance to 'get the bastards' or even just to score a point in a difficult meeting I would go at it like a rocket, blood rushing to my face, heart racing. I was quick to react, and primed for fighting. This is a pattern that I have been stuck in, and I have my own reasons for that, but it is also the pattern that a lot of the activism I have been attracted to is stuck in. There was a reason that I thought getting the bastards mattered, and it wasn't only strategic. It made me feel more comfortable to be operating like that. And I wasn't the only one. I suspect that it is the people who are drawn to that kind of fight-y activism who are most noisy in defining what 'activism' is. Perhaps even people who are not activists, but who are nevertheless reacting strongly – fightingly, we could say – to the fight-y kind of activism, are also helping to define 'activism' through their reactivity to it. This is to the detriment of activism's appeal to people who do not feel called by being in fight mode, as I explored in Chapter 4. It may be drowning out the voices of those who are doing activism in other ways.

I used to keep an informal mental log, at the NGOs I worked in, of the use of military and violent metaphor by people who were working explicitly for peace. Included in this log were the dedicated and thoughtful people I worked with on gun control who would get awfully interested in the specifications of weapons systems, one of whom kept back copies of *Jane's Defence* in the pile of reading material next to the loo. Also included was the human rights advocate – and from anecdotal stories I've heard, I'm fairly sure this person will not be the only one to have done this – who posed for a photograph with a borrowed automatic weapon and a grin on a research trip to a conflict zone. 'We'll take them outside and bayonet them in the eye,' said in jest while planning tactics for a difficult diplomatic negotiating room, won the prize for worst military-metaphor offender. I used to groan, many of us did, at how utterly, inappropriately violent it sounded, but I now think it was pointing to the underlying frame we were all acting from. And how different were such utterances, anyway, from the 'let's get the bastards' that I was happy to join in with?

Activists are caught. We might be able to see that the bromides about relentless competition promoted by the neoliberal imaginary are not really the common sense that they are painted as. We might comprehend with our intellect that humans are evolutionarily primed for both competition and cooperation, but that we have created an economic system which values one of these faculties over the other. It is less apparent, however, that other unremarked behaviours we consider to be common sense – the competitive and aggressive ways in which we may behave among ourselves, or the way that it feels wrong not to be in rapid-fire-reaction mode – have been constructed by the same forces that shape the systems we want to change. It makes me wonder about the adrenaline highs that can be experienced in 'cancel culture', Twitter pile-ons and the shouting down of those who are trying to make their point, and about the competitiveness among activists for purest status, whatever the metric. Being stuck in these frames also requires certainty. Psychotherapists I spoke to noted that trauma can bring a flattening of perception that makes it hard to perceive nuance. Our survival needs, when we are stuck in trauma patterns, require us to make quick decisions about what is safe and what needs fighting. This pattern brings a false certainty and a rightness, a sense derived from our heightened perception of safety versus danger, that things must inevitably fall into binary oppositions of right and wrong, us and them.

The rapid-fire reactivity of 'fight' or 'flight', then, frames and conditions activists' response to problems. It triggers us into action-panic mode; heightens anger; promotes jumping in with a solution. The urgent reactivity of 'flight' mitigates against the possibility of sitting still, perhaps even in silence, to find the best response, a way of acting in solidarity rather than trying to be the saviour, and a way of acting that avoids burnout. The instincts of 'fight' can increase the competition for victim status, and heighten criticism of other activists who we think are getting it wrong. In this scarcity pattern, there is never enough time to do anything but act fast and keep going. The dominance-seeking of 'fight' leads to having to know best, assuming we are right, getting into conflict with those on the same side and, for those who are trying to help, riding obliviously over the sensibilities, voices and needs of anyone we think we are helping. And all of this fighting and running is helping those activists with privilege to avoid unbearable feelings of inadequacy, helplessness or shame. Those of us who have been doing activism to help cannot hope to minimise the impact of these trauma frames on our behaviour unless we face the feelings of powerlessness and shame that can be hiding behind them.

The other side of trauma perception, however, is numbness, and this too, running deeply in cultural patterns, has an effect on how we do activism. Trauma feelings are overwhelming so we will do anything to avoid feeling them, and one way to protect ourselves is through not feeling at all: through numbness and dissociation.[261] These states can alternate with moments of heightened threat perception. If we have experienced trauma we can find ourselves in 'freeze', with its paralysis and loss of agency, where the parasympathetic nervous system overrides arousal and we 'play dead' because we cannot fight or run. We can also find ourselves in a learned state of helplessness that comes from repeatedly being in situations of harm that cannot be avoided. This is not to suggest that everyone who is harmed loses their agency, just as not everyone who suffers trauma acts out the harm they have experienced on others. Resistance movements can be a healthy restoration of agency, and activist resistance as a means of recovery is a recurrent theme in decolonial approaches to understanding trauma.[262]

But numbness is a helpful frame to understand the dominant imaginary that activists want to change. When those with privilege are operating from these cultural trauma patterns, are shutting down feelings in order to go on at any cost, and are prone to seeing things in terms of power, then there are costs for everyone else. They are more likely to make decisions that will preserve their privilege by preventing them having to acknowledge it, in case they have to experience the intolerable feelings that it helps to hide. They are more likely to make decisions that will result in those intolerable feelings being felt by those who are more vulnerable. Numbness, then, is a tangible phenomenon that links the split within us (our tendency to deny what we can't bear to feel in ourselves and to project it onto others) to the split in the dominant imaginary's conception of the world (its separation of the world into people who are subject and people who are object; people who are subject and non-human beings who are object). Numbness is deeply implicated, therefore, in privilege of all kinds, and in the deep-running patterns of whiteness and patriarchy.

Numbness is entangled, too, with the dominant imaginary's privileging of reason. Emotions and emotional pain are experienced in our bodies, and so we can avoid them by disconnecting from our bodies and retreating to our minds. The Eurocentric imaginary that Descartes helped to found is notoriously disembodied: mind is separated from body, feelings from thinking. *Ideas* such as Cartesian duality help to create our cultural frames and patterns, but so do our very real *feelings* of numbness that derive from emotional wounds. The two come together when the dominant culture promotes and encourages reason over feeling. It becomes very easy to avoid feeling by filling our minds with thinking, analysis and intellectualising. Indeed, that has been a risk in my whole enquiry. Turning to theory – as I have been doing to shed light on my questions about activism – can be a form of distancing, of turning away from the difficulty.[263] I like the feeling of coherence and intellectual pleasure when it all hangs together, when it all seems to make sense, when somebody else's idea speaks and sparks across time and space to illuminate my own questions. For those who like thinking, theory can be a retreat into the certainties of the intellectual sphere, a retreat from the discomfort of the feeling realm.

Numbness from our own feelings, however, is what allows us to be numb to the feelings of others. Together with the desire to split off the internal discomfort and displace it onto someone else, numbness is what allows us to harm others, or to be complicit in harm, and not to feel the impact of what we are doing. It switches us off, so that difficult information about the suffering of others, human and non-human, does not land. It gets in the way of emotional expression: George Lakey, an American trainer who has been supporting activists since the civil rights movement, writes about the difficulties, for middle-class activists who have been socialised to suppress emotions, in harnessing the emotions necessary for social movements to flourish and grow.[264] It also leads to insensitivity and an inability to notice their effect upon others. Combined with privilege and access to power, emotional numbness heightens the potential to replicate oppressive behaviours within activism.

Now, harmful behaviour is not going to manifest in an unaware activist in exactly the same way that it manifests in, let's say, a politician who orders refugee boats to be turned away from port and then prosecutes their captains, or in a director of a company that profits from contracts to run detention centres for migrants. Progressive activists like to differentiate ourselves from such people, and indeed, we are obviously making some different choices. But cultural trauma patterns in unaware activists may cause us to act out patterns that cause harm and that perpetuate existing systems. That is why trauma patterns are worth talking about as the activists try to welcome the boats, close the detention centres and unseat the politicians.

This is relevant to the scandals of Oxfam staff paying for sex in Haiti and the organisation failing to disclose allegations of child abuse, and sexual harassment of female staff by Save the Children managers in London.[265] But it also applies to cultures of overwork, to treating administrative staff differently to those staff working on 'the issue', to the use of aggressive language. 'Whatever dynamics come at the centre of your movement are there to teach you what your movement is about,' Banks warns. 'Where you're destructive internally – between individuals or in relationships within your organisation – is where you will be destructive in your movement. It shows you where your shadow is: what you haven't yet been able to understand about your mission. It's showing up because you can't see it. If you're not curious about it, it will fundamentally harm your mission.' The overwork and burnout culture of many activists mirrors the relentless activity of the industrial growth economy we may be trying to change. The silencing of grassroots activists, often people of colour, within coalitions dominated by well-funded, mostly middle-class, mostly white NGOs mirrors the silencing of people oppressed by the structures of colonialism or globalised capitalism.[266] The activation, by activists, of panicky fear about climate change and ecological breakdown risks pushing people further into the extreme nervous system states that are already part of the problem.

Trauma matters for entangled activists because it explains, at an embodied level, how we can end up 'running' the system we want to change through us, and manifesting it once again in our own behaviour. The point is not necessarily that everyone is traumatised, although many may be, but that we are all living in a culture that is running on trauma patterns. Even if we aren't actually traumatised ourselves, the social norm is to act as if we are. Nor is the point that everyone will act out their power over others, or be numb to the harm that we are causing or are complicit in. But a culture that has been structured by trauma around a dominance frame, and that is characterised by emotional numbness, will make it much more likely that any of us will do so.

Whether we describe jockeying for dominance in the terms of trauma, as Banks is doing, or of a failure of 'mutual recognition', in Benjamin's terms, the result is the same: it is a deep metaphorical frame, a disposition on the world, a political outlook, that emerges from the imperatives of control, force and knowing-best. We have come to confuse dominance and control with power itself rather than understanding it as just one form that power can take, because it's the only kind of power – manifesting in the state or patriarchy, for example – that we usually see. The cognitive linguist George Lakoff, who built on his work on embodied metaphors to see that the frames underpinning politics in the US correspond to two different and deeply held understandings of the family, calls it 'strict father' (albeit he is not speaking explicitly in terms of trauma). In his terms, this is the conservative approach that values firm punishment and early 'independence' from both mother's knee and the state. He contrasts this with the 'nurturant parent' approach of progressive political outlooks, which in both parenting and the social sphere can tolerate the idea of vulnerability and dependence (although Banks's point is that those arguing for progressive politics are as likely to be run by cultural trauma patterns as anybody else).[267] The author Riane Eisler, in search of the roots of patriarchal domination, calls this frame 'dominator culture', which she contrasts with the possibility of 'partnership culture'.[268] The author Charles Eisenstein's explorations of intersubjectivity, for which he uses the Buddhist monk Thich Naht Hanh's term 'interbeing', see its opposite in terms of the 'programme of control'. He means the deep-rooted programme of dominance, force and control that manifests in politics, business, debates on the evening news, our food supply systems, our relations with the natural world, and, through parenting styles, with our children. Eisenstein's book *The More Beautiful World Our Hearts Know is Possible*, which encourages activists to move out of this 'programme', was part of the inspiration for my own enquiry.[269] I wanted to explore how his ideas looked in the light of the particular form of activism that I had been doing, and my questions about it.

Looking at activism through a trauma frame has helped me to make further sense of the instinct with which I began my enquiry: that trying to persuade people to change through rational argument alone was profoundly insufficient. Talking, exchange of ideas, new stories, new policies, new agendas, will not be enough when our behaviour is conditioned by the habits of our nervous systems and the patterns of cultural expectations that these habits have formed. Our bodily responses are implicated in our every interaction, and carry the weight of long histories. Looking at activism through a trauma frame also helped me make sense of the behaviour that I had observed within activism. It suggests a deep set of reasons for why activists might be finding it hard to achieve the mutual recognition and equal co-creation of real intersubjectivity. Neither running fast, nor armouring ourselves to fight, nor numbing ourselves to feeling is conducive to developing the sensitivity to others that we need to relate to each other in a truly mutual way. So we don't find that place of 'betweenness' where we relate to each other as fellow human subjects, each party open to being altered by the other and by the relationship.

What does this mean for our activism? We need to slow down enough to notice what is going on. We need to notice where our own actions fit the trauma survival patterns of power-seeking, running and numbness, and see if we are able to make any shifts ourselves. Where we have been influenced by cultural habits, we may be able to alter some aspects of our responses through our own attentiveness. But first we must slow down. The great divide that can open in activist groups – between those who want to focus on action plans and strategy, and those who first or simultaneously want to do the necessary work to come into good relationship with each other – can sometimes map on to the divide between those people who are on the run or numbed and keeping busy so they don't have to acknowledge it, and those who have experienced trauma and recognise it or who have done enough work to be able to acknowledge that its patterns may at least be in play. Being on the run can manifest in thoughts like 'this is all very well but we need to get on with business', or 'this sounds like nonsense'. Slowing down doesn't mean we can't do our activist work. But it does mean we don't hurl ourselves at each task. That we take time for some stillness between the tasks. That we pay attention to difficulties that emerge in and between our groups. And, perhaps, that we are more compassionate with ourselves than we have been before.

And where we are on the run ourselves, we may need some help. I have had several experiences where my earnest attempts at stillness, including through meditation, scared the life out of me. Intellectually, I knew they were necessary, because I couldn't keep running any longer, but they triggered such frightening feelings that I needed to seek support. Stillness, unsupported, if we have been running or fighting for a long time, can be existentially terrifying. Learning to tolerate the feelings that have been hiding behind anger, control and speed is a slow and difficult task, but at least I am now learning what the task is. And while I still need much practice, my growing awareness of what has been *running me* leaves me feeling freer to respond differently; to approach my activism in a different way.

10 Reaching over the gap

I'S NOT that activists don't appreciate the workings of dualities that separate some humans from other humans, our minds from our bodies, humans from nature. But without awareness of how deep these splits run, it is hard to prevent ourselves acting from them. It was my own growing awareness of these splits as they manifested in me that caused me to start questioning the ways in which I was fighting as a campaigner for new laws. This awareness was seeded in me when, in the years before my children were born, I would go camping, hill-walking, rock-climbing and river-swimming almost every weekend to recover from the campaigning work I was doing during the week. I began to notice that I was a different self in the wild. Weekdays were dominated by a thinking, arguing, hurling myself around the world on aeroplanes self that felt as if it operated from the upper reaches of my skull and left the rest of me desiccated, stiff-necked and migrainous. In the wild, at weekends, I was a porous, mossy, expansive, soft, bodily self. It's not that I stopped thinking. But I was also delighting in green river water and reeds stroking my skin as I swam; in gusts of cold air and hard, sharp edges of rock under my scoured fingertips as I picked my way, swearing, up a vertical limestone crag; in the enormity of widened and softened perception that can be experienced on a mountain ridge under a huge sky towards the end of several hours of quiet walking. In experiencing how whole it was possible to feel, I was noticing how disembodied I was feeling the rest of the time. I was, I realised, a physical creature, and the boundary between me and the non-human world was not so firm as I had thought. I was experiencing an awareness of my own split between mind and body, between psyche and nature, a split that seemed related to the gap between the restricted form of consciousness that I brought to work and the more expansive consciousness that was brought forth when I was in the hills.

I reached for books, fiction and non-fiction, that made sense of it – this split of modernity, and arguably a split that is much older, that separated humans from the matrix of existence. I inhaled Natalie Merchant's ecofeminist classic *The Death of Nature*, and fell for D.H. Lawrence's observation about love in *The Rainbow*:

> Oh, what a catastrophe, what a maiming of love when it was made personal, merely personal feeling. This is what is the matter with us: we are bleeding at the roots because we are cut off from the earth and sun and stars. Love has become a grinning mockery because, poor blossom, we plucked it from its stem on the Tree of Life and expected it to keep on blooming in our civilised vase on the table.

My being drawn to that green door of awareness was a pull away from a mode of consciousness that helped to create the problems I was fighting: a dry, rationalistic, atomistic approach that counts only the things that can be counted and sees the economic bottom line as the 'real' world.[270]

I started, dimly, to intuit that my replication of this mode of consciousness in my work to undermine these economic systems was less than optimal. But instead of following the glimmering thread of this intuition – which was rather fainter than my observations of the more practical ways in which our tactics were mirroring the systems we wanted to change – I got excited about what I was only just beginning to learn, and raced straight into ownership of it. Instead of building on the transformative state that I had been cultivating in the wild, participating in the ancient pan-cultural understanding that meditating and sleeping out alone on mountaintops will bring visions (and not always benign ones), I turned away and dived into action.[271] The conditioning was strong, for sure. Delighted with my new knowledge, but without having fully taken on the extent of my ongoing deep entanglement in split, dualistic thinking – including, of course, the very possibility that I could consider such knowledge 'mine' – I went back into campaigner mode. I condemned this dualism that was causing us to stand by while we destroyed the basis of life on earth. What we need is more connection with nature! More connection with our feelings! More connection with each other! All of which is true. But an unthinking condemnation of dualism can, like so much activism that unthinkingly condemns an ideology, start to sound forced and strident.

There is a subtlety here: to recognise that the desire to fight a polarity without mitigating for the impact of our own internally polarised way of understanding the world leaves us reaching across the gap, forcefully. We recognise, as we start to wake up, those of us who have been asleep, that the problem – we are split – must be fixed. But we may not immediately recognise that our internalisation of the split in our culture unconsciously shapes *how* we might to try to heal that split. When we reach across the gap forcefully – the gap between how things are and how we want them to be, as well as the gap that we perceive between those of us who see that things could be different, and those who seem not to see it – we can overreach. When we lean across the gap forcefully, we can entrench the difference. This is to say, in different terms, what I was suggesting in Chapter 4: that activists who speak about and to their opponents in projective ways will magnify the gap between them. All of this is hard to perceive, however, when we are overreaching out of a habit of trying-too-hard or of fight-and-control that feels normal, or that has become a way of surviving. It is hard to perceive, too, when we are up against people and forces that do need opposing. Power never gives up its privileges without a fight, and frightening social forces do not feel too far away. The point is not to avoid confrontation, resistance and opposition, as they are an inevitable part of activism, but to look at the nature of the forcefulness we are bringing to them.[272]

In a conversation with one of my former colleagues, Annie Dunnebacke, described what would happen to her when she was 'on' as a campaigner.

> I would get louder, shutting off from myself, not looking at the connection between how I was acting and how I felt, cutting off from a relationship with the person in front of me. More argumentative, more confident, more certain, probably fake. In this mode, there was a risk of asserting things far more strongly than the facts – or my true feelings – warranted. It's such an awful feeling: complete dissonance. There's something very masculine about the persona I felt I had to create. I felt it very acutely when I was the only woman and had to negotiate agreements round a tableful of men. If I became unsure of myself for any reason I would veer back into that masculine stuff.

In speaking so forcefully in these situations, in trying to take on what she was seeing as the prevalent male way of speaking, Dunnebacke was reinforcing the gap between herself as an activist and the others round the table who were representing existing structures of 'power'. She was also reinforcing the gap between herself as a woman, and all of those men. By the time we had this conversation, she had become so uncomfortable with the performance of that certainty that she had stepped away from that form of activism.

'In almost all forums there's an implicit expectation that the male voice has authority. Wherever you start from, you'll have absorbed that in your cells. Most women entering male territory will feel they are on the back foot because they are a woman,' says Judith Seelig, who I will describe as a spiritual teacher of exceptional depth and insight, but who wouldn't dream of labelling herself as such. Women activists who want to change patriarchal structures, she is saying, often try to compensate. We assert strongly, become strident, especially when that back-footedness is compounded by our activist status, our sense of being external to power structures. The stridency costs us valuable energy, and can leave us feeling that we are not being 'ourselves'. It also means we are not well heard, and we amplify the gap between ourselves and our audience. 'I'm talking about the back foot, but it's literal,' says Seelig:

> It's like medieval warfare, there's a ditch, an embankment between you. Lots of women lean forward. They lean forward over the gap. If you're going to be a woman speaking, you mustn't be the supplicant, or you're already less-than. If you're not going to be strident, you've got to find some neutral self-authority that says, 'this is what I have to say'. From a place of stillness, and the security of being powered by whatever it is that funds and nourishes you. That's not so easy to push to one side.[273]

This insight, I think, is applicable to any activist who feels, for whatever reason, on the back foot.

Opposition that is fuelled by a forceful approach feels like force to those receiving it, even if it is not physically violent. Nadine Andrews, a psychosocial researcher who uses cognitive linguistics as part of her work, is interested in the meaning of 'direct action' contained in the etymology of the word 'activist'.[274] In activist terminology 'direct action' refers to physically blocking public space, or physically entering corporate or government space. It's 'direct' because it is putting activist bodies directly in the way of business as usual; it's not the more roundabout method of trying to engage power in conversation, such as the policy advocacy that many of the well-known NGOs do. But the 'directness' that interests Andrews, as a practitioner of Taoist physical arts, is at the level of force meeting force and, in this sense, what she says can apply to many other forms of activism than the variety that activists call direct action. 'If you meet force with force, it takes up a lot of energy, and you can't do that forever without something having to give, which is burnout,' she says. And on the recipient's side, that force is received as something requiring a defensive reaction. Andrews notes that 'duality in Taoism is not about absolutes, it's about the interplay between the opposites. So it's a different way of thinking about duality than in the West, which tends to be either this, or that.' She is suggesting that resistance does not have to be forceful, as well as that a duality does not have to become polarised. The problem is that our imaginary tends to see dualities that way, and this encourages our habitual way of responding to them with forcefulness.

Dunnebacke's description suggests another reason why activists are leaning across the gap forcefully. It's not just because we might, like many people in our culture, be stuck in the heightened nervous system state that helps to structure our imaginary, in which we keep ourselves feeling safe through keeping busy or keeping on top. Nor is it just because we are caught in a way of thinking: the everything-is-knowable, polarised subject-and-object, doer and done-to terms that are at the heart of the individualistic liberal imaginary. It is that we feel we *have* to know, which in itself can be a product of these other reasons for leaning across the gap. Knowing and being certain are a defence, a way of feeling safe and in control when our nervous system is aroused. Our dualistic epistemology, meanwhile, casts us as the 'knower' and those with other epistemologies – or indeed, sometimes just different views – as the not-knowing 'other'. Dunnebacke describes it as:

> the difference between lobbying someone when you're
> trying to impose a viewpoint you're convinced of – there's
> a forcefulness, righteousness – as opposed to coming to
> a conversation with actual true openness. You may have
> strong feelings but you are completely open to different
> truths or what someone else might feel. But there's so
> little space for uncertainty. Why are we attached to what
> we think needs to happen? Are we certain it does? How
> can we move forward and act even though we're beset by
> uncertainty and panic? How can we move forward even
> if we haven't got a clue? These are the questions, and
> we don't have the answers. Why do we find it so hard to
> accept that we don't have the answers?[275]

'The problem of how to find a voice that has credibility on the topic of uncertainty is enough to keep a person up at night,' writes the filmmaker and author Nora Bateson.[276] A willingness to acknowledge uncertainty is missing from our imaginary, demonstrably missing from our politics, and is almost inevitably, therefore, missing from activism. The need for openness to what is not known, a willingness to be more uncertain, came up frequently in my interviews with activists. Men and women spoke about it, some but not all making an explicit connection to the missing quality of the 'feminine'. Those who made a connection to the 'feminine' were doing so in an archetypal sense, as a way of describing a quality that is present in both women and men. I don't want to get too stuck on this being an attribute of the feminine because it can be inflammatory, either to those whose feminism has worked for decades to escape determinist attributions about what being female or feminine is, or to those whose activism is now working to escape binary determinations at all. The point remains that there is a quality of uncertainty that is missing in our public and interior lives. This missing quality of not-knowing is Keats's 'negative capability', where, he said, 'a Man is capable of being in uncertainties, mysteries, doubts, without any irritable reaching after fact and reason'.[277] I've tried to bear this in mind throughout the process of writing this book; to hold at arm's length my activist tendency to have to sound entirely certain, while remaining clear enough to convey what I – at this point – understand.

There's another reason why we sometimes lean across the gap so forcefully, and why we think we have to know the answer. It's that we're so desperate for the sense of meaning that activism is giving us. The need for meaning is human, and in some accounts stands at the very core of us. The mythologist and wilderness guide Martin Shaw suggests that 'as we age, the desire for meaningful work can descend on us almost as strongly as romantic love. The soul reveals the desire for significance, for heft, for some psychic resonance over and over, and will crash our lives against the rocks until we take notice.'[278] Viktor Frankl, the psychologist and Holocaust survivor whose description of his experience of the concentration camps stands alongside Primo Levi's, took from the horror that meaning, and our free choice in how to find it, is the one thing that cannot be taken away from us.[279] 'Terror management' theory, built on the foundations laid by anthropologist Ernest Becker in his book *Denial of Death*, suggests that humans are the only animal with conscious awareness that we will inevitably die, and that the strategies we have developed to avoid thinking about this fact revolve around cultural meaning-making.[280]

But while the need for meaning is part of what defines us as humans, one of the defining features of the modern imaginary is its sense of alienation from meaning. This alienation is not just in Marxist terms, where we are disconnected from what we are producing and consuming (although that is part of it), but is in the broader meaning of a spiritual crisis. The crisis is that we no longer know how to relate to the world around us and to feel that we have a meaningful place in it. We don't know what our purpose is or where we belong. Modernity's disenchanting of the world began with the Copernican revolution and accelerated with the death of God, through the Enlightenment and the scientific revolution. The author and broadcaster Mark Vernon illustrates this shift with a 16th-century illustration of the Copernican universe, the sun enthroned in its new place at the centre with planets circling around. Outside of that circle, in the corners created by the circular universe placed within a rectangular picture frame, are people. We had become separate observers, outside the universe, separated from everything else that is.[281] Processes of 19th-century urbanisation and industrialisation were followed by late 20th-century and 21st-century de-industrialisation and casualisation of labour, which undermined even the communities of solidarity and meaning that had formed around work in the industrialised world.

In this alienated context, our need for meaning has been cleverly co-opted and fulfilled by consumer capitalism and its endless quest for growth, and this is part of what activists are reacting against when we become activists. We're not only reacting to the deleterious practical impacts of capitalism's excesses, but to its implicit assertion that this is all that life should be about. Activism is a massive great meaning generator for those who do it. It's a way of re-embedding ourselves in a community, in a society, in the world. It provides purpose, fellowship, solidarity, position and voice. The risk, however, is that this is so very appealing, in a world of alienation and lack of meaning, that we over-do it. We are coming from this place of desperate thirst in an unhealthy culture whose public imperatives and institutions don't support us to find good meaning, and we find, in activism, a way of making meaning. We are trying to make up for so much that the effort can make us strident. We overreach, shout ourselves hoarse and burn out. Our desperate need for a meaningful life gets woven, too, into the other status-chasing and identity-policing aspects of activism, as well as into the anger and projections onto those we're battling with. The author and activist Jonathan Smucker suggests that activists who retreat into the carefully defended identities of subgroups are trying, desperately, to regain the 'psychic completion' that participation in a revitalised lifeworld of intact community – even if it is a small marginal one – offers.[282]

Our reaching over the gap, between how things are and how we want them to be, can also come from a displacement of our desperate desire to solve something that cannot be solved in our own lives. We take on these huge tasks, like halting the arms trade, shutting down the oil industry, changing the voting system, or reforming the tax regime, and many people we meet who are not activists feel that these are incomprehensible choices: why would we make life so difficult for ourselves? But these intractable problems can seem more bearable and easier to face than the prospect of mending the wound in ourselves or in our difficult relation with a family member. Our own hurt may not be exactly the same as the hurt 'in the world' that we are trying to fix, but the enormity of the task that we have taken on for ourselves can match the depth of the hurt and the sadness within us. The 'wounded healer' is a term that we might already be familiar with, but I'm wondering if we should become more familiar with the idea of the 'wounded activist'. If we can acknowledge that we are part of the unhealthy system we are trying to fix, we can acknowledge that we have been hurt by it, too. And there is a gift, of sorts, in that. The sensitivity that comes with our awareness of how we have been wounded by the system allows us to understand the extent of the problem. We're not always going to solve the personal problem *before* we can work on the external problem, but it helps to reduce our striving and forcefulness to at least acknowledge both the connections and the differences.

The point, then, is not to avoid bringing any force to activism. Bad things are happening and activists want to resist them, and when we do so, we may encounter counter-resistance in turn from those who want to keep things the way they are. Resistance requires some force, in the sense of energy and strength applied in a particular direction. We can't just go floppy and acquiescent. But nor do we want to hurl ourselves against it in fear and fury. We need to be able to think clearly to make good decisions and use our limited resources well. The forcefulness we want to avoid is the forcefulness that comes from bringing all of our own desperate needs to our activism. Just as we may need to burn down our anger about the issue into a steady flame that can fuel us without rasping our throats and burning us out, we may also need to burn down our need for meaning, our need to reach over the split that we sense within us and within our culture, our need to solve, to know and to control, and to assuage our own hurt.

Part 3

Starting in a different place

11 Learning to sing again

IN MARCH 2015 John Ashton, a former UK diplomat to the international climate talks, gave an extraordinary speech to an energy conference. It took the form of an open letter to the CEO of Shell, Ben van Beurden, who the previous month had explicitly rejected calls for a transformation to a low- or no-carbon economy. You can see the practised diplomat at work. Ashton recognised that people in the oil industry must feel unappreciated by those whose lives still depend on oil yet who heap 'the sins of the world at your door'. He honoured van Beurden's work in providing fuel for an energy-hungry world. Then, gently, he started to unpick the oil man's resistance. He pointed out the difference between the 'mask' that van Beurden wore in his CEO role, and the real face underneath. The mask emits positive noises about the industry's 'moral obligation' but concludes that fossil fuels will be needed for decades. The face underneath tells a different story: fear of change. If van Beurden could accept that the old business model is dying, and manage its decline while building a new one, then, Ashton suggested, 'there would be no need for a mask. The face could look the world in the eye and see itself reflected back.'[283]

The letter was published in *The Guardian* and was shared on one of the campaigners' mailing lists I subscribe to, and I was astounded. I had recently stepped away from my 'getting the bastards' job, and this was the first time I had noticed an activist trying to stand in the shoes of the person they were criticising when asking them to do something different. Ashton didn't hold back: he wondered whether he was seeing a 'touch of narcissism, a touch of paranoia, a touch of psychopathy'. Re-reading it now, I suspect some readers may have found his tone patronising. But he was not doing that outright dismissal of the opponent's viewpoint and inner life that so often happens when campaigners complain about someone's actions and call on them to act differently – as I had so often done. He was acknowledging that there might be reasons for van Beurden's stance, that his job might put him in conflict with his real self, but that the times were overtaking him and he nonetheless needed to shift. Van Beurden did not respond and Shell is still drilling for oil, so I obviously cannot hold this up, on its own, as a success story. Yet it is interesting – a glimpse of doing it differently. I had a conversation with Ashton when I first started researching this book because I was intrigued to hear the story behind his approach. He'd left the diplomatic service in 2012 'without a plan' and for similar reasons, he said, to the ones that had driven me out of campaigning NGOs. His view of the changes that were needed was becoming more radical, and when he wrote that speech he was gradually coming to the view 'that we need to learn to sing again. We can talk about how to do that, what should the song be and what should the notes be … But what's much harder is to sing at all.'

Why might activists not be able to 'sing'? Why might our voices not ring true, nor easy or clear to hear? What constrained my voice in that TEDx talk that made me so uncomfortable? As I have argued throughout this book, we are unable 'to sing' because we are not acknowledging our entanglements. We are not speaking the whole story when we project all wrongdoing onto the other side and do not acknowledge our own complicity in the systems we want to change. We are not being entirely true when the intensity driving our speech is rooted in what we are hiding from in ourselves: our need to be right, to be in charge, to be the saviour, to be heard. Our voices can crack when we are striving to reach over the gap that has held us back, trying to find meaning in a world that is lacking it. Our voices can break when we are hurt by our entanglements in a system that for so long has caused trauma. We might be tensed and running on fear, of the outside world or of not being enough in ourselves. We might be too numb to feel the impact of our words and actions, or too numb to act effectively. When we do these things, and live from these constrictions, it can be heard in our voices. I mean this both metaphorically and literally. Literally because, if we are splitting off part of ourselves, striving too hard, living in our minds to avoid feeling what is in our body, the very resonance of our voice is altered.

My friend Briony Greenhill is – among many talents – a musician who teaches vocal improvisation. Her students are amateurs and those using voice to explore self-development, as well as professional singers who are more accustomed to singing notes already composed. When confronted with the prospect of extemporised singing, many students experience fear, alarm and, for some, involuntary constrictions in the body that restrict the voice. What suppresses the voice? 'I would say it's part of this whole suppression of the heart and the body in white culture,' Greenhill says.

> The thing about truth and the true voice is you need a
> kind of alignment of logos, mythos and eros, of the mind,
> heart and body. You feel it in your body, it feels true in
> your heart, you believe it with your mind, it comes out of
> your voice and it rings true because you're aligned behind
> it. I think when we enter into ourselves, our sensations,
> our voices, our bodies, a lot of what can constrict is either
> present fear, fear deriving from past trauma, or a terror
> of what we might reveal should we open the Pandora's
> box of our inner life and broadcast it via a free voice.
> When you explore your shadow you might find your own
> violence, your own greed, your own limitations, fear,
> incompetence, your own place in a long lineage and large
> system of violence.[284]

The self-compassion that we have to cultivate for our own healing, she is suggesting, leads not only to a clearer voice for those wanting to improvise in song, but becomes the foundation of the compassion that allows us to speak as an activist without dehumanising our opponent, for instance, the fearful human who wears the mask of the CEO. The Quakers would call it 'answering that of God in everyone'.[285] Finding that compassion is a form of growing up, too, that will help us in our developmental task, as Robert Kegan puts it, of 'developing an empathy for the coherence of the other's position and the costs that leaving it might entail … in fashioning a bridge that is more respectfully anchored on both sides of the chasm, instead of assuming that such a bridge already exists and wondering why the other has not long ago walked over it.'[286]

I have been thinking about what may have got in the way of my voice sounding clearly; what may have been behind my stridency. The conversations I've had while writing this book, with activists, scholars, psychologists and therapists, have helped to surface in me an acknowledgement of what had long been an 'unthought known', to use Christopher Bollas' resonant term from psychoanalysis.[287] In seeking to persuade all of the targets of my activism of my point of view, I was also seeking to persuade my own father. I was never going to change his values; he was comfortable in his economically right-wing outlook and saw no reason to alter it. But maybe I could instead persuade some of the right-wing men who ran banks, companies and other institutions of power to do what I was demanding. In the absence of explicit approval of my worldview from my Dad, any changes I was able to make in the outside world would constitute an implicit form of approval, from men (for it was nearly always men) with similar views, for my opinions, values and chosen identity. This does not mean that the specifics of what I was doing were misplaced, or that my critique of the shadow financial system was not sound.[288] The laws that I helped to get changed still needed changing. I was standing on the broad shoulders of those who had worked on it before I did,[289] and what I was saying has been amplified and vindicated many times since I started working on the issue.[290] But there was an extra component to what I was doing, an intensity, forcefulness and drivenness that might have been felt by those who experienced my campaigning, even if it couldn't be explained.

In the light of this realisation, there is also probably no coincidence in the timing of my personal motivation for this enquiry. My questions about the activism I was doing had long been present, but I suppressed them until, I later realised, the time when Dad was dying. He had a form of cystic fibrosis, and by late summer of 2014 we knew his time was running out. He died a year later. I now wonder if his long death was releasing me from my impossible task of trying to gain an approval that – he would have said – was already implicitly given. The reasons for me to have been seeking approval in this way, inasmuch as I currently understand them, are beyond the scope of this book. But the release from that powerful form of approval-seeking left a space in which I could look at activism with a widened perspective. It offered an opportunity to start reconciling my powerful sense of the need and potential for change with a realisation of my own entanglements in activism. Perhaps, too, I was being released from a reactivity-to-his-views in which I would always take the reactive position of standing against, rather than the potentially more generative position of *standing for*. In discussions within our family I would adopt the 'against' position and, locked into it by habit, I would find it hard to perceive that there could be an alternative approach. The alternative was, and is, to stand on my own ground, stand for what I believe in and resist what I don't, but without my actions and speech being shaped by my *reactivity* against what I am resisting.

We are entangled, then, in an imaginary that says we are separate from everyone and everything else: *an imaginary that insists we are not entangled*. No wonder it can be so hard to see our predicament. And even if we do see it, is there anything we can do about it? Alain Touraine, a French scholar of social movements, thought that activists had to 'deintegrate' from society in order to see its hold on them. Debra King's study of emotions in activist movements observed the cognitive and emotional dissonance that this deintegration creates for activists. We try to disengage from aspects of the world we live in, yet are not able to fully reconstitute ourselves in the world that we are trying to create.[291] What I have seen through this enquiry is that to whatever extent activists are at all able to 'deintegrate' ourselves in order to 'see' what we want to change, it is only in a way that is partial and uneven. We remain held by some aspects of the imaginary while developing clear critiques of others.

I have seen, too, how this partial and uneven process is structured by our personal stories and psychologies; by our responses to our own and collective traumas; by our positions, anger and defences in relation to traumatic political histories. All of these factors affect our epistemologies, our allergies, our unacknowledged habits. They trip us up as we try to identify and avoid the master's tools. This uneven gaining of perspective on the imaginary helps to explain a phenomenon that can look like culture wars *within* activism. It helps to explain the polarisation that can occur between those committed to personal improvement and those who are chained to the railings: the many competitions for purest status that take place; the way that some white middle-class campaigners will insist that the urgency of 'climate' outranks the urgency of the social justice questions that are, for many people, so obviously and utterly entangled with our shared climate catastrophe.

These entanglements go so deep that it would be easy to become discouraged and step away, despairing at how existing forms of power will always infect our efforts. But to recognise our entanglement, to see that the master's tools are everywhere, is not the same as turning away. Nor is it an invitation – as it can sometimes seem – to turn away. Yes, we participate in and are partly made by the system we try to change. But we are not performing, here, the solely dismantling move of the 'deconstructive' or 'anti-modern' postmodernist who sees that they are always a 'participant observer', and who stops after unpacking the impossibility of finding any un-influenced ground from which to understand any phenomenon. I am not saying there is no point trying to change anything. At the end of Chapter 8 I was suggesting that we can transcend the limitations of modernity by putting its thinking on an equal footing with other ways of thinking and knowing, and Chapter 9 showed how, for some people, this task may require a difficult reckoning with their embodied selves and with what they may have hidden and projected. Now, in facing up to our entanglement, we are faced with the classic limitation of postmodernity – a potential cul-de-sac in which we cannot reach a clear perspective from which to understand, nor clear ground from which to act because we are so entangled.[292] But we can transcend the potential limitation of this way of thinking on our actions, by acknowledging our entanglement and *then starting from a different place*. We are not stepping away. Yet nor are we under the illusion that it is possible to disentangle ourselves from our context. Indeed, if we think we *can* disentangle ourselves, then we're probably still entangled in modernity's delusion: in the very idea that we can be separate from everyone and everything else that is.

There is a constructive way forward. But it requires getting real about entanglement; about where we're starting from and what we're bringing, and where anybody else might be coming from. And this can be painful to acknowledge. One long-standing activist told me that she had had to grieve when she let go of the hope that she would ever find an organisation or group or movement that is free of mirroring the unhealthy systems it wants to change. We might need to grieve, in such realisations – and some of us might need to apologise – for all the difficulty and pain that is caused when activism reinforces problems while trying to solve them. But perhaps we are also grieving for the loss of certainty of what we had always been told was our place in the world: the idea that we are an independent actor, free of constraints. Where *are* we starting from, then? The starting place becomes a different place when we approach it differently.

1. Knowing ourselves

One of the features of this different starting place is that we are open to knowing ourselves better. If the injunction for healers is 'physician, heal thyself', then the injunction for activists should perhaps, like that for philosophers, be 'activist, know thyself'. Therapists who are trying to heal people must, in addition to training, undergo therapy themselves, so that they can recognise when their own issues are arising in the interaction with their patient. Social researchers who are trying to understand the world must investigate and account for their own position and assumptions. But activists who want to understand and heal the problems of the world often just dive in. I'm not suggesting that everyone wanting to do some activism should embark on years of therapy, which can be hard to access and expensive. Many activists are young people with energy, time and freedom from responsibilities, who understand the urgency of the moment and want to act. The gaining of understanding about our own shadows, meanwhile, is a slow process that can take a lifetime.

I am suggesting, however, that activist organisations and movements could explicitly develop cultures of reflection in which – alongside the planning for action – we can talk openly about the ways in which we can be part of the problem ourselves. About our anger and our desire for control and status and saviourhood and being right and everything else that we are seeking. Activist organisations and movements could explicitly develop cultures that normalise checking in and support in terms of what we are bringing of ourselves to the tasks in the outside world, that develop our capacities to relate to each other across difference, without trying to assimilate everyone to our own point of view. They could develop cultures that encourage activists to relinquish as well as reclaim. Relinquish, for some, the need to know best, or to be right; while others relinquish their silence. Reclaim, for some, the humility that would allow them to risk sharing their vulnerability, so that the silence around it becomes neither armour nor complicity; while others reclaim their power.

2. Thinking is not enough

Another characteristic, then, of this different place from which we are starting, is that thinking is not enough. We can convince ourselves of anything if we cut ourselves off from the information and empathy that comes from our body through our feelings, and that comes through our intuition when we practise stillness. Of course reason is necessary. This is not a baby-and-bathwater move of chucking out 300 years of Enlightenment influence. But in entanglement terms, activism that claims to operate *only* on reason is caught in the liberal imaginary. We need this 'something' that we sense is missing. This was one of Martin Luther King Jr's insights when he was forming his outlook and methods.[293] It was obvious to him that reason on its own could lead to atrocities, and his response was that reason needed to be tempered with faith. In the communities he was working in, Christian faith was a key bond and a moral orientation. Decades later and in more diverse contexts, shared faith cannot be relied upon in the same way. But there are many other possible counterweights to the dubious power of thinking alone. (Many of them, as keen observers note, have become more popular in the absence of religion.) There is turning to the wisdom of the body, as some activists are starting to see, through trauma, healing and shared ritual, music and dancing. There is turning to the power of contemplative stillness, as practitioners of meditation and activists on behalf of meditation's benefits know. Meditative traditions offer the stillness in which we can begin to notice our feelings, intuitions, connections to other beings – everything that our reasoning mind finds hard to fathom.

3. Activism as a practice not a goal

Spiritual approaches to activism suggest that it is best pursued as a practice and not a goal, and this, too, creates a very different starting place. 'I am 81, and I don't feel any lack of enthusiasm, any lack of energy, any burnout or anything of that kind which many people suffer,' says Satish Kumar, a long-standing peace and environmental activist and magazine editor.

> If you ask me what sustains you, without feeling frustrated or disappointed or despondent, I would say that for me, activism is not about achieving results, activism is about being engaged in the process, because process itself has its own value. There is no utopia out there which we can establish. It's always a process of living. Every day, we have to shower – there's no utopia that you can have one shower and the rest of your life you are clean. Every day you get hungry, and there is no utopia that one day you eat, and for the rest of your life you are not hungry. It's a process. Activism is every day doing something that is worth doing.[294]

This may be the only way to keep going when we realise that – in the Nigerian philosopher Bayo Akomolafe's words – 'there is no *there* there. We are not going to go the whole way. We are not going to get there. Activism needs to leave the age of mastery.'[295] We are not going to fix everything. We may have as much impact on the world by raising a child, or sitting at our grandmother's feet, he suggests. This may well be true, particularly in the light of attachment theory, although Akomolafe is not speaking about what he calls 'post-activism' in such instrumental terms. But realising there is no achievable 'there' to aim for can also be the point at which activists give up entirely. Hearing Satish Kumar say it is 'not about achieving results' can be very hard to hear. I still find it hard to hear, at the same time as I recognise the truth in it. This may say something about where I still am. Attachment to outcome can be an attachment to the importance of our own role in the process. If activists are invested in being able to do it ourselves, and then realise that the problems are too deep and we cannot solve them, even in our lifetime, this can be a bad ego blow. It might be more comfortable to turn away.

This is the other 'getting real' sequence, which we need to understand once we've done the initial 'getting real' of acknowledging that we are entangled. Here's how this one goes: activists are told by our opponents to 'get real', in the sense of 'there is no alternative'. 'Do stop being fanciful, it's time to be realistic,' we are told, often by those who are invested in things staying as they are, and almost as often by people who can't bear to think about it at all. Activists respond, in turn, 'No! We reject your "getting real"; people suffer from your views about what has to be real (a world based only on profit values, let's say), and it's in our power to change what is seen as realistic.' But deep underneath all that, there is another form of *getting real* for activists. When we realise the depth of the problems, and that we are ourselves deeply implicated, we start to see how long it might take. It might take longer than our lifetimes. And it might never happen. There really might be no 'there' there, as Akomolafe puts it. This had already come as a devastating realisation for activists who are invested in the idea of our own agency and effectiveness, and now, in the light of carbon deadlines and potential systemic global collapse, it is even worse. We really might run out of time. We really might be up against adaptation to collapse, as indeed many people in the world already are. Awareness of death can be helpful in cutting to the chase about what is important, as the evolving public conversation during the Covid-19 pandemic has shown. As Jamie Kelsey-Fry, an activist and journalist puts it, 'The only chance our species has got is a revolution in our answer to the question: "What the fuck are we here for?"'[296]

But still, the hardest thing is to keep going when it is not clear what the outcome of your efforts will be. *That* is really getting real, and that is where seeing activism as a practice helps. Activists who have had to struggle for their own existence, in the dailiness of facing obstacles, have a longer experience of it than those who discover it by running into the wall while trying to help. Vanessa Faloye, a facilitator and trainer for activist organisations, said she has had

> a very deep grieving and awakening in understanding that
> I will not achieve my big dreams of collective liberation in
> my lifetime. It is capitalism – quick fix, everything as quick
> as possible – that taught me to believe that it was actually
> possible to solve the world's problems by the time I was
> 33. ... tapping into my ancestral lineage and knowing
> that I work on the shoulders of giants, on the shoulders of
> ancestors who fought for their dreams and my liberation,
> has been the quiet assurance I've needed to know that I
> am working for a liberatory future that I can't see now, or
> even imagine right now, and that's ok. Activism, for me,
> has been redefined as trying everything in my power to sit
> in the tension of living that future now, and knowing that
> I will never see that future.[297]

We must let go of one vision of progress, then, while holding on to the one we are fighting for. The one we must let go of has ourselves at its heart, as causal agents, participating in a grand narrative of progress by helping to bring some of it about. When we are attached to the idea that we will create progress, we make ourselves more prone to burnout at the many times when we are not experiencing forward movement on the things we are working on.[298] Yet letting go of this attachment is hard, because at the same time, we are motivated to make things better. We *can* imagine something better, and we refuse to let go of that possibility. It's why we are doing activism rather than watching TV. When I got arrested with Extinction Rebellion with no clear idea of whether it would work, that lack of clarity felt something of a relief after so many years of having to justify the likelihood of success of my interventions to my NGOs' funders. When we stop trying to save the world, we become substantially freer to do something that could be useful.[299] The decision to take part in activism, in this light, is one of virtue ethics, where the important thing is doing it because it is the right thing to do, not because we think it will or will not work. Questions of what will or won't work are necessary but second order, in the realm of strategy.

It is not that the practice of activism without attachment to outcome will itself prevent us replicating what we seek to change. It is more that in order to detach ourselves from outcomes – which is a subversive and difficult move in our instrumentally focused imaginary – it helps to become aware of the beyond-the-issue factors that have been driving us and helping to make us so attached to outcomes in the first place. These beyond-the-issue factors can be personal shadows or societal ones or both, and an appreciation of entanglements can help us to identify them. This is where my personal enquiry into my hectic and strident activist persona meets the story of entanglements that I have been following. I feel substantially if not entirely freed from the drivenness, forcefulness and need for control that used to characterise my activism – my acting from the heightened place. (I must admit, I am still learning – and regularly failing – how not to act from that place when my children are doing my head in.) Much of that freedom comes from starting to understand that these behaviours were rarely to do with my commitment to the issues I was working on.

4. Not starting with ourselves

The biggest difference in terms of starting point is that we don't start with ourselves: another subversive act in an imaginary centred on the individual. In her work on 'doer and done-to' dynamics, Jessica Benjamin proposes a radical surrender of our attachment to the centrality of ourself, 'a certain letting go of the self' that 'also implies the ability to take in the other's point of view or reality'.[300] This is a precondition for developing epistemic humility: acknowledging other ways of knowing the world.[301] And if we have the privilege of choosing where to intervene with our activism, we can approach, as the facilitator Kat Wall suggests, with the question 'what service can I give' and not 'what's *my thing* going to be?' Surrender, then, is a good description of how activists can be truly alongside those we are trying to help as well as those we are trying to change. And we cannot be truly alongside others, or approach activism as a practice rather than something we personally have to win for it to be worthwhile, unless we *get over ourselves*. And all of these differences in where we start have implications for how we shape and run our activist organisations and movements.

It seems a paradox. We must start with ourselves and yet not start with ourselves. We must start with ourselves, in the sense that we cannot pretend the problem is nothing to do with us, and we cannot pretend that we are always only speaking about the problem. We must turn to ourselves in order to acknowledge our own entanglements, our own hidden longings, needs and troubles that we are bringing to our activism, and which will get us into difficulties if we let them run us. But starting with ourselves in that sense is only the first step towards the transformation that might really change our activism, and maybe everything else. As we turn to the activism we are doing, whatever that work is, *not* starting with ourselves is the difference in how we can proceed. Not starting with ourselves gives us a chance of breaking the bonds of our entanglement in the dominant culture's habits of exceptionalism, extraction and assuming that we are the subject and everyone else is object. Not starting with ourselves means surrendering our need to know, in order to listen to the knowledge and experience and plans of those whom we want to help. Surrendering our need to be right, so that we can acknowledge the viewpoint and humanity of everyone we're dealing with. Surrendering our need to put ourselves at the centre. Both aspects of this double move are necessary. We have to be able to acknowledge ourselves and our needs and position in order to then put ourselves to one side and offer service. Otherwise, we risk being the narcissist who needily covers their own vulnerability by acting in a way that claims to be helping, but whose purpose is to attract attention that deflects from what we want to hide.

I have been learning about not starting with myself (and my teacher, Judith Seelig, might say that I have a lot to learn) in an intentional group where we practise, through speaking honestly about what we feel, relating to each other as equals and not beginning with ourselves when we speak. Some of it is done by email and some when we meet a few times a year. It is sometimes difficult because we are so unpractised. But the 'alongsidedness', which is what we call the feeling that emerges from this practice, is never less than glorious and delightful. It feels genuinely and joyfully revolutionary, even if the material being discussed is sometimes difficult, and I understand that feeling to be the opposite of the individualist habit of trying to be the subject at the expense of everyone else. Bringing joy into activism matters; without it, one campaigner warned me, 'only the self-flagellating will want to be involved'. The point is, getting over ourselves is best practised with others – including by doing activism, in the broadest possible application of that word. So, too, is singing clearly. 'You're in a field you share with others, you're in a collective life field and so truth isn't only your own,' says Greenhill, the vocal improvisation teacher. 'You're seeing a piece of something bigger and you're giving voice to the piece you can see.'[302]

We can practise bringing to activism, too, the states that can help us go beyond our thinking, rationalising ways of being – let's invoke T.S. Eliot and call them the stillness and the dancing.[303] The stillness of contemplation, meditation or time sitting in nature, that may be required for us to recognise our entanglements and interconnections with all other people and life forms. The dancing of ritual, music and embodiment that can help wake us from the emotional numbness that has been part of the problem. My contention is that these states are not only useful for the practice of activism. I do appreciate the irony of my instrumental approach here, but they are also useful to help us better appreciate some of the lessons of activist entanglement, and become more conscious of what we are bringing to our task. I am suggesting that even activism itself offers opportunities to practise ways of being that can teach us, in turn, to approach activism differently; that can help us to start it from a different place. We don't need to run away and sort ourselves out. We can learn on the job. Both the stillness and the dancing can bring us to a point where we understand, in our bodies as well as our minds, that we are not separate from everyone and everything else. This can be the starting point for any form of activism. We can see that we are not trying to save a world that is over there, but are engaged in the business of life in a world that is right here, in us as well as outside of us.

What does this look like in practice? It is one thing to read or hear about something and understand it mentally, another to experience it. There are activist cultures that are already trying to put some of these principles into action, and circles of campaigners getting together to think about the shadows they may be bringing to their work. There are training courses that are starting to weave, into their teaching of political tactics, opportunities for deep personal reflection and for experiencing the emotions attached to those things that activists have found hard to think about.[304] There are networks of practitioners of 'inner' development and healing and 'contemplative activism' who are offering their skills to activist organisations, teaching them the value of stillness before even thinking about action. There are activists talking about 'unlearning' the deep ways of being that create the problem. This can involve turning to our bodies, and starting to recognise the sensations that tell us our nervous systems are aroused and we are becoming uncomfortable. It can involve learning to recognise, as Sophy Banks and others are teaching, that discomfort – in our bodies, or in a group's dynamics – can be a feedback loop providing information that we need to do something differently. Some of this work has been going on for a while, and some of it is new, and to showcase specific examples of it is beyond the scope of this book. But a process of emergence is underway, in the sense of emergence as a principle by which something novel arises from the whole that is not present in any of its constituent parts. What is emerging from the combination of these flowerings is activism that is aware of itself, and the potential of that is only just unfolding.

Writing this book has changed me. My political and ecological outlook, and my commitment to social and ecological justice have not swerved, only deepened and formed more connections. But the quality of drive I apply to whatever I'm doing feels different, as do the feelings I experience about people who are not doing activism. I am still regularly baffled by people's choices, but I feel less judgemental, less likely to indulge in ideological descriptions of my opponents or targets or audience. I can think that somebody is wrong without dehumanising them. All right, let's be honest: when I am triggered to anger by someone's behaviour, my first reaction is still to think they're an arsehole. But my immediate second reaction is to wonder why they behaved as they did; perhaps they are defending themselves, or perhaps they got triggered too, by something I said, and they have not been supported to acquire the skills to respond differently. I am more likely to acknowledge, in situations where previously I would have rushed to judgement, that there are ways in which I am not so different. And I am more likely to acknowledge that sometimes I can't face it. That I want to turn away, too. That I don't want to think about my own complicity. Gandhi is not without his problems, but re-reading him, I found an observation that I wish I had framed on my NGO desk: 'It is quite proper to resist and attack a system, but to resist and attack its author is tantamount to resisting and attacking oneself.'[305] I wish, too, that I had worked some of this out before my Dad died and I could have created a new stage of my relationship with him in which I was not casting myself as the 'activist', and casting him, whenever we had political conversations, as the 'not-activist' who was wrong. I wish that there had been some other catalyst for this shift than his death.

I don't yet know what kind of activism I will do next, though I do know that this is not a time to be falling asleep.[306] My experience of raising children so far is that I can do only two big things well. Looking after children in their pre-school years has, up until now, been one of them. The work of writing this book has, for a while, been the other. Whatever I get involved in will be an opportunity to put into practice some of what I have learned. For now I am talking to people, cooking ideas and stirring a few pots. But my sense of what constitutes activism has widened. It is now much clearer: anything that helps to alter the imaginary is activism. Anything that helps to heal the dominant culture as well as those whom it hurts is activism, including work to heal the brittleness and exceptionalism of those of us who are hiding our vulnerability behind privilege and power within it.

I am still full of respect for the people who are doing the types of activism that I was doing before: investigating the things that are going wrong, working in the thick of policy fires, running in and out of radio and TV interviews all day. Anything I have said in this book about what I was doing when I was in those kinds of organisations isn't a dig at those organisations or anyone who works for them. The same problems emerge across many forms of activism, and I am using my experiences in them only as examples. And the work they are doing still needs doing, even if they sometimes need to approach it differently. The reporting on the terrible things that happen to people who are trying to defend their homes and land. The naming and holding to account of those who misuse power. The analysis of policy and its gaps and the suggestions of what is needed instead – even if new policies won't solve the whole problem on their own. It is by no means guaranteed, but I might even find myself doing some version of those tasks again one day, if I can see an intervention that makes systemic sense. That would certainly be a test of what I have learned. Would I be able to do investigative reporting, which can be so full of hero vibes, without succumbing to the temptation of getting heroic about my findings? Could I point out abuses of power without making 'us and them' distinctions and projecting my own shadows onto the people who are most directly responsible? How would I support the work of other activists in solidarity, without any personal agenda? Whatever I end up doing next, it will be with a sense of the 'movement ecology' of which I am a part. I will have the awareness that whatever I am doing is a small piece of the puzzle and not the entire answer, which means that what everyone else is doing is contributing to the puzzle too.

And of course, I'll not escape my entanglements entirely. My old patterns are a hungry ghost who is never very far away. While there's part of me that has enjoyed stepping back and being reflective about activism, there's another part of me that reads something outrageous in the news and still wants to get the bastards, and I email my friends and collaborators who I suspect may already be devising plans to do so. (They often are.) I enjoy being able to put what I have learned into words, yet at the same time I know that intellectualising and word-smithing is my own ongoing entanglement in a culture that has devalued feeling and sensing to catastrophic effect, as well as a strategy to avoid my own painful feelings. Part of me senses that I may be offering something of intrinsic value to the world to come, and another part of me still cares about what other activists might think of me, and whether by thinking, and trying to share my thinking, I have been 'doing enough' for a world that is in trouble.

I'm still sometimes caught between my old idea of what an activist is, my old way of understanding activism as only action, and the more capacious sense of activism that has been forming throughout the writing of this book, that includes reflection as well as action. I'm in regular conversations about these questions with at least three groups of people who do activism in the broadest sense of the term, and perhaps in another five years I would write a different book. This book is where I've got to now. I am writing these words during a week in 2020 when the June temperature in Siberia has reached 38 degrees, and the streets and social media are full of anti-racist activism along with criticism of how it is being done. The work continues … and so will this conversation.

Ten questions for entangled activists

1. What are the stories that have helped to shape you?

2. How have your perceptions of 'how to do activism' been shaped by your experiences?

3. What are you bringing to your activism that may not be to do with the problem you want to fix?

4. What might you need to reclaim?

5. What might you need to relinquish?

6. What practices would support your body's knowing and intuition?

7. What have you overlooked about what may need to change?

8. Who are you going to ask for their opinion about what really needs to change?

9. Who would you like to be in conversation with about being entangled?

10. Do you need to start from a different place and, if so, what might it look like?

Endnotes

1 Karen Barad, Quantum Entanglements and Hauntological Relations of Inheritance: Dis/continuities, SpaceTime Enfoldings, and Justice-to-Come, *Derrida Today*, 3.2, 2010, p. 251. Barad is a physicist who plays fruitfully across disciplinary boundaries with philosophy, feminism and queer studies, among others. I am conscious of her warnings about the many erroneous applications of ideas from quantum theory, which is about sub-atomic microparticles, to phenomena in the macro and social world: 'In the popular literature quantum physics is often positioned as the scientific path leading out of the West to the metaphysical garden of Eastern mysticism. Paralleling these popular renditions, one can find suggestions in the feminist literature that quantum physics is inherently less androcentric, more feminine, and generally less regressive than the masculinist tendencies found in Newtonian physics. But those who naively embrace quantum physics as some exotic Other that will save our weary Western souls forget too quickly that quantum physics underlies the workings of the A-bomb, that particle physics (which relies on quantum theory) is the ultimate manifestation of the tendency towards scientific reductionism, and that quantum theory in all its applications continues to be the purview of a small group of primarily Western-trained males.' (Barad, Meeting the Universe Halfway, in Lynn Hankinson Nelson and Jack Nelson, eds, *Feminism, Science, and the Philosophy of Science*, 1995, Dordrecht/Boston, pp. 161–194.) Nonetheless, the concept of entanglement remains highly suggestive in multiple contexts, as artists, poets and thinkers continue to explore. In quoting her words here, I am using them in a metaphorical sense to awaken intimations of entanglement's possibilities, rather than as any direct analogy.

2 Octavia Butler, *Parable of the Sower*, Headline, 1993.

3 John Muir, *My First Summer in the Sierra*, Boston: Houghton Mifflin, 1911.

4 Bill Torbert is a researcher and consultant on adult development and leadership. Adam Kahane, *Collaborating with the Enemy: How to Work with People You Don't Agree with Or Like Or Trust*, Berrett-Koehler, 2017, p. 95.

5 Kettling is a controversial police tactic to contain demonstrators in a limited area.

6 My thanks to the facilitator and psychotherapist Sophy Banks for this framing of the question.

7 Francis Spufford, *Unapologetic: Why, despite everything, Christianity can still make surprising emotional sense*, Faber, 2012.

8 It can be applied in the management of organisations and change processes across business, government and social change … although it often isn't. See Dave Snowden's explanations of his Cynefin Framework, videos of which can be easily found online.

9 'In urgent times, many of us are tempted to address trouble in terms of making an imagined future safe … Staying with the trouble does not require such a relationship to times called the future. In fact, staying with the trouble requires learning to be truly present', Donna J. Haraway, *Staying with the Trouble: Making Kin in the Chthulucene*, Duke University Press, 2016, p. 1.

10 Carolyn Ellis, Tony E. Adams and Arthur P. Bochner, Autoethnography: An Overview, *Historical Social Research* vol. 36 no. 4 (138), 2011, pp. 273–290.

11 Audre Lorde, The Master's Tools Will Never Dismantle the Master's House, *Sister Outsider: Essays and Speeches*. Berkeley, CA: Crossing Press, 1984, pp. 110–113.

12 According to the Etymonline etymology dictionary, which is considered reliable if not definitive by scholars. See Mart Kuldkepp, Sweden's Historical Mission and World War I, *Scandinavian Journal of History*, 39:1, 2014, pp. 126–146.

13 This figure was correct at time of going to press.

14 Joanna Macy and Chris Johnstone, *Active Hope: How to face the mess we're in without going crazy*, New World Library, 2012, Chapter 1.

15 In a notorious and closely watched case in the High Court a few years later, which generated legal costs of up to £100 million, Berezovsky unsuccessfully sued Abramovich for £3 billion in damages. The court dismissed his claim that Abramovich had intimidated him into selling his shares in the Russian oil giant Sibneft, as well as his claims about a broken promise over the aluminium company RusAl. *Boris Abramovich Berezovsky v. Roman Arkadievich Abramovich* (2012) High Court of Justice, Chancery Division, EWHC 2463 (Comm). BBC News, 'Roman Abramovich wins court battle against Berezovsky', 31 August 2012.

16 Global Witness has recently begun to explicitly modify its stance: see its CEO's blog on 24 September 2020, 'On the climate crisis, more of the same won't work. We need a revolution'.

17 Katrine Marçal, transl. Saskia Vogel, *Who Cooked Adam Smith's Dinner? A story about women and economics*, Granta, 2016.

18 We sort-of won, and sort-of still haven't. I was interviewed about this campaign for *Granta* magazine: Oliver Bullough, The Second Career of Michael Riegels, *Granta*, issue 150, February 2020.

19 Donella Meadows, *Thinking in Systems*, Chelsea Green, 2008, p. 4.

20 DeRay Mckesson wrote about Black Lives Matter, 'When a message is spoken loud and clear and in unison, when formerly there were whispers or collections of disparate rumblings, it is easy to think of people as finally having found their voices, as if those voices had been lost. That they are being heard now, though, is more an indictment of the listener, not the speaker. We the protesters have never been the voiceless. We have been the unheard.' DeRay Mckesson, 'I learned hope the hard way': on the early days of Black Lives Matter, *The Guardian*, 12 April 2019.

21 Jürgen Habermas, *Theory of Communicative Action, Volume 2, Lifeworld and System, A Critique of Functionalist Reason*, transl. Thomas McCarthy, Beacon Press, Boston, 1981, pp. 352 and

392; Jürgen Habermas, New Social Movements, *Telos*, September 21, 1981, no. 49, pp. 33–37.

22 Kalpana Wilson, Race, Gender and Neoliberalism: changing visual representations in development, *Third World Quarterly*, vol. 32 no. 2, 2011, pp. 315–331.

23 This was the suggestion in 1989 by Francis Fukuyama, then a US State Department official, that at the end of the Cold War, and with the 'total exhaustion of viable systematic alternatives', Western liberalism had won the day. Francis Fukuyama, The End of History? *The National Interest*, Summer 1989.

24 My thanks to the campaign strategists Natasha Adams and Jim Coe for this image.

25 Civil Society Futures, The Independent Inquiry, November 2018 https://civilsocietyfutures. org/wp-content/uploads/sites/6/2018/11/Civil-Society-Futures__The-Story-of-Our-Future.pdf

26 Audre Lorde, Learning from the 1960s, *Sister Outsider: Essays and Speeches*. Berkeley, CA: Crossing Press, 1984, pp. 134–144.

27 Francesca Polletta, Katt Hoban, Why Consensus? Prefiguration in Three Activist Eras, *Journal of Social and Political Psychology*, 2016, vol. 4(1), pp. 286–301.

28 http://guerrillafoundation.org/why-we-do-what-we-do/

29 Catherine Eschle, Troubling Stories of the End of Occupy: Feminist narratives of betrayal at occupy Glasgow, *Social Movement Studies* 17:5, 2018, pp. 524–540.

30 This point was argued by many observers, including the journalist and author Nafeez Ahmed, The flawed science behind Extinction Rebellion's change strategy, 28 October 2019   https://medium.com/insurge-intelligence/the-flawed-science-behind-extinction-rebellions-change-strategy-af077b9abb4d

31 Mind as process is the insight of Humberto Maturana and Francisco Varela's 'Santiago theory' of cognition. A helpful summary can be found in Fritjof Capra and Pier Luigi Luisi, *The Systems View of Life: A Unifying Vision*, Cambridge University Press, 2014, Chapter 12. That soul and matter are two sides of the same coin, two ways in which the universe realises itself, is also the contention of 'reflexive monism', a position on the philosophy of mind that seeks to resolve the question of what the universe is made of without resorting either to dualism or reductionism (in which one aspect is reduced to a function of the other). Max Velmans, Reflexive Monism, *Journal of Consciousness Studies*, vol. 15, Number 2, 2008, pp. 5–50(46).

32 Nadia Gilani, Why I'm No Longer Talking to White People About Yoga, *Huffington Post*, 26 January 2020; Rumya Putcha, Yoga Becky and the Politics of Silence, *Namaste Nation blog*, 9 May 2020.

33 Paolo Freire, *Pedagogy of the Oppressed*, Pelican, 1972, pp. 27–8.

34 My thanks to the mediator and facilitator Sophie Docker for this observation.

35 My gratitude to Sophy Banks who has schooled me in this awareness over several years.

36 Jonathan Haidt, *The Righteous Mind: Why Good People are Divided by Politics and Religion*, Penguin, 2012, chapters 7 and 8.

37 From Michel Foucault's introduction to Gilles Deleuze and Félix Guattari, *Anti-Oedipus*, 1972, quoted in Natasha Lennard, *Being Numerous: Essays on Non-Fascist Life*, Verso, 2019, p. 15.

38 Summary for Policymakers of IPCC Special Report on Global Warming of 1.5°C, 8 October 2018.

39 Some of the ample research on this link is summarised in Michele Gelfand, Authoritarian leaders thrive on fear. We need to help people feel safe, *The Guardian*, 2 January 2020.

40 Kimberlé Crenshaw, Demarginalizing the Intersection of Race and Sex: A Black Feminist Critique of Antidiscrimination Doctrine, Feminist Theory and Antiracist Politics, *University of Chicago Legal Forum*, 1989, iss. 1, pp. 139–167.

41 Nick Shaxson, *Treasure Islands: Tax havens and the men who stole the world*, Vintage, 2012; Nick Shaxson, *The Finance Curse: How global finance is making us all poorer*, Bodley Head, 2018; Guy Shrubsole, *Who Owns England? How we lost our green and pleasant land, and how to take it back*, Indibooks, 2018.

42 Robert Booth, UK social security payments 'at lowest level since launch of welfare state' *The Guardian*, 18 November 2019. 'The figures come as a senior government adviser said economic insecurity had become "the new normal" and polling showed a third of middle-class voters feared a slump in living standards in the next decade.'

43 Mary Annaïse Heglar, Climate Change Ain't the First Existential Threat, 18 February 2019, https://medium.com/s/story/sorry-yall-but-climate-change-ain-t-the-first-existential-threat-b3c999267aa0

44 I am grateful to the geography scholar Paul Chatterton whose paper describing the interactions on an activist road blockade introduced me to the idea of the 'not'-activist. Paul Chatterton, 'Give up Activism' and Change the World in Unknown Ways: Or, Learning to Walk with Others on Uncommon Ground, *Antipode*, March 2006.

45 Climate Outreach and Global Call for Climate Action, *Climate Visuals: Seven principles for visual climate change communication*, 2018.

46 Nadia Y. Bashir, Penelope Lockwood, Alison L. Chasteen, Daniel Nadolny and Indra Noyes, The ironic impact of activists: Negative stereotypes reduce social change influence, *European Journal of Social Psychology*, 43, 2013, pp. 614–626.

47 George Bernard Shaw, Epistle Dedicatory to Arthur Bingham Walkley, *Man and Superman*, 1903.

48 Lauren E. Duncan and Abigail J. Stewart, Personal political salience: The role of personality in collective identity and action. *Political Psychology* 28, 2007, pp. 143–164.

49 Theorists include Mancur Olson, William A. Gamson, and Charles Tilly; see discussion in Nick Crossley, *Making Sense of Social Movements*, Open University Press, 2002; Edward L. Rubin, Passing through the Door: Social Movement Literature and Legal Scholarship, *University of Pennsylvania Law Review*, vol. 150 no. 1, Nov 2001, pp. 1–83.

50 Theorists include Alain Touraine, Manuel Castells and Donatella Della Porta; see discussion in John A. Hannigan, Alain Touraine, Manuel Castells and Social Movement Theory: a Critical Appraisal, *The Sociological Quarterly*, vol. 26 no. 4, Winter 1985, pp. 435–454; Edward L. Rubin, Passing through the Door: Social Movement Literature and Legal Scholarship, *University of Pennsylvania Law Review*, vol. 150 no. 1, Nov 2001, pp. 1–83.

51 Theorists include Derrick Bell, Patricia J. Williams, Kimberlé Crenshaw; and Catherine MacKinnon, Martha Minow, Robin West.

52 Cristina Flesher Fominaya, Collective Identity in Social Movements: Central Concepts and Debates, *Sociology Compass* 4/6, 2010, pp. 393–404.

53 Daniel K. Cortese, I'm a 'good' activist, you're a 'bad' activist, and everything I do is activism: parsing the different types of 'activist' identities in LBGTQ organizing, *Interface*, vol. 7 (1) May 2015, pp. 215–246.

54 Laura Portwood-Stacer, *Lifestyle Politics and Radical Activism*, Bloomsbury, 2013.

55 Ron Eyerman, How Social Movements Move: Emotions and Social Movements, in Helena Flam and Debra King (eds), *Emotions and Social Movements*, Routledge, 2005.

56 Alberto Melucci, The Symbolic Challenge of Contemporary Movements, *Social Research*, vol. 52 no. 4, Winter 1985, pp. 789–816.

57 George Lakey, To Succeed, Movements Must Overcome the Tension Between Rationality and Emotion, *Open Democracy*, 10 September 2015.

58 Nick Crossley, *Making Sense of Social Movements*, Open University Press, 2002, Introduction; James M. Jasper, The Emotions of Protest: Affective and Reactive Emotions in and Around Social Movements, *Sociological Forum*, vol. 13 no. 3, Sep 1998, pp. 397–424.

59 James M. Jasper, The Emotions of Protest: Affective and Reactive Emotions in and Around Social Movements, *Sociological Forum*, vol. 13 no. 3, Sep 1998, pp. 397–424; Gavin Brown, Jenny Pickerill, Space for Emotion in the Spaces of Activism, *Emotion, Space and Society* 2, 2009, pp. 24–35; Debra King, Sustaining Activism Through Emotional Reflexivity, in Helena Flam and Debra King (eds), *Emotions and Social Movements*, Routledge, 2005; Ron Eyerman, How Social Movements Move: Emotions and Social Movements, in Flam and King (eds) *Emotions and Social Movements*; Chris Barker, Brian Martin and Mary Zournazi, Emotional self-management for activists, *Reflective Practice: International and Multidisciplinary Perspectives*, 9:4, 2008, pp. 423–435. Colin Barker, however, noted that the emotions of activism are hard to disentangle from the 'understandings and purposes of which they are an inherent part'. Colin Barker, Crises and Turning Points in Revolutionary Development: emotion, organization and strategy in Solidarnosc, 1980–81, *Interface*, vol. 2 (1) May 2010, pp. 79–117.

60 William Davies, *Nervous States: How Feeling Took over the World*, Vintage, 2018, p. xiv.

61 Carl Jung, The Archetypes and the Collective Unconscious, *Collected Works*, vol. 9, p. 284 (from the glossary in Jung, *Memories, Dreams, Reflections*, Fontana Press, 1961).

62 While some psychoanalytic theories suggest that innate and existential demands cause us to split off parts of our self, others claim that social forces and the withholding of social approval motivate splitting.

63 Connie Zweig and Jeremiah Abrams, The Shadow Side of Everyday Life, in Zweig and Abrams (eds), *Meeting the Shadow: The Hidden Power of the Dark Side of Human Nature*, Tarcher/ Penguin, 1991, pp. xviii–xix; Robert Bly, *A Little Book on the Human Shadow*, Harper & Row, 1988.

64 Fanny Brewster, The Racial Shadow of American Politics, *ARAS Connections*, 2016; Thomas Singer, A Jungian approach to understanding 'us vs them' dynamics, *Psychoanalysis, Culture & Society* 14, 2009, pp. 32–40; Jerome S. Bernstein, The US-Soviet Mirror, in Zweig and Abrams (eds), *Meeting the Shadow: The Hidden Power of the Dark Side of Human Nature*, Tarcher/ Penguin, 1991.

65 Audre Lorde, The Uses of Anger: Women Responding to Racism, *Women's Studies Quarterly*, 9:3, Fall 1981, pp. 7–10.

66 I am grateful to the ecopsychologist and psychotherapist Mary-Jayne Rust, with whom I had a fruitful conversation and correspondence about anger and hatred in campaigning.

67 Personal communication.

68 bell hooks, *The Will to Change: Men, Masculinity and Love*, Washington Square Press, 2004, p. 7.

69 Alastair McIntosh and Matt Carmichael, *Spiritual Activism: Leadership as Service*, Green Books, 2016, pp. 150–151.

70 Mary Douglas, *Purity and Danger*, Routledge, 1966, p. 193.

71 Personal communication.

72 For example, Daniel K. Cortese, I'm a 'good' activist, you're a 'bad' activist, and everything I do is activism: parsing the different types of 'activist' identities in LBGTQ organizing, *Interface*, vol. 7 (1) May 2015, pp. 215–246; Chris Bobel, 'I'm not an activist, though I've done a lot of it': Doing Activism, Being Activist and the 'Perfect Standard' in a Contemporary Movement, *Social Movement Studies* 6, 2007, pp. 147–159; Frances Lee (ed), *Toward an Ethics of Activism: A Community Investigation of Humility, Grace and Compassion in Movements for Justice*, 2018.

73 Frances Lee, Excommunicate me from the church of social justice, blog, 2017.

74 Jonathan Smucker, *Hegemony How-To*, AK Press, 2017, pp. 69–70.

75 Jonathan Haidt, *The Righteous Mind, Why Good People are Divided by Politics and Religion*, Penguin, 2012, pp. 124 and 173.

76 My thanks to Vanessa Faloye for this formulation.

77 Martha Nussbaum, *Upheavals of Thought: The Intelligence of Emotions*, Cambridge University Press, 2001, pp. 193 and 221.

78 This research is readably summarised in Sue Gerhardt, *Why Love Matters: How affection shapes a baby's brain*, Routledge, 2004.

79 Philip Larkin, 'This Be The Verse', *Collected Poems*, Faber and Faber, 2003; Oliver James, *How Not to F*** Them Up*, Vermilion, 2010.

80 Sarah Blaffer Hrdy, *Mothers and Others: The Evolutionary Origins of Mutual Understanding*, Harvard University Press, 2009.

81 https://systems-souls-society.com/the-oldest-story-how-parenting-and-politics-are-linked/
A practical point for activists is that if the challenge for society is to produce people who can live with their humanity in all its vulnerability, and one of the keys to that is what happens in infancy, then this suggests that a key task for activists interested in systemic intervention points should be ensuring a lot more support for parents of babies and small children.

82 Alice Miller, *For Your Own Good: The roots of violence in child-rearing*, Virago, 1987; Sue Gerhardt, *The Selfish Society*, Simon & Schuster, 2010.

83 The phrase 'good-enough mother', popular in psychotherapeutic circles in the 1980s, is analytically powerful in its conception of inevitable failures in the parent–child bond that, in the context of good attachment, allow a child to develop a secure sense of themselves. It remains, too, a much-appreciated gift to exhausted parents who are trying to remain calm and complete the day's tasks while several feet beyond the end of their tether. It can refer to a good-enough father or any other carer as well as a mother.

84 My thanks to the psychotherapist, author and broadcaster Mark Vernon for this observation.

85 Martha Nussbaum, *Hiding from Humanity: Disgust, shame and the law*, Princeton, 2004; Martha Nussbaum, *From disgust to humanity: sexual orientation and constitutional law*, OUP, 2010.

86 Jan Haaken, Riding the waves of feminism: Psychoanalysis and women's liberation. *Psychoanalysis, Culture & Society*, 2016, 21, pp. 223–231.

87 bell hooks, *The Will to Change: Men, Masculinity and Love*, Washington Square Press, 2004; Robert Bly, *A Little Book on the Human Shadow*, Harper & Row, 1988.

88 Blake E. Ashforth, Ronald H. Humphrey, Emotion in the workplace: a reappraisal, *Human Relations*, vol. 48 no. 2, 1995, pp. 97–125.

89 Nadine Andrews noted that she found both of these in her research: people in their work roles having to reduce their emotionality about the subject they are dealing with, and projecting their discomfort onto others. Personal communication. See Nadine Andrews, Psychosocial Factors Influencing the Experience of Sustainability Professionals, *Sustainability Accounting, Management and Policy Journal*, vol. 8 iss. 4, pp. 445–469.

90 Renée Lertzman, *Environmental Melancholia, Psychoanalytic Dimensions of Engagement*, Routledge, 2015. She covers some of the arguments in the blogs on her website.

91 These denial strategies include 'shoot the messenger' (focus on negative information about the organisation providing the information), 'the medium is the message' (focus on the alleged manipulative strategy behind the appeal), and 'babies and bathwater' (focus on questioning the validity of the actions recommended in the appeal, so that the 'baby' of responsible action is thrown out with the 'bathwater' of the partial truth in the audience's assumptions about the effectiveness of the possible action). Irene Bruna Seu, 'Doing denial': audience reaction to human rights appeals, *Discourse and Society*, vol. 21 no. 4, July 2010, pp. 438–457.

92 Personal communication. The 'Stansted 15's' conviction was quashed on appeal in January 2021, with the judge commenting that there was 'no case to answer.

93 https://www.goodtherapy.org/learn-about-therapy/types/existential-psychotherapy

94 I am grateful to Sarah Stein Lubrano for alerting me to this dimension of agency.

95 Reni Eddo-Lodge, *Why I'm No Longer Talking to White People About Race*, Bloomsbury, 2017; Guilaine Kinouani's writing is at www.racereflections.co.uk and on Twitter at @KGuilaine.

96 Sara Ahmed, *Living a Feminist Life*, Duke University Press, 2017, p. 38.

97 Ahmed, *Living a Feminist Life*, p. 155.

98 Tom Crompton and Tim Kasser, *Meeting Environmental Challenges: The Role of Human Identity*, 2009, WWF/Green Books. Chapter 3 has a concise summary of the literature on threat and coping, as applied to the threat of climate change.

99 Robin DiAngelo, White Fragility, *International Journal of Critical Pedagogy*, vol. 3 (3), 2011, pp. 54–70.

100 Alan G. Vaughan, A Conversation between Like-Minded Colleagues and Friends: Alan Vaughan and Andrew Samuels, *Jung Journal*, 12:2, 2018, pp. 118–137.

101 Personal communication.

102 Valeria Pecorelli, Wondering While Wandering: living between academia and activism, *Interface*, vol. 7 (2) Nov 2015, pp. 145–160.

103 Paul Chatterton, 'Give up Activism' and Change the World in Unknown Ways: Or, Learning to Walk with Others on Uncommon Ground, *Antipode*, March 2006.

104 Lynne Layton, Editor's introduction to special issue on 'Us vs Them', *Psychoanalysis, Culture & Society*, 2009, 14, pp. 1–3.

105 Joanna Macy and Chris Johnstone, *Active Hope: How to face the mess we're in without going crazy*, New World Library, 2012, p. 65.

106 Nadine Andrews, Psychosocial factors influencing the experience of sustainability professionals, *Sustainability Accounting, Management and Policy Journal*, vol. 8 iss. 4, 2017, pp. 445–469.

107 Another account of this can be found in the 'mean green meme' proposed by the theorist of consciousness Ken Wilber, which I look at in Chapter 7.

108 'I have rendered and explored this conundrum in almost every book I have written.' Toni Morrison, *The Origin of Others*, Harvard University Press, 2017, p. 30.

109 Toni Morrison, *The Origin of Others*, p. 38.

110 The KonTerra Group, *Amnesty International Staff Wellbeing Review*, 2019.

111 According to *The Guardian*, the review by a QC into the death of Gaëtan Mootoo found that 'a serious failure of management' at Amnesty had contributed. A separate inquiry into the death of Rosalind McGregor found that Amnesty bore no responsibility. Karen McVeigh, Amnesty 'failed to support and value' Paris worker who killed himself, *The Guardian*, 19 November 2018; Karen McVeigh, Amnesty International has toxic working culture, report finds, *The Guardian*, 6 Feb 2019.

112 Jem Bendell, Deep Adaptation: A Map for Navigating Climate Tragedy, *IFLAS Occasional Paper 2*, July 2018. His website includes rebuttals to the criticisms that were made of his reading of the climate science.

113 Quoted in his blog: https://jembendell.com/2020/02/06/what-activism-next-ideas-for-climate-campaigners/

114 Stephen Hopgood, *Keepers of the Flame: Understanding Amnesty International*, Cornell University Press, 2006.

115 Another campaigner who worked with NGOs that were campaigning on the Copenhagen summit told me that the atmosphere among those doing this work was a 'kind of collective insanity of hope', a wilful turning away from the increasingly obvious realisation that it was going to be very hard to achieve anything meaningful there.

116 One staff member told the investigation after the staff suicides: 'It's very challenging to read what one human being can do to another. Nobody in my whole career has ever asked, are you okay reading this stuff?' The KonTerra Group, *Amnesty International Staff Wellbeing Review*, 2019.

117 Cher Weixia Chen and Paul C. Gorski, Burnout in Social Justice and Human Rights Activists: Symptoms, Causes and Implications, *Journal of Human Rights Practice*, vol. 7 iss. 3, Nov 2015, pp. 366–390.

118 Personal communication. See his blog on this: http://www.coeandkingham.org.uk/planning/we-like-to-think-were-stevie-wonder-we-plan-like-were-the-jesus-but-were-not-even-the-band-in-ricks-bar-in-casablanca/

119 I explored this in an essay, From Hyde Park to Wembley, A journey in activism, *Dark Mountain*, iss. 16: Refuge, October 2019.

120 I learned this excellent phrase from Judith Seelig.

121 Open Letter from the Wretched of the Earth bloc to the organisers of the People's Climate March of Justice and Jobs, 17 January 2016.

122 There are many easily accessible explanations of it online.

123 Stephen Karpman, Fairy Tales and Script Drama Analysis, *Transactional Analysis Bulletin*, 7 (26) 1968, pp. 39–43.

124 Judith Herman, *Trauma and Recovery: The Aftermath of violence – from domestic abuse to political terror*, Basic Books, 1992, pp. 142–143.

125 See the work of 'No White Saviours', a Ugandan advocacy group. Radi-Aid, a Norwegian initiative, seeks to overturn clichéd images and saviourism. It's named for their launch film, a Band Aid spoof called *Radiators for Norway*.

126 Robtel Neajai Pailey, De-centring the 'White Gaze' of Development, *Development and Change*, Oct 2019.

127 Personal communication.

128 Nesrine Malik, Where are Clooney and Co Now that Sudan Needs Them? *The Guardian*, 21 January 2019.

129 George Clooney and John Prendergast, We're not silent on Sudan – we're going after the regime's loot, *The Guardian*, 24 January 2019.

130 Pailey cites Eric Williams's *Capitalism and Slavery* (1944), and Manning Marable's *How Capitalism Underdeveloped Black America (1983)*.

131 Kimberlé Crenshaw, Demarginalizing the Intersection of Race and Sex: A Black Feminist Critique of Antidiscrimination Doctrine, Feminist Theory and Antiracist Politics, *University of Chicago Legal Forum*, 1989, iss. 1.

132 Personal communication.

133 Personal communication.

134 Personal communication.

135 Personal communication.

136 Rosetta Thurman and Trista Harris, *How to Become a Nonprofit Rockstar*, lulu.com, 2011.

137 https://www.hgi.org.uk/human-givens/introduction/what-are-human-givens

138 Viktor Frankl, *Man's Search for Meaning: An Introduction to Logotherapy*, transl. Ilse Lasch, Beacon Press, 1959.

139 Their website, selfdeterminationtheory.org, explains their work for a non-academic audience.

140 Deci and Ryan's self-determination theory suggests that there is no simple polarisation between extrinsic and intrinsic motivations, as many extrinsic motivations become 'internalised' to varying degrees; instead it is more of a spectrum.

141 Tim Kasser, Materialistic Values and Goals, *Annual Review of Psychology*, 2016, 67, pp. 489–514; Tim Kasser, Steve Cohn, Allen D. Kanner, Richard M. Ryan, Some Costs of American Corporate Capitalism: A Psychological Explanation of Values and Goal Conflicts, *Psychological Inquiry*, vol. 18 no. 1, 2007, pp. 1–22.

142 Tom Crompton, *The Case for Working with our Cultural Values*, WWF, 2010.

143 Nora Bateson, Liminal Leadership, *Kosmos*, Fall/Winter 2017.

144 https://www.ted.com/participate/ted-prize/prize-winning-wishes/global-witness

145 Cameron Anderson, John Angus D. Hildreth, and Laura Howland, Is the Desire for Status a Fundamental Human Motive? A Review of the Empirical Literature, *Psychological Bulletin*, March 2015. (The other criteria were that the need for status appears universal across age, culture and gender; that its absence causes ongoing and not just temporary negative health, well-being and psychological outcomes; and that it induces behaviour designed to satisfy status needs.)

146 Laura Portwood Stacer, *Lifestyle Politics and Radical Activism*, Bloomsbury, 2013.

147 Personal communication.

148 Tiffany Lethabo King and Ewuare Osayande, The Filth on Philanthropy, in INCITE! (eds), *The Revolution will not be Funded: Beyond the Non-Profit Industrial Complex*, Duke University Press, 2017.

149 Anand Giridharadas, *Winners Take All: The Elite Charade of Changing the World*, Allen Lane, 2018.

150 Iain McGilchrist, *The Master and his Emissary: The Divided Brain and the Making of the Western World*, Yale, 2009, pp. 143.

151 Donella Meadows, *Thinking in Systems*, Chelsea Green, 2008, pp. 162–163.

152 I am adopting here the approach of the feminist philosopher Kate Manne, who sees misogyny less as 'hatred' of women (although that also exists) than a system of policing women who refuse to meet patriarchal requirements. Kate Manne, *Down Girl: The Logic of Misogyny*, OUP USA, 2017.

153 Jürgen Habermas, transl. Thomas McCarthy, *Theory of Communicative Action, Volume 2: Lifeworld and System, A Critique of Functionalist Reason*, Beacon Press, Boston, 1981, p. 125.

154 His interest was in forms of communication, and his work contrasted the forms of communication that take place in the 'lifeworld' with the communications that emerge from people when they are operating from their adopted role in the system, which are instrumental and intended to get people to do something the system wants.

155 Habermas, *Theory of Communicative Action*, vol. 2, p. 312.

156 Habermas, *Theory of Communicative Action*, vol. 2, Chapters VI and VIII.

157 Peter Levine, Habermas with a Whiff of Tear Gas: Nonviolent Campaigns and Deliberation in an Era of Authoritarianism, *Journal of Public Deliberation*, vol. 14 iss. 2, Dec 2018.

158 Charles Taylor, *Modern Social Imaginaries*, 2004, Duke University Press, p. 23.

159 Sam Earle, Deep Social Change: the flawed logic of 'Reducitarianism', blog post, https://blog.usejournal.com/deep-social-change-the-flawed-logic-of-reducitarianism-3eafcb79d97c; personal communication.

160 Charles Taylor, *Modern Social Imaginaries*, p. 33.

161 Stephen Frosh, Psychosocial studies with psychoanalysis, *Journal of Psychosocial Studies*, 12(1–2) 2019, pp. 101–114.

162 Personal communication. Andrew Simms, (ed), *There was a Knock at the Door: 23 folk modern folk tales for troubled times*, New Weather Institute, 2016; *Knock Twice: 25 modern folk tales for troubling times*, 2017; *Knock Three Times: 28 modern folk tales for a world in trouble*, 2019.

163 Terry Pratchett, *Witches Abroad*, Corgi, 2005, quoted in Alex Evans, Why progressives should worry about the myth gap, *Open Democracy*, 11 January 2017.

164 Ben Okri, *A Way of Being Free*, Head of Zeus, 1997, p. 46.

165 Personal communication. See Martin Shaw, *Scatterlings: Getting Claimed in the Age of Amnesia*, White Cloud Press, 2016, p. 178.

166 R.H. Tawney, *Religion and the Rise of Capitalism*, 1926; Max Weber, *The Protestant Ethic and the Spirit of Capitalism*, 1905.

167 Bruno Latour comments, of environmentalism's failings: 'The difference between the environmental movement and the history of social movements is so striking. From the mid-19th century to the mid-20th century, socialists as well as communists have tried to rethink the entirety of Western philosophy to frame fights against inequalities and injustice .... The work of political ecology was never developed to that extent. They have swallowed hook, line, and sinker the perverse notion of nature – especially its exteriority to politics – the notion of the global, and the whole ideal of objective science, in a way that has ensured that social movements and ecological movements remain separate.' Bruno Latour, Denise Milstein, Isaac Marrero-Guillamón and Israel Rodríguez-Giralt, Down to earth social movements: an interview with Bruno Latour, *Social Movement Studies*, 17:3, 2018, pp. 353–361. Latour's book *Down to Earth: Politics in the New Climate Regime, Polity*, 2018, explores this question in more detail.

168 Mark Vernon, *A Secret History of Christianity: Jesus, the Last Inkling, and the Evolution of Consciousness*, John Hunt, 2018.

169 The *Stanford Encyclopedia of Philosophy* webpage on 'Law and Ideology' has an overview of approaches to understanding ideology.

170 This was the work of the Mont Pèlerin Society, see Philip Mirowski and Dieter Plehwe, (eds) *The Road from Mont Pèlerin: The Making of the Neoliberal Thought Collective*, Harvard University Press, Cambridge, MA, 2009.

171 Hannah Arendt, *The Origins of Totalitarianism*, Penguin, 1951, p. 615.

172 Hannah Arendt, *The Origins of Totalitarianism*, pp. 615–622.

173 George Kateb, Ideology and Storytelling, *Social Research*, vol. 69 no. 2, Summer 2002, pp. 321–357.

174 Frederic Laloux, *Reinventing Organizations*, Nelson Parker, 2014, p. 14.

175 Ken Wilber, Introduction to Frederic Laloux, *Reinventing Organizations*, p. x.

176 Colour-coded diagrams of Don Beck and Christopher Cowan's Spiral Dynamics model and its adaptation by Ken Wilber, including how they relate to each other, can easily be found online. See Don Edward Beck, Christopher C. Cowan, *Spiral Dynamics: Mastering Values, Leadership and Change*, Wiley-Blackwell, 2005; Ken Wilber, *Sex, Ecology, Spirituality*, Shambhala, 1995. Frederic Laloux's book *Reinventing Organizations* (Nelson Parker, 2014) has a clear summary.

177 A good short summary of Kegan's developmental model is available online: Jennifer Garvey Berger, *Key Concepts for Understanding the Work of Robert Kegan*, Kenning Associates, 2006.

178 See Jonathan Rowson, The Unrecognised Genius of Jean Piaget, *Medium*, 19 December 2016.

179 Robert Kegan, *In Over our Heads: The Mental Demands of Modern Life*, Harvard University Press, 1998, p. 342.

180 Robert Kegan, *In Over Our Heads*, pp. 344–345, 351. His elaboration of the 'self-transforming' mind is less detailed than his focus on the shift from 'socialised' to 'self-authoring', which is where the majority of people are. At the point he was writing in the nineties, he thought 1 per cent of people reached the 'self-transforming' stage; Ken Wilber, writing in 2017, thought 5 per cent of people were at what he or others call 'integrated', 'systemic' or 'integral' thinking. Ken Wilber, *Trump and a Post-Truth world*, Shambhala, 2017.

181 Jonathan Haidt, *The Righteous Mind: Why Good People are Divided by Politics and Religion*, Penguin, 2012, p. 129.

182 Jeremy Gilbert, Psychedelic Socialism, *Open Democracy*, 22 September 2017.

183 Foucault's Collège de France lectures weren't published in French for more than 20 years. They were published in English a few years later by Palgrave Macmillan.

184 Michel Foucault, *The Birth of Biopolitics, Lectures at the Collège de France, 1978–79*, transl. Graham Burchell, Palgrave Macmillan, 2008.

185 Ayeisha Thomas-Smith, Radicalising Homo-Economicus; or Rethinking Neoliberal Subjectivity and 'Radical Labour', unpublished thesis.

186 Ronald Butt, Mrs Thatcher: The First Two Years, *Sunday Times*, 3rd May 1981.

187 Antonio Gramsci, *Selections from the Prison Notebooks of Antonio Gramsci*, Lawrence and Wishart, 1976.

188 Tina Wallace, NGO Dilemmas: Trojan Horses for Global Neoliberalism? *Socialist Register*, vol. 40, 2004, pp. 202–219. Liam Barrington-Bush wrote a good analysis of how this plays out in the internal management of NGOs in his book *Anarchists in the Boardroom*, morelikepeople.org, 2013.

189 INCITE! (eds), *The Revolution Will Not Be Funded: Beyond the Non-Profit Industrial Complex*, Duke University Press, 2004 and 2017.

190 Amara H. Pérez, Between Radical Theory and Community Practice, Sisters in Action for Power, pp. 91–99, in INCITE! (eds) *The Revolution Will Not Be Funded*.

191 Personal communication.

192 Personal communication.

193 Useful references can be found without a paywall in Feyzi Ismail, Sangeeta Kamat, NGOs, Social Movements and the Neoliberal State: Incorporation, Reinvention, Critique, *Critical Sociology*, vol. 44 iss. 4–5, 2018, pp. 569–577. The following paper is open access via LSE Research Online: Irene Bruna Seu, Frances Flanagan and Shani Orgad, The Good Samaritan and the Marketer: public perceptions of humanitarian and international development NGOs, *International Journal of Nonprofit and Voluntary Sector Marketing*, 30 April 2015.

194 Roopali Mukherjee and Sarah Banet-Weiser, (eds) *Commodity Activism: cultural resistance in neoliberal times*, NYU Press, 2012.

195 Jonathan Smucker, *Hegemony How-To: A Roadmap for Radicals*, AK Press 2017, pp. 72–73.

196 Sara Ahmed, Selfcare as Warfare, Feminist Killjoy blog, 2014.

197 Timothy Morton, Poisoned Ground, *symplokē*, vol. 21 no. 1–2, 2013, pp. 37–50.

198 Hilary Prentice, Cosmic Walk: Awakening the Ecological Self, www. hilaryprenticepsychotherapy.net/article%203%20cosmic%20walk.htm

199 Laura Naegler, 'Goldman-Sachs doesn't care if you raise chicken': the challenges of resistant prefiguration, *Social Movement Studies*, 17:5, 2018, 507–523.

200 Laura Portwood Stacer, *Lifestyle Politics and Radical Activism*, Bloomsbury, 2013, p. 22.

201 Personal communication.

202 Mark Whitehead, Rhys Jones, Rachel Lilley, Rachel Howell, Jessica Pykett, Neuroliberalism: Cognition, context, and the geographical bounding of rationality, *Progress in Human Geography*, vol. 43 issue 4, 2018, pp. 632–649.

203 The term comes from Gayatri Chakravorty Spivak's influential essay, Can the Subaltern Speak? in Cary Nelson and Lawrence Grossberg (eds), *Marxism and the Interpretation of Culture*, University of Illinois Press, 1988.

204 Semiotics is the study of the patterns that underlie language and communication.

205 Walter Mignolo, Decoloniality and Phenomenology: The Geopolitics of Knowing and Epistemic/Ontological Colonial Differences, *The Journal of Speculative Philosophy*, vol. 32 no. 3, 2018, pp. 360–387.

206 Paul Gilroy, *The Black Atlantic: Modernity and Double Consciousness*, Verso, 1992, pp. 39, 70.

207 This phrase is from the psychoanalyst Jessica Benjamin, and I explore it in more depth in Chapter 9.

208 Iain McDaniel's concise overview of political resistance offers useful context: Resistance in intellectual history and political thought, *History of European Ideas* 44:4, 2018, pp. 397–403.

209 Aníbal Quijano, Coloniality and Modernity/Rationality, *Cultural Studies* 21: 2, 2007, pp. 168–78.

210 Aníbal Quijano, Coloniality and Modernity/Rationality, *Cultural Studies* 21: 2, 2007, p. 172. In saying this, Quijano is talking about the influence of Cartesian thinking on European thought: the 'I' of Descartes, 'I think, therefore I am', is an isolated individual, and any object that this 'I' can know is external to it. European thought is not without mention of intersubjectivity. It was a tool in the work of Edmund Husserl, who appeared briefly in my description of the 'lifeworld' in Chapter 6. Husserl was trained in Cartesian philosophy and scientific methodology, but found them insufficient to describe the nature of experience. He wanted to get beyond the duality of subject and object, and the field of phenomenology that he helped to found tried to study conscious experience objectively, but from a first-person standpoint. Husserl's tool to achieve this was intersubjectivity – a way of understanding ourselves in relation to the world and as mutually constituting each other, founded on empathy. Walter Mignolo discusses Husserl in the light of Quijano's argument in his paper Decoloniality and Phenomenology: The Geopolitics of Knowing and Epistemic/Ontological Colonial Differences, *The Journal of Speculative Philosophy* , vol. 32 no. 3, Special Issue with the Society for Phenomenology and Existential Philosophy, 2018, pp. 360–387. See also *Stanford Encyclopedia of Philosophy* on Husserl; and Iain McGilchrist, *The Master and his Emissary: The Divided Brain and the Making of the Western World*, Yale, 2009, pp. 143–144.

211 Dan Hocoy, Aaron Kipnis, Helene Lorenz, Mary Watkins, *Liberation Psychologies: An Invitation to Dialogue*, Pacifica Graduate Institute, 2017. Liberation psychology was developed by Ignacio Martín-Baró, a Salvadorean scholar and psychologist who was murdered by a US-trained death squad in 1989.

212 Iain McGilchrist, *The Master and His Emissary: The Divided Brain and the Making of the Western World*, Yale, 2010. He summarises his argument in this short animation: https://www.thersa.org/discover/videos/rsa-animate/2011/10/rsa-animate---the-divided-brain. There is also a documentary film about his work, *The Divided Brain* (2019).

213 McGilchrist, *The Master and His Emissary*, p. 170.

214 Republic of South Africa, White Paper for social welfare: principles, guidelines, recommendations, proposed policies and programmes for developmental social welfare in South Africa. August 1997, cited in David A. McDonald, Ubuntu bashing: the

marketisation of 'African values' in South Africa, *Review of African Political Economy*, June 2010, vol. 37 no. 124, pp 139–152.

215 Mogobe B. Ramose, Globalization and *ubuntu*, in P.H. Coetzee and A.P.J. Roux (eds), *The African Philosophy Reader*, Routledge, 1998, pp. 732–762.

216 Pheng Cheah, The Limits of Thinking in Decolonial Strategies, newsletter of Townsend Center for the Humanities at University of California, November 2006, Berkeley, https://townsendcenter.berkeley.edu/publications/limits-thinking-decolonial-strategies

217 As Judith Butler elaborates this question: 'Is the norm first "outside", and does it then enter into a pre-given psychic space, understood as an interior theater of some kind? Or does the internalization of the norm contribute to the production of internality?' Judith Butler, *The Psychic Life of Power: Theories in Subjection*, Stanford, 2007, p. 19.

218 Gayatri Chakravorty Spivak, Can the Subaltern Speak? 1988, in Cary Nelson and Lawrence Grossberg (eds), *Marxism and the Interpretation of Culture*, University of Illinois Press, 1988; Claire Cosquer, Altering Absence: From race to empire in readings of Foucault, *Foucault Studies*, no. 26, June 2019 pp. 1–20. In Judith Butler's words, Foucault was 'notoriously taciturn on the topic of the psyche'. Judith Butler, *The Psychic Life of Power: Theories in Subjection*, Stanford, 2007, p. 18.

219 In 2001 Farhad Dalal surveyed the psychoanalytical clinical literature on race and found systematic assumptions that differences between races are essential rather than constituted historically; and that psychoanalytical explanations of racial prejudice keep the external reality of actual racism at bay because of white guilt. Farhad Dalal, Insides and Outsides: a review of psychoanalytic renderings of difference, racism and prejudice. *Psychoanalytic Studies*, 3(1) 2001, pp. 43–66. See also Farhad Dalal, Jung: A racist. *British Journal of Psychotherapy*, 4(3), 1988, pp. 63–279.

220 For example, Open letter from a group of Jungians on the question of Jung's writings on and theories about 'Africans', *British Journal of Psychotherapy*, 34, 4, 2018, pp. 673–678. See also Guilaine Kinouani's writings about her experiences of racism within the professional field of psychology on her website, Race Reflections.

221 Mary-Jayne Rust, personal communication. See Mary-Jayne Rust, *Towards an Ecopsychotherapy*, Karnac, 2020; and James Hillman, A Psyche the Size of the Earth, in Roszak et al (eds), *Ecopsychology: Restoring the Earth, Healing the Mind*, Sierra Club Books, 1995.

222 Akwugo Emejulu and Francesca Sobande, On the Problems and Possibilities of European Black Feminism and Afrofeminism, in Emejulu and Sobande, (eds), *To Exist is to Resist: Black Feminism in Europe*, Pluto, 2019.

223 Guilaine Kinouani, Difference, Whiteness and the Group Analytic Matrix: An integrated formulation, *Group Analysis*, vol. 53 issue 1, 2019, pp. 60–74; Fanny Brewster, The Racial Shadow of American Politics, *ARAS Connections*, 2016 Presidency Papers Special Issue; Frantz Fanon, *Black Skin, White Masks*, 1952 (transl. Charles Lam Markmann, Grove Press, 1967).

224 Jessica Benjamin, *Beyond Doer and Done To: Recognition Theory, Intersubjectivity and the Third*, Routledge 2018, p. 23.

225 Iris Murdoch, The Sublime and the Good, *Chicago Review* 13, Autumn 1959, p. 51.

226 Toni Morrison, T*he Origin of Others*, Harvard, 2017, p. 38.

227 Benjamin, *Beyond Doer and Done To*, p. 39.

228 She has also worked with it in the context of the conflict in Israel/Palestine.

229 Jessica Benjamin, 'Moving Beyond Violence': What We Learn from Two Former Combatants about the Transition from Aggression to Recognition, in Pumla Gobodo-Madikizela (ed), *Breaking Intergenerational Cycles of Repetition: A Global Dialogue on Historical Trauma and Memory,* Verlag Barbara Budrich, 2015.

230 See Molly Merson, Whiteness and the Problem of Mutual Recognition, blog, 10 May 2020.

231 Judith Herman, *Trauma and Recovery: The aftermath of violence – from domestic abuse to political terror*, 1992, Basic Books, p. 33.

232 Bessel van der Kolk, *The Body Keeps the Score: Mind, Brain and Body in the Transformation of Trauma*, Penguin, 2014, p. 2.

233 Bessel van der Kolk, *The Body Keeps the Score*, p. 77.

234 Judith Herman, *Trauma and Recovery*, p. 237.

235 See, for example, the Race Reflections website run by Guilaine Kinouani, a scholar and therapist focusing on racial trauma.

236 Michael Rothberg, Decolonizing Trauma Studies: A Response, *Studies in the Novel*, 40, 2008, pp. 224–234. Sonya Andermahr, (ed) *Decolonising Trauma Studies, Trauma and Postcolonialism,* (Special Issue of *Humanities*), 2016; Irene Visser, Decolonizing Trauma Theory: Retrospect and Prospects. *Humanities*, 2015, 4, pp. 250–265; Norman Saadi Nikro, Situating Postcolonial Trauma Studies, *Postcolonial Text*, vol. 9 no. 2, 2014.

237 Vincent J. Felitti, Robert F. Anda, Dale Nordenberg et al, Relationship of childhood abuse and household dysfunction to many of the leading causes of death in adults. The Adverse Childhood Experiences (ACE) Study, *American Journal of Preventative Medicine* 1998, 14(4) pp. 245 –258.

238 Bessel van der Kolk, *The Body Keeps the Score*, p. 148.

239 Bessel van de Kolk and Robert S. Pynoos, Proposal to include a developmental trauma disorder diagnosis for children and adolescents in DSM-V, 2009; Bessel van der Kolk, *The Body Keeps the Score*, pp. 164–166; Catherine Frogley, Developmental Trauma: How useful is this framework? The Association for Child and Adolescent Mental Health website, 3 August 2018.

240 From his interview with Krista Tippett on the podcast 'On Being', 4 June 2020.

241 She blogs at https://healthyhumanculture.wordpress.com/

242 A good place to start is Stephen Porges, *The Polyvagal Theory: Neurophysiological Foundatons of Emotions, Attachment, Communication, and Self-Regulation*, Norton, 2011.

243 'Traumatic symptoms are not caused by the "triggering" event itself. They stem from the frozen residue of energy that has not been resolved and discharged' when we have to enter the 'freeze' state of immobility. Peter A. Levine, *Waking the Tiger: Healing Trauma, The Innate Capacity to Transform Overwhelming Experiences*, North Atlantic Books, 1997.

244 In the account of the Marxist feminist Silvia Federici, one of the links between the colonial violence and dispossession inflicted on people elsewhere, and the violence and dispossession inflicted on people within the UK, is that both were essential to the beginnings of capitalism. She extends Marx and Foucault's observations about the subjugation of bodies into work machines or 'biopower' to an analysis of how women's

power was broken through the witch hunts, and how hierarchies of gender, race and age were built to divide the working class. Silvia Federici, *Caliban and the Witch: Women, the body and primitive accumulation*, Autonomedia, 2004.

245 C. Fred Alford, *Trauma, Culture and PTSD*, Palgrave Macmillan, 2016, p. 1.

246 My thanks to Briony Greenhill for this observation.

247 Martha Henriques, Can the legacy of trauma be passed down the generations? *BBC Future*, 26 March 2019; Bessel van der Kolk, *The Body Keeps the Score*, p. 152.

248 C. Fred Alford, *Trauma, Culture and PTSD*, pp. 2–3.

249 *Office for National Statistics*, 'People who were abused as children are more likely to be abused as an adult', 27 September 2017. Child abuse, in this analysis, included psychological and physical abuse, sexual abuse, and witnessing domestic abuse.

250 M. Glasser, I. Kolvin, D. Campbell, A. Glasser, I. Leitch, S. Farrelly, Cycle of child sexual abuse: Links between being a victim and becoming a perpetrator. *British Journal of Psychiatry*, 179 (6), 2001, pp. 482–494; Judith Herman, *Trauma and Recovery*, pp. 112–113.

251 Bessel van der Kolk, *The Body Keeps the Score*, p. 147.

252 Sue Gerhardt, *Why Love Matters: How affection shapes a baby's brain*, Routledge, 2004.

253 Joy Schaverien, Boarding School Syndrome: Broken attachments and hidden trauma, *British Journal of Psychotherapy*, vol. 27 iss. 2 May 2011, pp. 138–155.

254 George Monbiot, Boarding schools warp our political class – I know because I went to one, *The Guardian*, 7 November 2019.

255 Nick Duffell, *Wounded Leaders, British Elitism and the Entitlement Illusion*, Lone Arrow Press, 2014.

256 Editorial, *Journal of Psychosocial Studies*, vol. 11 iss. 2, October 2018.

257 Jeffrey C. Alexander, Toward a Theory of Cultural Trauma,' pp. 1–30 in Jeffrey C. Alexander, Ron Eyerman, Bernhard Giesen, Neil J. Smelser and Piotr Sztompka (eds) *Cultural Trauma and Collective Identity*, Berkeley: University of California, 2004. See also Angela Onwuachi-Willig, The Trauma of the Routine: Lessons on Cultural Trauma from the Emmett Till Verdict, *Sociological Theory*, vol. 34 no. 4, Dec 2016, pp. 335–357, which describes how cultural trauma arises not only when 'normal' events are interrupted by horror, but when repeated horrific events are given official sanction; and John Hughson and Ramón Spaaij, 'You are always on our mind': The Hillsborough tragedy as cultural trauma, *Acta Sociologica*, vol. 54 no. 3 Sep 2011, pp. 283–295, which describes the impact of conflicting representations of a traumatic event.

258 Menakem defines cultural somatics as 'an area of study and practice that applies our knowledge of trauma and resilience to history, intergenerational relationships, institutions, and the communal body'. Resmaa Menakem, *My Grandmother's Hands: Racialized Trauma and the Pathway to Mending our Hearts and Bodies*, Central Recovery Press, 2017, p. 22.

259 The psychoanalytic term for this is 'projective identification', which is a more complex process than the projections that I talked about in Chapter 2, where we can 'see' things that we have suppressed in ourselves in others. The term comes from Melanie Klein, and built on Freud's ideas about projection.

260 Resmaa Menakem, *My Grandmother's Hands*, p. 26.

261 Bessel van der Kolk, *The Body Keeps the Score*, Penguin, 2014, pp. 67–73.

262 Irene Visser, Decolonizing Trauma Theory: Retrospect and Prospects. *Humanities*, 2015, 4, pp. 250–265.

263 Stephen Frosh, Beyond Recognition: The Politics of Encounter, *Psychoanalysis, Culture & Society*, 20, 2015, pp. 379–394.

264 George Lakey, To succeed, movements must overcome the tension between rationality and emotion, *Open Democracy*, 10 September 2015.

265 Oxfam criticised over Haiti sex claims, *BBC*, 11 June 2019; Karen McVeigh, Save the Children 'let down staff and public' over sexual misconduct claims, *The Guardian*, 5 March 2020.

266 Open Letter from the Wretched of the Earth bloc to the organisers of the People's Climate March of Justice and Jobs, 16 December 2015; Wretched of the Earth, *An Open Letter to Extinction Rebellion*, Red Pepper, 3 May 2019.

267 George Lakoff, *Moral Politics: What Conservatives Know that Liberals Don't*, University of Chicago Press, 1996, and *Don't Think of an Elephant: Know your values and frame the debate*, Chelsea Green, 2004.

268 Riane Eisler, *The Chalice and the Blade*, HarperCollins, 1998.

269 Charles Eisenstein, *The Ascent of Humanity*, 2007; *The More Beautiful World Our Hearts Know is Possible*, 2013, North Atlantic Books.

270 Thanks to the American wilderness guides Bill Plotkin and Geneen Marie Haugen for this resonant term, the 'green door'. It was Bill's book *Soulcraft: Crossing into the mysteries of nature and psyche*, (New World Library, 2003) that first helped me make sense of what I was experiencing in the wild.

271 The wilderness guide and mythologist Martin Shaw explains one of the ways in which I went wrong in his book *Wolf Milk: Chthonic Memory in the Deep Wild*, Cista Mystica Press, 2019. The re-integration after such experiences is longer and harder than the experience itself, he cautions, and must be treated with respect.

272 'My study of Gandhi convinced me that true pacifism is not nonresistance to evil, but nonviolent resistance to evil,' wrote Martin Luther King Jr in *My Pilgrimage to Nonviolence*, 1 September 1958.

273 Personal communication.

274 She uses the online etymological resource Etymonline in her research.

275 Personal communication.

276 Nora Bateson, *Small Arcs of Larger Circles: Framing through other patterns*, Triarchy Press, 2016, p. 40.

277 Feminist criticism, while pointing out the obvious – that Keats was referring only to a man – discusses the multiple ways in which Keats' poetry has been associated with the feminine. Some associations rely on particular assumptions about what these characteristics might be: 'praising that in him which resembles what they have defined as feminine'. See Margaret Homans, Keats Reading Women, Women Reading Keats, *Studies in Romanticism* 29, Fall 1990, pp. 341–370.

278 Martin Shaw, *Scatterlings: Getting Claimed in the Age of Amnesia*, White Cloud Press, 2016, p. 58.

279 He oriented his psychotherapeutic approach around this understanding. Viktor Frankl, *Man's Search for Meaning: An Introduction to Logotherapy*, transl. Ilse Lasch, Beacon Press, 1959.

280 Ernest Becker, *The Denial of Death*, The Free Press, 1973; Sheldon Solomon, Jeff Greenberg, Tom Pyszcynski, *The Worm at the Core: On the role of death in life*, Allen Lane, 2015, pp222-4.

281 Copperplate engraving from Andreas Cellarius' 'Atlas Coelestis seu Harmonia Macrocosmica', published in 1660 in Amsterdam.

282 Jonathan Smucker, *Hegemony How-To: A Roadmap for Radicals*, AK Press, 2017, pp. 112–115.

283 John Ashton, Open letter to Shell's Ben van Beurden from John Ashton, *The Guardian*, 30 March 2015.

284 Personal communication.

285 I am grateful to Laurie Michaelis of Quaker Living Witness for explaining to me the Quaker principles relevant to activism.

286 Robert Kegan, *In Over Our Heads: The Mental Demands of Modern Life*, Harvard University Press, 1998, p. 332.

287 Christopher Bollas, *The Shadow of the Object: Psychoanalysis of the Unthought Known*, Free Association Books, 1987.

288 For example, Global Witness: *Undue Diligence: How banks do business with corrupt regimes*, 2009; *Secret Life of a Shopaholic, An African dictator's playboy son and a multi-million dollar shopping spree in the US*, 2009; *International Thief Thief: How British Banks are Complicit in Nigerian Corruption*, 2010.

289 I owe bottomless thanks for their generous sharing of knowledge and experience over several years to a group of extraordinary, big-hearted people: John Christensen and Richard Murphy, founders of the Tax Justice Network, Jack Blum, an American lawyer and anti-corruption investigator, Elise Bean, who was Chief Counsel to the US Senate Permanent Subcommittee on Investigations under Sen. Carl Levin, and the late Joy Geary, an Australian lawyer, anti-money laundering expert, bad-ass road cyclist and much-missed friend.

290 UK government papers released under the 30-year secrecy rule in 2017 showed that when the global anti-money laundering framework was being set up under US influence in the 1980s, UK officials had actively worked behind the scenes to prevent it being effective in its aims at stopping dirty money and preserve the City of London's pre-eminence as a financial centre. This was what we had long suspected, and it was gratifying as well as ghastly to see it proven. Mary Alice Young and Michael Woodiwiss, A World Fit for Money Laundering: the Atlantic alliance's undermining of organized crime control, *Trends in Organized Crime*, April 2020.

291 Debra King, Sustaining activism through emotional reflexivity, in Helena Flam and Debra King, eds), *Emotions and Social Movements*, Routledge, 2005.

292 Ken Wilber calls it 'aperspectival madness'; Ken Wilber, *Trump and a Post-Truth World*, Shambhala, 2017; *Sex, Ecology, Spirituality*, Shambhala, 1995, pp. 746–749.

293 Stephen B. Oates, The Intellectual Odyssey of Martin Luther King, *The Massachusetts Review*, vol. 22 no. 2, Summer, 1981, pp. 301–320.

294 Personal communication.

295 Personal communication.

296 Personal communication. My friend Jack Blum, who has been a campaigning lawyer and anti-corruption expert in the US since the sixties, said exactly the same thing, minus the profanity.

297 Personal communication.

298 Nadine Andrews' research into the psychosocial factors influencing sustainability professionals' work commitment noted this phenomenon. Nadine Andrews, Psychosocial factors influencing the experience of sustainability professionals, *Sustainability Accounting, Management and Policy Journal*, vol. 8 iss. 4, pp. 445–469.

299 I explored this in more detail in an essay for Dark Mountain about Extinction Rebellion. Anthea Lawson, Hyde Park to Wembley: A Journey in Activism, *Dark Mountain* iss. 16: Refuge, 2019.

300 Jessica Benjamin, *Beyond Doer and Done To: Recognition Theory, Intersubjectivity and the Third*, Routledge 2018, pp. 23–24.

301 The philosopher José Medina suggests that the 'epistemic virtues' worth adopting are humility, curiosity/diligence and open mindedness, in contrast to the 'epistemic vices' of arrogance, laziness and closed-mindedness. José Medina, *The Epistemology of Resistance, Gender and Racial Oppression, Epistemic Injustice, and Resistant Imaginations*, Oxford University Press, 2013.

302 Personal communication.

303 T.S. Eliot, 'East Coker', *Four Quartets, Faber & Faber, 1943*.

304 For example, the Ulex Project: http://ulexproject.org/courses_events/

305 Louis Fischer (ed), *The Essential Gandhi: An anthology of his writings on his life, work and ideas*, Vintage, 1962, p. 93.

306 I use this metaphor with due respect to the excellent work of the people who advocate for more rest as an ongoing strategy to dismantle the extractive working patterns of capitalism, whiteness, and 'grind culture'. See, for example, the work of Tricia Hersey, aka 'The Nap Ministry'.

Acknowledgements

THIS BOOK has been a collaborative effort, borne out of conversation upon conversation. Some of those conversations took place in the research interviews that I conducted for the book, others during my years of campaigning, and yet others with friends. Some people have influenced my thinking more than the text might suggest; others have influenced me but asked not to be named. I am grateful to all of the activists and scholars, living and gone, from whom I have learned about activism. People I have worked with, been inspired by, or whose words I have read and from whose legacies I continue to learn with gratitude.

Thank you, for your sharing of experiences, expertise, teaching, information and perspectives; for your stories, time, energy, and spirit; for introductions, reading suggestions, and writing advice, to Aiah Kungbana, Alex Evans, Amy Barry, Anders Lustgarten, Andres Fossas, Andrew Samuels, Andrew

Simms, Anita Lewis, Ayeisha Thomas-Smith, Bayo Akomolafe, Bertie Cairns, Bill Plotkin, Brendan O'Donnell, Caroline Howard, Charlie Cory Wright, Charlotte Millar, Dave Key, David Fuller, David Young, Delphine Mascarene de Rayssac, Dickens Kamugisha, Elise Bean, Eliza Kenyon, Emilia Roig, Erica Thompson, Eva Okunbor, Gaia Harvey Jackson, Gail Bradbrook, George Boden, Guppi Bola, Hilary Prentice, Imani Robinson, Indra Adnan, Iris Andrews, Jack Blum, James Turner, James Marriott, Jamie Kelsey-Fry, Johnny Chatterton, Jem Bendell, Jenny Ross, Jess Holliday, John Ashton, John Christensen, Jude Allen, Justine Huxley, Katherine Wall, Larch Maxey, Laurence Cox, Laurie Michaelis, Liam Kavanagh, Lindsay Alderton, Liz Slade, Lucia Nader, Mark Vernon, Martin Kirk, Martin Shaw, Mary-Jayne Rust, Megan MacInnes, Mike Davis, Naomi Fowler, Natasha Adams, Nick Shaxson, Oli Courtney, Pippa Evans, Rob Nash, Robert Palmer, Romy Kraemer, Ronan Harrington, Ruth Ben Tovim, Ruth Hunt, Ruth Potts, Sam Earle, Sarah Woods, Satish Kumar, Sehin Teferra, Simon Bramwell, Sophia Pickles, Sophie Docker, Stu Basden, Tom Crompton, Vanessa Faloye, Winnie Ngabiirwe and many others. Any mistakes or omissions are entirely mine.

Thank you to Jonathan Rowson for the challenge and the support, without which this book would not have happened. Jonathan saw something in the questions about activism with which I turned up on his doorstep in 2017, and offered support from Perspectiva, the research organisation that he had recently founded, for me to start investigating them. His own searching questions about activism helped to provoke my thinking, and his close readings of my drafts sharpened it. Perspectiva has been a forum for stimulating conversations with an extraordinary group of big-hearted and sharp-minded people. It has also been a home from which I was able to raise a grant from the Emergence Foundation to run some exploratory workshops and support my writing during 2019. I'm extremely grateful to Simon Town and the Emergence Foundation board and stakeholder group for their support, and to everyone who participated in and brought their experiences, wisdom and questions to the events.

Thank you to my editor, Minna Salami, whose editorial suggestions were transformative, whose rigour pushed me beyond what I had thought were my limits, and whose enthusiasm for the project has been life-giving. I read her book *Sensuous Knowledge*, which I recommend, just as I'd finished my last draft, and was struck by the correspondences between the stories they tell. Thank you to my proofreader, Johanna Robinson, for picking up problems that I'd been looking at yet not noticing for months, to Alison Shakspeare, for making the text look beautiful, and to David Hirst, for generous help with my legal questions. Thank you to Vanessa Faloye, whose attentive reading of the manuscript broadened the scope of many points and gave me faith in the necessity of the endeavour. Thank you to Caspar Henderson, who offered valuable editorial guidance, and to Annie Dunnebacke, Tom Gaisford, Polly Trenow and Jim Coe for their insightful responses to the manuscript. Thank you to Briony Greenhill, Laurence Cox, Nadine Andrews, Nili Sigal, Sam Earle, Sarah Stein Lubrano, Simon Christmas and Sophy Banks, who read early drafts of individual chapters and offered valuable advice. Thank you to Michael Edwards, who commissioned an article based on some of the material in Chapter 4 for openDemocracy, and to Charlotte Du Cann, who commissioned an essay on activism and despair for Dark Mountain that I composed in my mind while in a police cell, and that fed into Chapter 11.

Thank you to Bayo Akomolafe, who opened my eyes to the capaciousness of the concept of entanglement, introduced me to the thinking of Karen Barad and Donna Haraway, and whose thinking and conversation about 'post-activism' through his Emergence Network continues to fuel my own ongoing questions about activism. Thank you to everyone who took part in Bayo's course 'We Will Dance With Mountains', which I attended in late 2020 as I was completing the final edits to this book. I learned from you all how much further there is still to go in understanding my entanglements. Thank you to Alastair McIntosh, whose books *Soil and Soul* and *Spiritual Activism* opened my eyes to the inner life of activism, and to Charles Eisenstein, whose book *The More Beautiful World Our Hearts Know is Possible* gave shape to some of my emerging questions about the campaigning I was doing.

Thank you to Judith Seelig, from whom I continue to learn so much, and to Anu Arasu, Araminta and Tim Littlehales, Arnaud Czaja, Belinda Lawson, Colin Goldman, Elaine Cox, Elisabeth Braun, Guillermo Rozenthuler, Jeff Cruz, Judy Thomson, Kate Jacoby Seelig, Lucia

Bardoul, Marilyn Homer, Maymay Knight, Michael McGurran, Nat Torr, Prashant Nair, Rida Hysenbelli, Robbie Burns, Rus Victory, Simone Coetzee, Tanya Clements, Veronica Needa and Victoria Hands, in whose company I am so happy to learn.

Thank you, for navigational guidance when I was lost and for always having my back, to Annie Dunnebacke, Briony Greenhill, Emily Spry, Emma Simpson, James Cook, Jilly Banwell, Kate Grange, Kate Landell, Laura Garforth, Matt Cain, Mira Katbamna, Miriam Nabarro, Natasha Iwowo and Polly Trenow.

Thank you to my mum, Gilly, for everything; and to Charlie and Liv for loving me despite decades of banging on at the dinner table. Thank you to George Kean for keeping at it, you are an inspiration.

Thank you to my husband Rob for unending love and support, including during the times when I was unable to describe what exactly I was doing. This book would not have been written without Rob's profound understanding that it is all work. By 'work' I mean the tasks that are done with children: cooking, shopping, nappies, laundry, the school run, cuddles, Lego, breaking up fights. And, too, the tasks that need to be done when somebody else is looking after the children: earning a living, voluntary commitments and pursuing such dreams as writing a book. To call any of these tasks 'work' is not to say that they are not enjoyable, for most of them can be (and we're now done with nappies, thank goodness). The point of designating them as work, though, is that they are all shared between us. I'm endlessly grateful to Rob for his commitment to experimenting with ways of putting this understanding into practice, and to my Mum and my in-laws, Shona and Terry, for backup childcare. And thank you Gwen and Fergus for keeping things real. There's something interesting about writing part-time while looking after children. Sticky paragraphs that couldn't be fixed with several hours of trying sometimes resolve themselves in unlikely moments of applying ketchup, pushing a swing or towing a small person home on a scooter.

Thank you, for your good company and projects and generous tea-making, to Jay Tompt and all of the users of the REconomy Centre, a local economic and social enterprise hub and co-working space in Totnes where I wrote the second half of the book.

Thank you, too, to the creatures and plants who live along the ancient trackway that leads up and over the steep hill behind where I live. In spring, at its loveliest, it is a bosky tunnel of celandines, wild garlic, bluebell and hart's-tongue fern under an entangled vault of oak, holly and sycamore. As I begin walking, my head is thick with an impenetrable amalgam of household tasks, children's arguments over breakfast, yesterday's writing, current affairs and whatever I have been reading or listening to. Within a few minutes of sinking into the green I start noticing who is newly unfurled and who has begun to fade, and I silently greet them. By the time I am turning for home twenty minutes later my mind is quiet of almost everything except the fully formed sentences that are leaping into my mouth.

Index

A

Abramovich, Roman 9
abuses 13, 127
  child 147, 151, 159
acceptability 91
access 92
achievement 29, 122
activism 5, 12, 18, 21, 22, 27, 37, 128. *See also lifestyle activism*; *See also grassroots activism*
  as a practice not a goal 185–188
  changes 18, 19, 20
  defining xxi–xxii, 6, 156
  imagery 103
  newcomers 18, 34
  over there-ness 12
activists 13, 15, 18, 25, 26
  creation 61–64